PENGUIN BOOKS

FEVER PITCH

Nick Hornby was born in 1957 and worked as a teacher before becoming a full-time writer. He is a regular contributor to British newspapers and magazines. His first novel, *High Fidelity*, was published in the U.S. in 1995. Hornby lives next to the Arsenal ground with his wife and son.

FEVER PITCH

NICK HORNBY

PENGUIN BOOKS

PENGUIN BOOKS

Published by the Penguin Group

Penguin Books USA Inc., 375 Hudson Street, New York, New York 10014, U.S.A.
Penguin Books Ltd, 27 Wrights Lane, London W8 5TZ, England
Penguin Books Australia Ltd, Ringwood, Victoria, Australia
Penguin Books Canada Ltd, 10 Alcorn Avenue, Toronto, Ontario, Canada M4V 3B2
Penguin Books (N.Z.) Ltd, 182–190 Wairau Road, Auckland 10, New Zealand

Penguin Books Ltd, Registered Offices: Harmondsworth, Middlesex, England

First published in Great Britain by Victor Gollancz Ltd 1992
First published in the United States of America in Penguin Books 1994

3 5 7 9 10 8 6 4 2

Grateful acknowledgment is made for permission to reprint extracts from
the following copyrighted works:
The Selected Stories of Andre Dubus. Reprinted by permission of Picador.
Out of His Skin by Dave Hill. Reprinted by permission of Faber and Faber.
The Hustler by Walter Tevis. Copyright 1959 Walter S. Tevis. By permission
of The Walter Tevis Copyright Trust. All rights reserved.

ISBN 0 14 02.3729 1
(CIP data available)

Printed in the United States of America
Set in Times Roman

I'd like to thank Liz Knights for her tremendous support, encouragement and enthusiasm; Virginia Bovell for her tolerance and understanding; Nick Coleman, Ian Craig, Ian Preece, Caroline Dawnay and Viv Redman.

For my mother, and for my father

INTRODUCTION

It's in there all the time, looking for a way out.

I wake up around ten, make two cups of tea, take them into the bedroom, place one on each side of the bed. We both sip thoughtfully; so soon after waking there are long, dream-filled gaps between the occasional remark – about the rain outside, about last night, about smoking in the bedroom when I have agreed not to. She asks what I'm doing this week, and I think: (1) I'm seeing Matthew on Wednesday. (2) Matthew's still got my *Champions* video. (3) [*Remembering that Matthew, a purely nominal Arsenal fan, has not been to Highbury for a couple of years, and so has had no opportunity to watch the more recent recruits in the flesh*] I wonder what he thought of Anders Limpar.

And in three easy stages, within fifteen, twenty minutes of waking, I'm on my way. I see Limpar running at Gillespie, swaying to his right, going down: PENALTY! DIXON SCORES! 2–0! . . . Merson's back-heel flick and Smith's right-foot shot into the far corner in the same match . . . Merson's little push past Grobbelaar up at Anfield . . . Davis's swivel and smash against Villa . . . (And this, remember, is a morning in July, our month off, when there is no club football of any kind.) Sometimes, when I let this dreamy state take me over completely, I go on and back, through Anfield '89, Wembley '87, Stamford Bridge '78, my whole footballing life flashing before my eyes.

'What are you thinking about?' she asks.

At this point I lie. I wasn't thinking about Martin Amis or Gérard Depardieu or the Labour Party at all. But then, obsessives have no choice; they have to lie on occasions like this. If we told the truth every time, then we would be unable to maintain relationships with anyone from the real world. We would be left to rot with our Arsenal programmes or our collection of original blue-label Stax records or our King Charles spaniels, and our two-minute daydreams would become longer and longer and longer until we lost our jobs and stopped bathing and shaving and eating, and we would lie on the floor in our own filth rewinding the video again and again in an attempt to memorise by heart the *whole* of the commentary, including David Pleat's expert analysis, for the night of 26th of May 1989. (You think I had to look the date up? Ha!) The truth is this: *for alarmingly large chunks of an average day, I am a moron.*

I would not wish to suggest that the contemplation of football is in itself an improper use of the imagination. David Lacey, the chief football correspondent for the *Guardian*, is a fine writer and an obviously intelligent man, and presumably he must devote even more of his interior life than I do to the game. The difference between Lacey and me is that I rarely *think*. I remember, I fantasise, I try to visualise every one of Alan Smith's goals, I tick off the number of First Division grounds I have visited; once or twice, when I have been unable to sleep, I have tried to count every single Arsenal player I have ever seen. (When I was a kid I knew the names of the wives and girlfriends of the Double-winning team; now, I can only remember that Charlie George's fiancée was called Susan Farge, and that Bob Wilson's wife was called Megs, but even this partial recall is terrifyingly unnecessary.)

None of this is *thought*, in the proper sense of the word. There is no analysis, or self-awareness, or mental rigour going on at all, because obsessives are denied any kind of perspective on their own passion. This, in a sense, is what defines an obsessive (and serves to explain why so few of them recognise themselves as such. A fellow fan who last season went to watch Wimbledon reserves against Luton reserves on a freezing January afternoon on his own – not in a spirit of one-upmanship or some kind of self-mocking, laddish wackiness, but because he was *genuinely interested* – recently strenuously denied to me that he was eccentric in any way).

Fever Pitch is an attempt to gain some kind of an angle on my obsession. Why has the relationship that began as a schoolboy crush endured for nearly a quarter of a century, longer than any other relationship I have made of my own free will? (I love my family dearly, but they were rather foisted on me, and I am no longer in touch with any of the friends I made before I was fourteen – apart from the only other Arsenal fan at school.) And why has this affinity managed to survive my periodic feelings of indifference, sorrow and very real hatred?

The book is also, in part, an exploration of some of the meanings that football seems to contain for many of us. It has become quite clear to me that my devotion says things about my own character and personal history, but the way the game is consumed seems to offer all sorts of information about our society and culture. (I have friends who will regard this as pretentious, self-serving nonsense, the kind of desperate justification one might expect from a man who has spent a huge chunk of his leisure time fretting miserably in the cold. They are particularly resistant to the idea because I tend to overestimate the metaphorical value of football, and therefore introduce it into conversations where it simply does not belong. I now accept that football has no relevance to the Falklands conflict, the Rushdie affair, the Gulf War, childbirth, the ozone layer, the poll tax, etc., etc., and I would like to take this opportunity to apologise to anyone who has had to listen to my pathetically strained analogies.)

Finally, *Fever Pitch* is about being a fan. I have read books written by people who obviously love *football*, but that's a

different thing entirely; and I have read books written, for want
of a better word, by hooligans, but at least 95 per cent of the
millions who watch games every year have never hit anyone in
their lives. So this is for the rest of us, and for anyone who has
wondered what it might be like to be this way. While the details
here are unique to me, I hope that they will strike a chord
with anyone who has ever found themselves drifting off, in the
middle of a working day or a film or a conversation, towards a
left-foot volley into a top right-hand corner ten or fifteen or
twenty-five years ago.

1968–1975

HOME DÉBUT

ARSENAL v STOKE CITY
14.9.68

I fell in love with football as I was later to fall in love with
women: suddenly, inexplicably, uncritically, giving no thought
to the pain or disruption it would bring with it.

In May '68 (a date with connotations, of course, but I am
still more likely to think of Jeff Astle than of Paris), just after
my eleventh birthday, my father asked me if I'd like to go with
him to the FA Cup Final between West Brom and Everton; a
colleague had offered him a couple of tickets. I told him that I
wasn't interested in football, not even in the Cup Final – true,
as far as I was aware, but perversely I watched the whole match
on television anyway. A few weeks later I watched the Man
Utd–Benfica game, enthralled, with my mum, and at the end
of August I got up early to hear how United had got on in the
final of the World Club Championship. I loved Bobby Charlton
and George Best (I knew nothing about Denis Law, the third
of the Holy Trinity, who had missed the Benfica match through
injury) with a passion that had taken me completely by surprise;
it lasted three weeks, until my dad took me to Highbury for
the first time.

My parents were separated by 1968. My father had met someone else and moved out, and I lived with my mother and my
sister in a small detached house in the Home Counties. This
state of affairs was unremarkable enough in itself (although I
cannot recall anyone else in my class with an absent parent

15

– the sixties took another seven or eight years to travel the twenty-odd miles down the M4 from London), but the break-up had wounded all four of us in various ways, as break-ups are wont to do.

There were, inevitably, a number of difficulties that arose from this new phase of family life, although the most crucial in this context was probably the most banal: the commonplace but nevertheless intractable one-parent Saturday-afternoon-at-the-zoo problem. Often Dad was only able to visit us midweek; no one really wanted to stay in and watch TV, for obvious reasons, but on the other hand there wasn't really anywhere else a man could take two children under twelve. Usually the three of us drove to a neighbouring town, or up to one of the airport hotels, where we sat in a cold and early-evening deserted restaurant, and where Gill and I ate steak or chicken, one or the other, in more or less complete silence (children are not great dinner conversationalists, as a rule, and in any case we were used to eating with the TV on), while Dad watched. He must have been desperate to find something else to do with us, but the options in a commuter-belt town between 6.30 and 9.00 on a Monday night were limited.

That summer, Dad and I went to a hotel near Oxford for a week, where in the evenings we sat in a deserted hotel dining room, and where I ate steak or chicken, one or the other, in more or less complete silence. After dinner we went to watch TV with the other guests, and Dad drank too much. Things had to change.

My father tried again with the football that September, and he must have been amazed when I said yes. I had never before said yes to any suggestion of his, although I rarely said no either. I just smiled politely and made a noise intended to express interest but no commitment, a maddening trait I think I invented especially for that time in my life but which has somehow remained with me ever since. For two or three years he had been trying to take me to the theatre; every time he asked I simply shrugged and grinned idiotically, with the result that eventually Dad would get angry and tell me to forget it, which was what I wanted him to say. And it wasn't just Shakespeare, either: I was equally suspicious of rugby matches and cricket matches and boat trips and days out to Silverstone and Longleat. I didn't want to do anything at all. None of this was intended to punish my father for his absence: I really thought that I would be happy to go anywhere with him, apart from every single place he could think of.

1968 was, I suppose, the most traumatic year of my life. After my parents' separation we moved into a smaller house, but for a time, because of some sort of chain, we were homeless and had to stay with our neighbours; I became seriously ill with jaundice; and I started at the local grammar school. I would have to be extraordinarily literal to believe that the Arsenal fever about to grip me had nothing to do with all this mess. (And I wonder how many other fans, if they were to examine the circumstances that led up to their obsession, could find some sort of equivalent Freudian drama? After all, football's a great game and everything, but what is it that separates those who are happy to attend half a dozen games a season – watch the big matches, stay away from the rubbish, surely the sensible way – from those who feel compelled to attend them all? Why travel from London to Plymouth on a Wednesday, using up a precious day's holiday, to see a game whose outcome was effectively decided in the first leg at Highbury? And, if this theory of fandom as therapy is anywhere near the mark, *what the hell is buried in the subconscious of people who go to Leyland DAF Trophy games?* Perhaps it is best not to know.)

There is a short story by the American writer Andre Dubus entitled 'The Winter Father', about a man whose divorce has separated him from his two children. In the winter his relationship with them is tetchy and strained: they move from afternoon jazz club to cinema to restaurant, and stare at each other. But

17

in the summer, when they can go to the beach, they get on fine. 'The long beach and the sea were their lawn; the blanket their home; the ice chest and thermos their kitchen. They lived as a family again.' Sitcoms and films have long recognised this terrible tyranny of place, and depict men traipsing round parks with fractious kids and a frisbee. But 'The Winter Father' means a lot to me because it goes further than that: it manages to isolate what is valuable in the relationship between parents and children, and explains simply and precisely *why* the zoo trips are doomed.

In this country, as far as I know, Bridlington and Minehead are unable to provide the same kind of liberation as the New England beaches in Dubus's story; but my father and I were about to come up with the perfect English equivalent. Saturday afternoons in north London gave us a context in which we could be together. We could talk when we wanted, the football gave us something to talk about (and anyway the silences weren't oppressive), and the days had a structure, a routine. The Arsenal pitch was to be our lawn (and, being an English lawn, we would usually peer at it mournfully through driving rain); the Gunners' Fish Bar on Blackstock Road our kitchen; and the West Stand our home. It was a wonderful set-up, and changed our lives just when they needed changing most, but it was also exclusive: Dad and my sister never really found anywhere to live at all. Maybe now that wouldn't happen; maybe a nine-year-old girl in the nineties would feel that she had just as much right to go to a game as we did. But in 1969 in our town, this was not an idea that had much currency, and my sister had to stay at home with her mum and her dolls.

I don't recall much about the football that first afternoon. One of those tricks of memory enables me to see the only goal clearly: the referee awards a penalty (he runs into the area, points a dramatic finger, there's a roar); a hush as Terry Neill takes it, and a groan as Gordon Banks dives and pushes the ball out; it falls conveniently at Neill's feet and this time he scores. But I am sure this picture has been built up from what I have long known about similar incidents, and actually I was aware of none of this. All I really saw on the day was a bewildering chain of incomprehensible incidents, at the end of which everyone around me stood and shouted. If I did the same, it must have been an embarrassing ten seconds after the rest of the crowd.

But I do have other, more reliable, and probably more meaningful memories. I remember the overwhelming *maleness* of it all – cigar and pipe smoke, foul language (words I had heard before, but not from adults, not at that volume), and only years later did it occur to me that this was bound to have an effect on a boy who lived with his mother and his sister; and I remember looking at the crowd more than at the players. From where I was sitting I could probably have counted twenty thousand heads; only the sports fan (or Mick Jagger or Nelson Mandela) can do that. My father told me that there were nearly as many people in the stadium as lived in my town, and I was suitably awed.

(We have forgotten that football crowds are still astonishingly large, mostly because since the war they have become progressively smaller. Managers frequently complain about local apathy, particularly when their mediocre First or Second Division team has managed to avoid a good hiding for a few weeks; but the fact that, say, Derby County managed to attract an average crowd of nearly seventeen thousand in 1990/91, the year they finished bottom of the First Division, is a miracle. Let's say that three thousand of these are away supporters; that means that among the remaining fourteen thousand from Derby, there were a number of people who went at least *eighteen times* to see the worst football of last or indeed most other seasons. Why, really, should anyone have gone at all?)

It wasn't the size of the crowd that impressed me most, however, or the way that adults were allowed to shout the word

'WANKER!' as loudly as they wanted without attracting any attention. What impressed me most was just how much most of the men around me *hated*, really *hated*, being there. As far as I could tell, nobody seemed to enjoy, in the way that I understood the word, anything that happened during the entire afternoon. Within minutes of the kick-off there was real anger ('You're a DISGRACE, Gould. He's a DISGRACE!' 'A hundred quid a week? A HUNDRED QUID A WEEK! They should give that to me for watching you.'); as the game went on, the anger turned into outrage, and then seemed to curdle into sullen, silent discontent. Yes, yes, I know all the jokes. What else could I have expected at Highbury? But I went to Chelsea and to Tottenham and to Rangers, and saw the same thing: that the natural state of the football fan is bitter disappointment, no matter what the score.

I think we Arsenal fans know, deep down, that the football at Highbury has not often been pretty, and that therefore our reputation as the most boring team in the entire history of the universe is not as mystifying as we pretend: yet when we have a successful side much is forgiven. The Arsenal team I saw on that afternoon had been spectacularly unsuccessful for some time. Indeed they had won nothing since the Coronation and this abject and unambiguous failure was simply rubbing salt into the fans' stigmata. Many of those around us had the look of men who had seen every game of every barren season. The fact that I was intruding on a marriage that had gone disastrously sour lent my afternoon a particularly thrilling prurience (if it had been a real marriage, children would have been barred from the ground): one partner was lumbering around in a pathetic attempt to please, while the other turned his face to the wall, too full of loathing even to watch. Those fans who could not remember the thirties (although at the end of the sixties a good many of them could), when the club won five Championships and two FA Cups, could remember the Comptons and Joe Mercer from just over a decade before; the stadium itself, with its beautiful art deco stands and its Jacob Epstein busts, seemed to disapprove of the current mob even as much as my neighbours did.

I'd been to public entertainments before, of course; I'd been to the cinema and the pantomime and to see my mother sing in the chorus of the *White Horse Inn* at the Town Hall. But that was different. The audiences I had hitherto been a part of had paid to have a good time and, though occasionally one might spot a fidgety child or a yawning adult, I hadn't ever noticed faces contorted by rage or despair or frustration. Entertainment as pain was an idea entirely new to me, and it seemed to be something I'd been waiting for.

It might not be too fanciful to suggest that it was an idea which shaped my life. I have always been accused of taking the things I love – football, of course, but also books and records – much too seriously, and I do feel a kind of anger when I hear a bad record, or when someone is lukewarm about a book that means a lot to me. Perhaps it was these desperate, bitter men in the West Stand at Arsenal who taught me how to get angry in this way; and perhaps it is why I earn some of my living as a critic – maybe it's those voices I can hear when I write. 'You're a WANKER, X.' 'The Booker Prize? THE BOOKER PRIZE? They should give that to me for having to read you.'

Just this one afternoon started the whole thing off – there was no prolonged courtship – and I can see now that if I'd gone to White Hart Lane or Stamford Bridge the same thing would have happened, so overwhelming was the experience the first time. In a desperate and percipient attempt to stop the inevitable, Dad quickly took me to Spurs to see Jimmy Greaves score four against Sunderland in a 5–1 win, but the damage had been done, and the six goals and all the great players left me cold: I'd already fallen for the team that beat Stoke 1–0 from a penalty rebound.

A SPARE JIMMY HUSBAND

ARSENAL v WEST HAM
26.10.68

On this, my third visit to Highbury (a goalless draw – I'd now seen my team score three times in four and a half hours), all the kids were given a free Soccer Stars album. Each page of the album was devoted to one First Division team, and contained fourteen or fifteen spaces in which to glue stickers of the players; we were also given a little packet of the stickers to start our collection off.

Promotional offers aren't often described thus, I know, but the album proved to be the last crucial step in a socialisation process that had begun with the Stoke game. The benefits of liking football at school were simply incalculable (even though the games master was a Welshman who once memorably tried to ban us from kicking a round ball even when we got home): at least half my class, and probably a quarter of the staff, loved the game.

Unsurprisingly, I was the only Arsenal supporter in the first year. QPR, the nearest First Division team, had Rodney Marsh; Chelsea had Peter Osgood, Tottenham had Greaves, West Ham had the three World Cup heroes, Hurst, Moore and Peters. Arsenal's best-known player was probably Ian Ure, famous only for being hilariously useless and for his contributions to the television series *Quiz Ball*. But in that glorious first football-saturated term, it didn't matter that I was on my own. In our dormitory town no club had a monopoly on support and, in any case, my new best friend, a Derby County fan like his father and uncle, was similarly isolated. The main thing was that you were a believer. Before school, at breaktime and at lunchtime, we played football on the tennis courts with a tennis ball, and in between lessons we swapped Soccer Star stickers – Ian Ure for Geoff Hurst (extraordinarily, the stickers were of equal value),

Terry Venables for Ian St John, Tony Hately for Andy Loch-head.

And so transferring to secondary school was rendered un-imaginably easy. I was probably the smallest boy in the first year, but my size didn't matter, although my friendship with the Derby fan, the tallest by several feet, was pretty handy; and though my performance as a student was undistinguished (I was bunged into the 'B' stream at the end of the year and stayed there throughout my entire grammar school career), the lessons were a breeze. Even the fact that I was one of only three boys wearing shorts wasn't as traumatic as it should have been. As long as you knew the name of the Burnley manager, nobody much cared that you were an eleven-year-old dressed as a six-year-old.

This pattern has repeated itself several times since then. The first and easiest friends I made at college were football fans; a studious examination of a newspaper back page during the lunch hour of the first day in a new job usually provokes some kind of response. And yes, I am aware of the downside of this wonderful facility that men have: they become repressed, they fail in their relationships with women, their conversation is trivial and boorish, they find themselves unable to express their emotional needs, they cannot relate to their children, and they die lonely and miserable. But, you know, what the hell? If you can walk into a school full of eight hundred boys, most of them older, all of them bigger, without feeling intimidated, simply because you have a spare Jimmy Husband in your blazer pocket, then it seems like a trade-off worth making.

DON ROGERS

Dad and I went to Highbury another half a dozen times that season, and by the middle of March 1969, I had gone way beyond fandom. On matchdays I awoke with a nervous churning in the stomach, a feeling that would continue to intensify until Arsenal had taken a two-goal lead, when I would begin to relax: I had only relaxed once, when we beat Everton 3–1 just before Christmas. Such was my Saturday sickness that I insisted on being inside the stadium shortly after one o'clock, some two hours before the kick-off; this quirk my father bore with patience and good humour, even though it was frequently cold and from 2.15 onwards my distraction was such that all communication was impossible.

My pre-match nerves were the same however meaningless the game. That season Arsenal had blown all chance of the Championship by about November, a little later than usual; but this meant that in the wider scheme of things it scarcely mattered whether they won the games I went to see. It mattered desperately to me, however. In these early stages, my relationship with Arsenal was of an entirely personal nature: the team only existed when I was in the stadium (I can't remember feeling especially devastated by their poor results away from home). As far as I was concerned, if they won the games I saw 5–0, and lost the rest 10–0, that would have been a good season, probably to be commemorated by the team travelling down the M4 to see me on an open-topped bus.

I made an exception for the FA Cup-ties; these I wanted Arsenal to win despite my absence, but we got knocked out 1–0 at West Brom. (I had been forced to go to bed before the result came through – the tie was played on a Wednesday night – and my mother wrote the score down on a piece of paper and attached it to my bookcase ready for me to look at in the morning. I looked long and hard: I felt betrayed by what she had written. If she loved me, then surely she could have come up with a better result than this. Just as hurtful as the score was the exclamation mark she had placed after it, as if it were . . . well, an exclamation. It seemed as inappropriate as if it had been used to emphasise the death of a relative: 'Gran died peacefully in her sleep!' These disappointments were still entirely new to me, of course, but like all fans, I've come to expect them now. At the time of writing, I have felt the pain of FA Cup defeat twenty-two times, but never as keenly as that first one.)

The League Cup I'd never really heard of, mainly because it was a midweek competition and I hadn't yet been allowed to attend a midweek game. But when Arsenal reached the final, I was prepared to accept it as a consolation for what had seemed to me to be a heartbreakingly poor season, although it had in fact been pretty run-of-the-mill for the sixties.

So Dad paid a tout way over the odds for a pair of tickets (I never found out exactly how much, but later, with justified anger, he led me to understand that they'd been very expensive) and on Saturday, 15th March ('BEWARE THE IDES OF MARCH' was the headline in the *Evening Standard*'s special colour supplement), I went to Wembley for the first time.

Arsenal were playing Swindon Town, a Third Division team, and no one seemed to have any real doubts that Arsenal would win the game, and therefore their first cup for sixteen years. I wasn't so sure. Silent in the car all the way there, I asked Dad on the steps up to the stadium whether he was as confident as everyone else. I tried to make the question conversational – sports chatter between two men on a day out – but it wasn't like that at all: what I really wanted was reassurance from an adult, a parent, my father, that what I was about to witness wasn't going to scar me for life. 'Look,' I should have said to him, 'when they're playing at home, in an ordinary League game, I'm so frightened they'll lose that I can't think or speak or even breathe, sometimes. If you think Swindon have any kind of chance at all, even a chance in a million, it's best if you take me home now, because I don't think I'd be able to cope.'

If I had come out with that, then it would have been unreasonable of my father to make me go inside the stadium. But I simply asked him, in an assumed spirit of idle curiosity, who he thought would win the game, and he said he thought Arsenal would, three or four nothing, the same as everyone else did, and so I got the reassurance I was looking for; but I was scarred for life anyway. Like my mother's exclamation mark, my father's blithe confidence later seemed like a betrayal.

I was so scared that the Wembley experience – a crowd of a hundred thousand, the huge pitch, the noise, the sense of anticipation – passed me by completely. If I noticed anything about the place at all it was that it wasn't Highbury, and my sense of alienation simply added to my unease. I sat shivering until Swindon scored shortly before half-time, and then the fear turned to misery. The goal was one of the most calamitously stupid ever given away by a team of professionals: an inept back-pass (by Ian Ure, naturally), followed by a missed tackle, followed by a goalkeeper (Bob Wilson) slipping over in the mud and allowing the ball to trickle over the line just inside the right-hand post. For the first time, suddenly, I became aware of all the Swindon fans sitting around us, with their awful West Country accents, their absurd innocent glee, their delirious disbelief. I hadn't ever come across opposing fans before, and I loathed them in a way I had never before loathed strangers.

With one minute remaining in the game, Arsenal equalised, unexpectedly and bizarrely, a diving header from a rebound off the goalkeeper's knee. I tried not to weep with relief, but the effort was beyond me; I stood on the seat and yelled at my father, over and over again, 'We'll be all right now, won't we? We'll be all right now!' He patted me on the back, pleased that something had been rescued from the dismal and expensive afternoon, and told me that yes, now, finally, everything would be OK.

It was his second betrayal of the day. Swindon scored twice more in extra time, one a scrappy goal from a corner, the other from Don Rogers after a magnificent sixty-yard run, and it was all too much to bear. When the final whistle went, my father betrayed me for the third time in less than three hours: he rose to his feet to applaud the extraordinary underdogs, and I ran for the exit.

When my father caught up with me he was furious. He delivered his ideas on sportsmanship with great force (what did I care about sportsmanship?), marched me to the car, and we drove home in silence. Football may have provided us with a new medium through which we could communicate, but that was not to say that we used it, or that what we chose to say was necessarily positive.

I don't remember Saturday evening, but I know that on the Sunday, Mother's Day, I elected to go to church rather than stay at home, where there was a danger that I would watch the highlights of the game on The Big Match and push myself over the edge into a permanent depressive insanity. And I know that when we got to church, the vicar expressed his pleasure in seeing such a large congregation given the competing temptations of a Cup Final on TV, and that friends and family nudged me and smirked. All this, however, was nothing compared to what I knew I would get at school on Monday morning.

For twelve-year-old boys permanently on the lookout for ways in which to humiliate their peers, opportunities like this were too good to miss. When I pushed open the door to the prefab, I heard somebody shout 'Here he is!', and I was submerged under a mob of screaming, jeering, giggling boys, some of whom, I noted darkly before I was knocked to the floor, didn't even like football.

It may not have mattered much in my first term that I was an Arsenal fan, but in my second it had become more significant.

Football was still, in essence, a unifying interest – nothing had changed in that way. But as the months passed, our allegiances had become much more defined, and we were much quicker to tease. This was easily anticipated, I suppose, but on that dreadful Monday morning painful nonetheless. As I lay in the grammar school dirt it occurred to me that I had made a grotesque mistake; it was my fervent wish that I could turn back the clock and insist that my father took me, not to Arsenal *v* Stoke, but to a deserted hotel dining room or the zoo. I didn't want to go through this once a season. I wanted to be with the rest of the class, trampling the hell out of some other poor heartbroken kid – one of the swots or weeds or Indians or Jews who were habitually and horribly bullied. For the first time in my life I was different and on my own, and I hated it.

I have a photograph from the game played on the Saturday after the Swindon tragedy, away at QPR. George Armstrong is just picking himself up, having scored the winner in a 1–0 win; David Court is running towards him, his arms triumphantly aloft. In the background you can see Arsenal fans on the edge of the stand, silhouetted against a block of flats behind the ground, and they too are punching the sky. I couldn't understand anything I saw in the picture at all. How could the players care, after the way they had humiliated themselves (and, of course, me) seven days – *seven days* – before? Why would any fan who had suffered at Wembley the way I had suffered stand up to cheer a nothing goal in a nothing match? I used to stare at this photo for minutes at a time, trying to detect somewhere within it any evidence of the trauma of the previous week, some hint of grief or of mourning, but there was none: apparently everyone had forgotten except me. In my first season as an Arsenal fan I had been betrayed by my mother, my father, the players and my fellow supporters.

ENGLAND!

Although the temptation to plunge into a warm bath containing dissolved essence of Kenneth Wolstenholme is always with me, I know in my heart that in the late sixties and early seventies, some things were better and some things were worse. The England team, of course, was better then: still the world champions, packed with great players, and looking as though they might be able to retain the World Cup in Mexico the following year.

I was proud of England, delighted that my father was taking me to see them play in a big game under floodlights at Wembley (and going back there so soon after the League Cup Final was therapeutic, a successful exorcism of demons that would otherwise have plagued me for years). And though there is no doubt that Colin Bell, Francis Lee and Bobby Moore were better than Geoff Thomas, Dennis Wise and Terry Butcher, it wasn't just the comparative quality that enabled me to feel unambiguous about that England side. The ambiguity came with age: by the time I was sixteen or seventeen, I knew better than the England manager.

A critical faculty is a terrible thing. When I was eleven there were no bad films, just films that I didn't want to see, there was no bad food, just Brussels sprouts and cabbage, and there were no bad books – everything I read was great. Then suddenly, I woke up in the morning and all that had changed. How could my sister not hear that David Cassidy was not in the same *class* as Black Sabbath? Why on *earth* would my English teacher think that *The History of Mr Polly* was better than *Ten Little Indians* by Agatha Christie? And from that moment on, enjoyment has been a much more elusive quality.

But in 1969, as far as I was concerned, there was no such thing as a bad England player. Why would Sir Alf pick someone who wasn't up to the job? What would be the point? I took it on trust that the eleven players who destroyed Scotland that night – two goals each for Hurst and Peters, Colin Stein replying for the Scots – were the best in the country. (Sir Alf had ignored everyone from Arsenal, which simply confirmed that he knew what he was doing.) And anyway the absence of any live football on television meant that we often didn't know who was much good or not: the highlights merely showed good players scoring goals, rather than bad players missing them.

By the early seventies I had become an Englishman – that is to say, I hated England just as much as half my compatriots seemed to do. I was alienated by the manager's ignorance, prejudice and fear, positive that my own choices would destroy any team in the world, and I had a deep antipathy towards players from Tottenham, Leeds, Liverpool and Manchester United. I began to squirm when watching England games on TV, and to feel, as many of us feel, that I had no connection whatsoever with what I saw; I might as well have been Welsh, or Scottish, or Dutch. Is it like this everywhere? I know that in the past the Italians have greeted their boys with rotten tomatoes at the airport when they return from overseas humiliations, but even that sort of commitment is beyond my comprehension. 'I hope they get stuffed,' I have heard Englishmen say on numerous occasions in reference to the England team. Is there an Italian or Brazilian or Spanish version of that sentence? It is difficult to imagine.

Part of this contempt may be related to the fact that we have too many players, all of indistinguishable dingy competence; the Welsh and the Irish have very little choice when it comes to putting out a team, and the fans know that their managers simply have to make do. In those circumstances, occasional poor performances are inevitable and victories are little miracles. Then of course there is the procession of England managers that has treated players of real skill and flair – Waddle and Gascoigne, Hoddle and Marsh, Currie and Bowles, George

and Hudson, footballers whose gifts are delicate and difficult
to harness, but at the same time much more valuable than a
pair of leather lungs – with the kind of disdain the rest of us
reserve for child molesters. (Which international squad in the
world would be unable to find a place for Chris Waddle, the
man who in 1991 ambled through the AC Milan back four
whenever he chose?) And finally there are the England fans
(discussed at greater length elsewhere), whose activities during
the eighties hardly encouraged identification with the team in
any of the rest of us.

It wasn't always thus with the fans at international matches.
It is impossible not to feel a little ache when one sees replays
of games in the 1966 World Cup that did not involve England,
for example. In the now-famous game between North Korea
and Portugal at Goodison Park (in which the unknown Asian
team took a 3–0 lead over one of the best sides in the competition before going out 5–3), you can see a thirty-thousand-plus
crowd, the vast majority of whom are Scousers, applauding
wildly after goals from each team. It is difficult to imagine the
same interest now; more likely, you'd get a couple of thousand
scallies making slanty eyes at the Asians in one team, and
monkey noises at Eusebio in the other. So, yes, of course I feel
nostalgic, even if I am longing for a time which never really
belonged to us: like I said, some things were better, some were
worse, and the only way one can ever learn to understand one's
own youth is by accepting both halves of the proposition.

The crowd that night contained none of these Goodison
saints, but they were no different from the crowds I had been
a part of during the rest of the season, with the exception of
an extravagantly emotional Scotsman in the row in front who
swayed precariously on his seat for the first half and failed to
reappear for the second. And most of us actively *enjoyed* the
game, as if for one night only football had become another
branch of the entertainment industry. Perhaps, like me, they
were enjoying the freedom from the relentless responsibility

and pain of club football: I wanted England to win, but they weren't *my* team. What, after all, did my country mean to me, a twelve-year-old from the Home Counties, compared to a north London side thirty miles from where I lived, a side I'd never heard of and never thought about nine months previously?

CAMPING

ARSENAL v EVERTON
7.8.69

For the opening game of my first full season I was at a scout camp in Wales. I hadn't wanted to go. I was never the most ging-gang-gooly gung-ho of scouts at the best of times and, shortly before our departure, I had discovered that my parents were finally getting divorced. Actually, this didn't disturb me unduly, at least consciously: after all, they had been separated for some time now and the legal process seemed to be a simple confirmation of the separation.

From the moment we arrived at the camp, though, I was dreadfully, overwhelmingly homesick. I knew that I was going to find it impossible to get through the ten days away; each morning began with a reverse charge call to my mother, during which I would sob pathetically and embarrassingly down the line back home. I was aware that this sort of behaviour was quite unbelievably feeble, and when an older scout was assigned to talk to me in order to discover what was wrong, I told him about the divorce with a shameless eagerness: it was the only explanation I could come up with that would in any way excuse my cissy longing to see my mother and my sister. It did the trick. For the rest of the holiday I was treated with a reverential pity by the rest of the campers.

I blubbed and dripped through the first week, but it wasn't

getting any easier, and on the Saturday my father was dispatched from his Midlands base down to see me. Saturday, of course, was the hardest day of all. I was stuck in some stupid Welsh field for the first home game of the season, and my sense of displacement was all the more acute.

I had missed football in the preceding months. The summer of '69 was the first in my life in which something seemed to be lacking. My dad and I were faced with pre-Arsenal problems; the sports pages no longer held any interest for me (in those days, before Gazza, before cynical and meaningless pre-season tournaments which somehow still offer a methadone alternative to the real competitions to come, before the ludicrous freneticism of the contemporary transfer market, the newspapers went weeks on end without even mentioning football); and we weren't allowed on to the tennis courts at school to kick a ball around. I had longed for and welcomed the previous summers, but this one destroyed so many routines I had come to rely on that it seemed to stifle rather than liberate – as if July and November had swapped places.

Dad arrived at the camp-site in mid afternoon. We walked over to a rock on the edge of the field and sat down; he talked about how little difference the divorce itself would make to our lives, and how we would be able to go to Highbury much more frequently next season. I knew he was right about the divorce (although to admit as much would have rendered his two hundred mile round-trip unnecessary), but the football promise seemed hollow. What, in that case, were we doing sitting on a rock in Wales when Arsenal were playing Everton? Quite a way back down the line my self-pity had got the better of me. I really did blame it all – the terrible food, the nightmarish walks, the cramped, uncomfortable tents, the revolting, fly-plagued holes we were supposed to crap into, and, worst of all, the two empty seats in the West Stand – on the fact that I was the child of estranged parents, the product of a broken home;

33

in fact, I was on a scout camp in the middle of Wales because I had joined the scouts. Not for the first time in my life, and certainly not for the last, a self-righteous gloom had edged out all semblance of logic.

Just before five, we went back to my tent to listen to the results. Both of us knew that to a large extent the success of my father's mission depended not on his ability to reassure or persuade but on the news from north London, and I think my father was praying even harder than usual for a home win. I hadn't really been listening to him for the previous twenty minutes anyway. He sat down on somebody else's sleeping bag, an incongruous figure in his immaculate sixties young executive casual gear, and we tuned in to Radio 2. The *Sports Report* theme made my eyes water again (in a different, better world we would be sitting on the hot leather seats of Dad's company car, trying to push through the traffic, and humming along); when it was over, James Alexander Gordon announced a 1–0 home defeat. Dad slumped back against the canvas, tired, knowing now that he'd been wasting his time, and I went back home the next afternoon.

BORING, BORING ARSENAL

ARSENAL v NEWCASTLE
27.12.69

'All those terrible nil–nil draws against Newcastle,' my father would complain in years to come. 'All those freezing, boring Saturday afternoons.' In fact, there were only two terrible nil–nil draws against Newcastle, but they occurred in my first two seasons at Highbury, so I knew what he meant, and I felt personally responsible for them.

By now I felt guilty about what I had got my father into. He had developed no real affection for the club, and would rather,

I think, have taken me to any other First Division ground. I was acutely aware of this, and so a new source of discomfort emerged: as Arsenal huffed and puffed their way towards 1–0 wins and nil–nil draws I wriggled with embarrassment, waiting for Dad to articulate his dissatisfaction. I had discovered after the Swindon game that loyalty, at least in football terms, was not a moral choice like bravery or kindness; it was more like a wart or a hump, something you were stuck with. Marriages are nowhere near as rigid – you won't catch any Arsenal fans slipping off to Tottenham for a bit of extra-marital slap and tickle, and though divorce is a possibility (you can just stop going if things get too bad), getting hitched again is out of the question. There have been many times over the last twenty-three years when I have pored over the small print of my contract looking for a way out, but there isn't one. Each humiliating defeat (Swindon, Tranmere, York, Walsall, Rotherham, Wrexham) must be borne with patience, fortitude and forbearance; there is simply nothing that can be done, and that is a realisation that can make you simply squirm with frustration.

Of course I hated the fact that Arsenal were boring (I had by now conceded that their reputation, particularly at this stage in their history, was largely deserved). Of course I wanted them to score zillions of goals and play with the verve and thrill of eleven George Bests, but it wasn't going to happen, certainly not in the foreseeable future. I was unable to defend my team's inadequacies to my father – I could see them for myself, and I hated them – and after each feeble attempt at goal and every misplaced pass I would brace myself for the sighs and groans from the seat next to me. I was chained to Arsenal and my dad was chained to me, and there was no way out for any of us.

PELÉ

BRAZIL v CZECHOSLOVAKIA
June 1970

Until 1970, people of my age and a good few years older knew more about Ian Ure than they did about the greatest player in the world. We knew that he was supposed to be pretty useful, but we had seen very little evidence of it: he had literally been kicked out of the 1966 tournament by the Portuguese, but he hadn't really been fit anyway, and nobody I knew could remember anything about Chile in 1962. Six years after Marshall McLuhan published *Understanding Media*, a good three-quarters of the population of England had about as clear a picture of Pelé as we'd had of Napoleon one hundred and fifty years before.

Mexico '70 introduced a whole new phase in the consumption of football. It had always been a global game in the sense that the whole world watched it and the whole world played it; but in '62, when Brazil retained the World Cup, television was still a luxury rather than a necessity (and in any case the technology required to relay the games live from Chile didn't exist), and in '66 the South Americans had performed poorly. Brazil were eliminated before the knock-out stage; Argentina went unnoticed until their elimination by England in the quarter-finals, when their captain Rattin was sent off but refused to walk, and Sir Alf referred to them as animals. The only other South American team in the last eight, Uruguay, got thumped 4–0 by Germany. In effect, 1970 was the first major confrontation between Europe and South America that the world had had the opportunity to witness. When Czechoslovakia went one up in Brazil's opening game, David Coleman observed that 'all we ever knew about them has come true'; he was referring to Brazil's sloppy defence, but the words are those of a man whose job it was to introduce one culture to another.

In the next eighty minutes, everything else we knew about

them came true too. They equalised with a direct free kick from Rivelino that dipped and spun and swerved in the thin Mexican air (had I ever seen a goal scored direct from a free kick before? I don't remember one), and they went 2–1 up when Pelé took a long pass on his chest and volleyed it into the corner. They won 4–1, and we in 2W, the small but significant centre of the global village, were duly awed.

It wasn't just the quality of the football, though; it was the way they regarded ingenious and outrageous embellishment as though it were as functional and necessary as a corner kick or a throw-in. The only comparison I had at my disposal then was with toy cars: although I had no interest in Dinky or Corgi or Matchbox, I loved Lady Penelope's pink Rolls-Royce and James Bond's Aston Martin, both equipped with elaborate devices such as ejector seats and hidden guns which lifted them out of the boringly ordinary. Pelé's attempt to score from inside his own half with a lob, the dummy he sold to the Peruvian goalkeeper when he went one way round and the ball went the other . . . these were football's equivalent of the ejector seat, and made everything else look like so many Vauxhall Vivas. Even the Brazilian way of celebrating a goal – run four strides, jump, punch, run four strides, jump, punch – was alien and funny and enviable, all at the same time.

The strange thing was that it didn't matter, because England could live with it. When we played Brazil in the second match, we were unlucky to lose 1–0; and in a tournament that provided dozens of superlatives – the best team of all time, the best player of all time, even the two best misses of all time (both Pelé's) – we chipped in with a couple of our own, the best save of all time (Banks from Pelé, of course) and the best, most perfectly timed tackle of all time (Moore on Jairzinho). It is significant that our contribution to this superlative jamboree was due to defensive excellence, but never mind – for ninety minutes England were every bit as good as the best team in the world. I still cried after the game, though (mainly because I had misunderstood the way the tournament worked – I thought we were out, and Mum had to explain the vagaries of the group system).

In a way Brazil ruined it for all of us. They had revealed a kind of Platonic ideal that nobody, not even the Brazilians, would ever be able to find again; Pelé retired, and in the five subsequent tournaments they only showed little flashes of their ejector-seat football, as if 1970 was a half-remembered dream they had once had of themselves. At school we were left with our Esso World Cup coin collections and a couple of fancy moves to try out; but we couldn't even get close, and we gave up.

THUMPED

ARSENAL v DERBY
31.10.70

By 1970 my father had moved abroad and a new Arsenal routine emerged, one which no longer relied on his more infrequent visits. I was introduced to another, older Arsenal fan at school, known as Rat, by the brother of my classmate Frog, and the two of us travelled up to Highbury together. The first three matches we saw were spectacular successes: 6–2 *v* West Brom, 4–0 *v* Forest and 4–0 *v* Everton. These were consecutive home games and it was a golden autumn.

It is stupid and unforgivably fogeyish to contemplate the prices in 1970, but I'm going to anyway: a return to Paddington cost 30p for a child; the return fare from Paddington to Arsenal on the tube was 10p; and admission to the ground was 15p (25p for adults). Even if you bought a programme it was possible to travel thirty miles and watch a First Division football match for less than 60p.

(Maybe there is a point to this banality after all. If I travel to see my mother on the train now the fare is £2.70 for a day return, a tenfold increase on 1970 adult prices; but in the 91/92 season it now cost £8 to stand on the terraces at Arsenal, a thirty-two-fold increase. For the first time ever, it was cheaper to go to the West End and see the new Woody Allen or Arnold Schwarzenegger – in your own seat – than to stand and watch Barnsley play for a nil–nil draw in the Rumbelows Cup at Highbury. If I were twenty years younger, I wouldn't be an Arsenal supporter in twenty years' time: it is not possible for most kids to find ten or fifteen quid every other Saturday, and if I had been unable to go regularly in my early teens then it is unlikely that my interest would have sustained.)

The art deco splendour of the West Stand was not possible without Dad's deeper pockets, so Rat and I stood in the Schoolboys' Enclosure, peering at the game through the legs of the linesmen. At the time the club disapproved of perimeter advertising and pre-match DJs, and so we had neither; Chelsea fans may have been listening to the Beatles and the Stones, but at Highbury half-time entertainment was provided by the Metropolitan Police Band and their vocalist, Constable Alex Morgan. Constable Morgan (whose rank never changed throughout his long Highbury career) sang highlights from light operettas and Hollywood musicals: my programme for the Derby game says that he performed Lehár's 'Girls Were Made To Love and Kiss' that afternoon.

It was a bizarre ritual. Just before the kick-off he would hit an extraordinary high note and sustain it as the climax to his performance: in the Lower East Stand, just behind him, the crowd would rise to their feet, while the North Bank would attempt to drown him out by whistling and chanting. The Schoolboys' Enclosure is the kind of quaint title that only Arsenal, with its mock opera, its Old Etonian chairman and its cripplingly heavy history, could have dreamed up, suggesting as it did a safe haven for Jennings and Darbishire, or William Brown, provided he behaved himself: skewiff caps and grubby blazers, frogs in pockets and Sherbet Fountains – an ideal spot, in fact, for two suburban grammar school boys up in town to watch the Big Game.

The reality of the Schoolboys' was somewhat different in 1970, just after number one crops and Doctor Martens had begun to appear on the terraces for the first time. The small, narrow section of terrace was in effect a breeding ground for future hooligans, tough kids from Finsbury Park and Holloway either too small or too poor to watch from the North Bank, where their big brothers stood. Rat and I didn't take any notice of them for the first few weeks; after all, we were all Arsenal fans together, so why should we be worried? Yet something separated us. It wasn't our accents – neither of us was particularly well-spoken. But it may have been our clothes, or our haircuts, or our clean, lovingly folded scarves, or our fervent pre-match scrutiny of the programme, which we kept spotless in an inside pocket or a duffle bag.

We left a couple of minutes before the end of the Derby game, when Arsenal were winning 2–0 (Kelly and Radford, one in each half). A couple of black boys (black boys! Flipping heck!), maybe our age, but yards taller and from a different planet – the planet Real Life, the planet Secondary Modern, the planet Inner City – jostled us as we walked past; my heart skipped a couple of beats and I made for the exit. They followed. We moved a little faster, anxious to get through the maze of alleyways and turnstiles that led out of the ground. Out in the street, I knew the kids wouldn't bother us in the middle of the crowd of grown-ups flooding away from the stadium.

The crowd didn't seem to perturb them in the slightest, however. We broke into a run towards the tube station; so did they. Rat made it, but they caught up with me, pushed me against the wall of the stadium, smacked me in the face a couple of times, stole my red-and-white scarf and left me in a crumpled, traumatised heap on the pavement. People – adults with a reassuring paternal demeanour – stepped over me or aroun me, just as I have walked around innumerable beatings outside grounds. I had been hit much harder at school (I was not only small but cheeky, a particularly unfortunate combination), but usually by people I knew, which made it somehow acceptable. This was different. This was much scarier: I didn't understand what the limits were – had I been lucky or unlucky? – and though I knew I was obsessed enough with the team to go back and stand in the same place again, the prospect of getting thumped once a fortnight at twenty to five was bleak.

I really don't think that I was aware of class then. A few years later, when I discovered politics, I would have felt that I deserved a smack in the mouth for being a privileged middle-class white male – indeed, in my late teens, when the chief source of my ideological input was the first Clash album, I probably would have delivered it myself – but then I just felt a deep sense of disappointment and shame. Disappointment because I had finally begun to suspect that some people didn't go to football for the Right Reasons (devotion to the Gunners, or at the least a yen for some sparkling wing play); shame because, despite my size and youth, I was still a male and there is something in males, something stupid and unreconstructed but powerful nonetheless, that simply refuses to tolerate anything that might be construed as weakness. (The above version of the afternoon's events is archetypally masculine: there were *two* of them against *one* of me; I was *tiny*, they were *huge*, and so on. It could well have been that I was assaulted by a blind seven-year-old with one arm, but my memory has properly protected me from any suspicion that I might have been a wimp from the sticks.)

Perhaps the worst of it was that I couldn't unburden the experience on to my mum. If I told her, I'd be banned from going to football unaccompanied by my father for years to come; so I kept it to myself, confessed that I'd left the scarf – a present

n – on the tube, endured endless complaints about
...ess and irresponsibility, and was denied my cus-
...day night trip to the chip shop. Any theories about
...g experience of urban deprivation would have
...wasted on me that night; I was only interested in suburban
deprivation, which seemed to me the cruellest deprivation of
them all.

CAN YOU SEE ME ON THE BOX?

SOUTHAMPTON v ARSENAL
10.4.71

On holiday in Bournemouth, where both my grandmothers
lived, and conveniently there is an away match at Southampton.
So I book a coach ticket, travel along the coast and squirm
through a packed Dell to the far edge of the terrace; and the
next day, when Southern show the highlights of the game on
TV, there I am on the bottom left of the screen every time a
corner is taken (McLintock scored from one of them, the first
in a 2–1 win): a sober lad, seven days short of my fourteenth
birthday, unmistakably pre-pubescent . . . but I'm not waving
or leering or shoving the boy standing next to me, just standing
there, a still point in the middle of all the juvenile hyperactivity
around me.

Why was I so serious? I was a *child* everywhere else: at home;
at school, where chronic fits of the giggles seized me well into
the sixth form; and out with my friends, one or two of whom
now had girlfriends, the most side-splittingly, gut-bustingly,
snot-dribblingly hilarious development the rest of us had ever
seen. (Symbolically, a nickname was altered. Larry, so-called
because of his physical and stylistic resemblances to Larry
Lloyd, the Liverpool centre-half, became Caz, because of the
interest he now shared with Casanova, the Italian striker. We

were delighted with the witticism.) But when I was watching Arsenal, I don't think I felt relaxed enough to laugh until I was well into my twenties; if I had been filmed by the corner flag at any time between 1968 and 1981 my expression would have been the same.

The simple truth is that obsessions just aren't funny, and that obsessives don't laugh. But there's a complicated truth here as well: I don't think I was very happy, and the problem with being a thirteen-year-old depressive is that when the rest of life is so uproarious, which it invariably is, there is no suitable context for the gloom. How can you express misery when people keep making you *snigger* all the time? There was no sniggering at Arsenal games, however – not from me, anyway. And even though I had friends who would have been happy to accompany me to matches, significantly my support soon became a solitary activity: the following season I watched around twenty-five games, seventeen or eighteen of them on my own. I just didn't want to have fun at football. I had fun everywhere else, and I was sick of it. What I needed more than anything was a place where unfocused unhappiness could thrive, where I could be still and worry and mope; I had the blues, and when I watched my team I could unwrap them and let them breathe a little.

HOW I WON THE DOUBLE

ARSENAL v NEWCASTLE
17.4.71

In a little over a year, things had changed. The team was still short of stars and pretty low on verve, but they suddenly became very hard to beat. In 1970 the dismal seventeen-year hunt for a trophy finally ended when Arsenal won the European Fairs Cup – amazingly, in some style. After thrashing Ajax,

Johann Cruyff and all, in the semi, they came from behind to beat Anderlecht of Belgium 4–3 in the final. They won 3–0 at Highbury in the second leg, and grown men danced on the pitch and wept with the relief of it all. I wasn't there. I wasn't allowed to go to a midweek match on a school night on my own.

1971 was Arsenal's *annus mirabilis*. They won the League Championship and the FA Cup in the same season, the famous Double that only three teams this century have managed. In fact, they won the trophies in the same week: on Monday night they won the Championship at Tottenham, and on the Saturday the Cup against Liverpool at Wembley. I wasn't there. I wasn't at Tottenham because I still wasn't allowed to go to a midweek match on a school night on my own; I wasn't at Wembley because Dad didn't come through with a ticket, despite promises to the contrary and, yes, I'm still bitter twenty years on.

So I wasn't there for anything. (I wasn't even there for the parade through Islington on the Sunday after the Cup Final. I had to go to see my Auntie Vi in Dulwich.) I missed it all. And as this book is about the consumption of football, rather than football itself, the Double year – Arsenal's finest season of the century – doesn't really have much place in my story, and how about that for impressionism? Sure, I threw a radio jubilantly against my bedroom wall when the final whistle blew at Tottenham; I literally went dizzy with joy when Charlie George scored the winner in the Cup Final and lay on his back with his arms outstretched; I strutted around school, trying to work out how I could humiliate my classmates in the same way they had humiliated me two years before, settling instead for a beatific smile which was understood by both teachers and boys. As far as they were concerned, I *was* Arsenal, and I was entitled to my triumphant bliss.

But I didn't think so, not really. I'd earned the pain against Swindon, but I hadn't contributed to the Double triumph in the same way, unless you counted a dozen or so League games, a school blazer groaning with lapel badges and a bedroom covered in magazine pictures as a contribution. The others, those who'd got hold of Final tickets and queued for five hours at Tottenham, they've got more to say about the Double than I.

I try now to hang on to the fact that a couple of weeks earlier, before all this glory, I had managed to place myself at the centre of the Double narrative. On my birthday Dad and I went to Arsenal *v* Newcastle (a terrible game, again); I sat clutching a radio that he had given me (the very radio, in fact, that I smashed on 3rd May), pocket-sized for Saturday afternoons. Leeds were top of the First Division, and that afternoon they had a home game against West Brom, fifth from bottom and without an away win all season. There used to be a comic strip called 'Billy's Boots', about a boy whose magic boots transformed their mediocre owner into a superstar; I suddenly seemed to be in possession of a radio which transformed the results of the most useless team into dramatic away victories. When I turned it on shortly after half-time, West Brom scored; when I did it again, they scored a second time. The tannoy at Highbury announced the news and the crowd went berserk; Charlie George scored the only goal and Arsenal went top of the League for the first time that season.

The gift I got that afternoon was priceless, like world peace or an end to Third World poverty, something that couldn't be bought for a million pounds – unless my dad had bought the referee at Leeds for a million pounds, the only possible explanation for some of his decisions that afternoon. One of West Brom's goals was by general consensus hundreds of yards offside, provoking the crowd into invading the pitch, which in turn resulted in Leeds being banned from their ground for the first few games of the following season. 'The crowd has gone mad and they have every right to do so,' Barry Davies pronounced memorably on *Match of the Day* that night; those were the days, when TV commentators actively encouraged riots rather than argued pompously for the return of National Service. If you did slip the ref something, then thanks, Dad. Brilliant idea. Would Leeds have lost at home to West Brom if it hadn't been my birthday? Would the game at Arsenal have finished nil–nil, as Arsenal *v* Newcastle games had always done before? Would we then have gone on to win the League? I doubt it.

ANOTHER CITY

CHELSEA v TOTTENHAM
January 1972

It is true to say that while I made a natural Arsenal supporter – I too was often dour, defensive, argumentative, repressed – my father belonged at Stamford Bridge. Chelsea were flamboyant, unpredictable and, it has to be said, not the most reliable of teams; my father had a taste for pink shirts and theatrical ties, and, stern moralist that I was, I think I felt that he could have done with a little more consistency. (Parenthood, George Graham would say, is a marathon, not a sprint.) Whatever the reason, Dad patently enjoyed going to Chelsea more than our trips to Highbury, and it was easy to see why. We once spotted Tommy Steele (or maybe it was John Alderton) coming out of the Gents in Chelsea's North Stand, and before the games we ate in one of the Italian restaurants on the King's Road. Once we went to look around the Chelsea Drugstore, where I bought the second Led Zeppelin album and sniffed the cigarette smoke in the air suspiciously. (I was as literal-minded as any Arsenal centre-half.)

Chelsea had Osgood and Cooke and Hudson, all flash and flair, and their version of football was bewilderingly different from Arsenal's (this League Cup semi-final, one of the best games I had ever seen, finished 2–2). But more importantly, the Bridge and its environs presented me with a different but still familiar version of *London*: familiar because the middle-class suburban boy has always been aware of it. It was not dissimilar to the London we already knew from trips to see pantomimes and films and museums, a busy, bright-lights-big-city London supremely aware that it was the centre of the world; and the people that I saw at Chelsea in those days were centre-of-the-world people. Football was a fashionable game, and Chelsea were a fashionable team; the models and actors and young executives who were cheering the Blues on were beautiful to look at and made the Bridge (the seats, anyway) an exquisitely exotic place.

But this wasn't what I came to football for. Arsenal and its neighbourhood was for me much more exotic than anything I would ever see around the King's Road, which was full of an old-hat ho-hum glitz; football had gripped me because of its *otherness*. All those quiet terraced streets around Highbury and Finsbury Park, all those embittered but still peculiarly loyal used-car salesmen . . . now that was *real* exoticism; the London that a grammar school boy from the Thames Valley could never have seen for himself no matter how many times he went to the Casino cinema to see films in Cinerama. We wanted different things, my dad and I. Just as he was starting to want a part of what Chelsea was all about (and just as he was, for the first time in his life, able to afford it), I wanted to go tearing off in the other direction.

ISLINGTON BOY

READING v ARSENAL
5.2.72

The white south of England middle-class Englishman and woman is the most rootless creature on earth; we would rather belong to any other community in the world. Yorkshiremen,

Lancastrians, Scots, the Irish, blacks, the rich, the poor, even Americans and Australians have something they can sit in pubs and bars and weep about, songs to sing, things they can grab for and squeeze hard when they feel like it, but we have nothing, or at least nothing we want. Hence the phenomenon of mock-belonging, whereby pasts and backgrounds are manufactured and massaged in order to provide some kind of acceptable cultural identity. Who was it that sang 'I Wanna Be Black'? The title says it all, and everybody has met people who really do: in the mid-seventies, young, intelligent and otherwise self-aware white men and women in London began to adopt a Jamaican patois that frankly didn't suit them at all. How we all wished we came from the Chicago Projects, or the Kingston ghettos, or the mean streets of north London or Glasgow! All those aitch-dropping, vowel-mangling punk rockers with a public school education! All those Hampshire girls with grand-parents in Liverpool or Brum! All those Pogues fans from Hert-fordshire singing Irish rebel songs! All those Europhiles who will tell you that though their mothers live in Reigate, their sensibilities reside in Rome!

Ever since I have been old enough to understand what it means to be suburban I have wanted to come from somewhere else, preferably north London. I have already dropped as many aitches as I can – the only ones left in my diction have dug themselves too far into definite articles to be winkled out – and I use plural verb forms with singular subjects whenever poss-ible. This was a process that began shortly after my first visits to Highbury, continued throughout my suburban grammar school career, and escalated alarmingly when I arrived at university. My sister, on the other hand, who also has problems with her suburban roots, went the other way when she went to college, and suddenly started to speak like the Duchess of Devonshire; when we introduced each other to our respective sets of friends they found the experience perplexing in the extreme. Which of us, they seemed to be wondering, had been adopted? Had she fallen on hard times or had I struck lucky? Our mother, born and bred in south-east London but a Home Counties resident for nearly forty years, cuts the accents neatly down the middle.

In a way nobody can blame any of us, the Mockneys or the cod Irish, the black wannabees or the pseudo Sloanes. The 1944 Education Act, the first Labour Government, Elvis, beatniks, the Beatles and the Stones, the sixties . . . we never stood a chance. I blame the eleven-plus. Before the war, maybe, our parents could have scraped the money together to send us to minor public schools, and we would have received our pisspoor cheapskate third-hand classical educations and gone to work in a bank; the eleven-plus, designed to create a meritocracy, made state schools safe for nice families again. Post-war grammar school boys and girls stepped into a void; none of the available cultures seemed to belong to us, and we had to pinch one quick. And what is suburban post-war middle-class English culture anyway? Jeffrey Archer and *Evita*, Flanders and Swann and the Goons, Adrian Mole and Merchant–Ivory, *Francis Durbridge Presents* . . . and John Cleese's silly walk? It's no wonder we all wanted to be Muddy Waters or Charlie George.

The Reading–Arsenal fourth-round Cup-tie in 1972 was the first and most painful of the many exposures to come. Reading was my nearest League team, an unhappy geographical accident that I would have done anything to change; Highbury was thirty-odd miles away, Elm Park a mere eight. Reading fans had Berkshire accents, and incredibly they didn't seem to mind; they didn't even *try* to speak like Londoners. I stood with the home supporters – the match was all-ticket, and it was much easier to go to Reading than to north London to get one – and while I waited my still customary ninety minutes for the game to begin, a whole family (a family!), mother, father and son, all kitted up in blue-and-white scarves and rosettes (rosettes!), started talking to me.

They asked me questions about my team and the stadium, made jokes – peasants! – about Charlie George's hair, offered me biscuits, lent me their programmes and newspapers. I was beginning to enjoy the conversation. My assumed Cockney sounded to my ears flawless against their loathsome burr, and our relationship was beginning to take on a gratifying city-slicker-meets-hicks-from-the-sticks hue.

It was when they asked me about schools that it all went terribly wrong: they had heard about London comprehensives, and wanted to know whether it was all true, and for what seemed like hours I weaved an elaborate fantasy based on the exploits of the half-dozen small-time thugs at the grammar. I can only presume that I had managed to convince myself, and that by this stage my town had, in my head, transmuted into a north London village somewhere between Holloway and Islington; because when the father asked where I lived, I told him the truth.

'Maidenhead?' the father repeated, incredulous. 'Maidenhead? But that's four miles down the road!'

'Nearer ten,' I replied, but he seemed unconvinced that the extra six miles made much difference, and I could see his point. I was blushing.

Then he finished me off. *'You shouldn't be supporting Arsenal this afternoon,'* he said. *'You should be supporting your local team.'*

It was the most humiliating moment of my teenage years. A complete, elaborate and perfectly imagined world came crashing down around me and fell in chunks at my feet. I wanted Arsenal to avenge me, to beat the Third Division team and their pedantic, dull-witted fans into a pulp; but we won 2–1 with a second-half Pat Rice deflection, and at the end of the game the Reading father ruffled my hair and told me that at least it wouldn't take me long to get home.

It didn't stop me, though, and it only took a couple of weeks to rebuild the London Borough of Maidenhead. But I made sure that the next time I went to an away game it was precisely that – far away, where people might believe that my Thames

Valley hometown had its own tube station and West Indian community and terrible, insoluble social problems.

HAPPY

ARSENAL v DERBY
12.2.72

For a match to be really, truly memorable back then, the kind of game that sent me home buzzing inside with the fulfilment of it all, these conditions had to be met: I had to go with my dad; we had to eat lunch in the chip shop (sitting down, no sharing of tables); we had to have seats in the Upper West Stand (the West Stand because you can see down the players' tunnel from there and so can greet the arrival of the team on the pitch before anyone in the ground), between the half-way line and the North Bank; Arsenal had to play well and win by two clear goals; the stadium had to be full, or nearly full, which usually implied an opposing team of some significance; the game had to be filmed, by ITV for *The Big Match* on Sunday afternoon rather than by the BBC for *Match of the Day* (I liked the anticipation, I guess); and Dad had to be wearing warm clothes. He often travelled over from France without an overcoat, forgetting that his Saturday afternoon was likely to be spent in sub-zero temperatures, and his discomfort was so violent that I felt guilty insisting that we stayed right until the final whistle. (I always did insist, however, and when we reached the car he was often so cold that he could hardly speak; I felt bad about it, but not bad enough to risk missing a goal.)

These were enormous demands, and it is hardly surprising that everything came together just the once, as far as I am aware, for this game against Derby in 1972, when an Alan Ball-inspired Arsenal beat the eventual League Champions 2–0 with two Charlie George goals, one a penalty and the other a superb diving header. And because there was a table for us in the chip shop, and because the referee pointed to the spot when Ball was brought down instead of waving play on, and because my dad remembered his coat, I have allowed this game to become something it wasn't: it now represents for me the whole works, the entire fixation, but that's wrong. Arsenal were too good, Charlie's goal was too spectacular, the crowd was too big and too appreciative of the team's performance . . . The 12th of February *did* happen, in just the way I have described it, but only its atypicality is important now. Life isn't, and has never been, a 2–0 home victory against the League leaders after a fish-and-chip lunch.

MY MUM AND CHARLIE GEORGE

DERBY COUNTY v ARSENAL
26.2.72

I begged and pleaded and nagged, and eventually my mother gave in and allowed me to travel to away games. Back then I was jubilant; now I'm indignant. What did she think she was *doing*? Didn't she ever read the papers or watch TV? Hadn't she heard of hooligans? Was she really unaware of what Football Specials, the infamous trains that carried fans all over the country, were *like*? I could have been *killed*.

Now that I think about it, my mother's part in all this was actually quite mysterious. She didn't like me spending my money on Led Zeppelin records, understandably, or on cinema tickets, and she didn't even seem that keen on me buying books. And yet somehow it was OK for me to travel to London or Derby or Southampton on an almost weekly basis and take my chances with any group of nutters that I happened upon. She has never discouraged my mania for football; in fact it was she who bought my ticket for the Reading Cup-tie, driving down a frozen, snow-covered A4 and queuing up while I was at school. And some eight years later I came home to find on our dining table an impossibly elusive ticket for the West Ham–Arsenal Cup Final that she had bought (for twenty quid, money she didn't really have) from a man at work.

Well, yes, of *course* it was something to do with masculinity, but I don't think that her usually tacit, occasionally active football support was supposed to be for my benefit; it was for hers. On Saturdays, it seems to me now, we enacted a weird little parody of a sitcom married couple: she would take me down to the station, I'd go on the train up to London, do my man's stuff and ring her from the forecourt call-box when I got back for a lift home. She would then put my tea on the table and I ate while I talked about my day and, sweetly, she would ask questions about a subject that she didn't know much about, but tried to take an interest in anyway, for my sake. If things had not gone well she would tiptoe around them; on a good day my satisfaction would fill the living room. In Maidenhead, this was exactly what happened from Monday to Friday, every single weekday evening. The only difference was that in our house we didn't get around to it until the weekend.

There is, I know, an argument which says that acting out the role of one's father with one's mother isn't necessarily the best way of ensuring psychic health in later years. But then, we all do it at some time or another, chaps, don't we?

Away games were my equivalent of staying late at the office, and the fifth-round Cup-tie at Derby was the first time I had got to do it properly. In those days there were no restrictions on travelling in the way there are now (British Rail eventually abandoned the Football Specials, and the clubs make their own travel arrangements): we could roll up at St Pancras, buy a dirt-cheap train ticket, and pile on to a dilapidated train, the corridors of which were patrolled by police with guard dogs. Much of the journey took place in darkness – light bulbs were shattered at wearyingly brief intervals – which made reading difficult, although I always, always took a book with me and spent ages finding the carriages which contained middle-aged men who would have no interest in attracting the attention of the alsatians.

At our destination we were met by hundreds and hundreds of police, who then escorted us to the ground by a circuitous route away from the city centre; it was during these walks that my urban hooligan fantasies were given free rein. I was completely safe, protected not only by the law but by my fellow supporters, and I had therefore been liberated to bellow along in my still-unbroken voice with the chanted threats of the others. I didn't look terribly hard, in truth: I was as yet nowhere near as big as I should have been, and wore black-framed Brains-style National Health reading glasses, although these I hid away for the duration of the route marches, presumably to make myself just that little bit more terrifying. But those who mumble about the loss of identity football fans must endure miss the point: this loss of identity can be a paradoxically enriching process. Who wants to be stuck with who they are the whole time? I for one wanted time out from being a jug-eared, bespectacled, suburban twerp once in a while; I loved being able to frighten the shoppers in Derby or Norwich or South-ampton (and they *were* frightened – you could see it). My opportunities for intimidating people had been limited hitherto, though I knew it wasn't *me* that made people hurry to the other side of the road, hauling their children after them; it was *us*, and I was a part of us, an organ in the hooligan body. The fact that I was the appendix – small, useless, hidden out of the way somewhere in the middle – didn't matter in the slightest.

If going to the ground was all glory and raw power, standing inside it, and getting back to the station afterwards, was less invigorating. Violence inside the grounds has all but dis-appeared now, for a variety of reasons: fans are separated properly (back then, if you fancied your chances in the opposition end, you could just walk through the turnstiles), away fans are usually kept back after games until the stadium has cleared, the policing is a lot more sophisticated, and so on. For the first half of the seventies, however, there was a fight at every single Arsenal game I attended. At Highbury they mostly took place on the Clock End, where the opposition's fans stood; usually they were brief flurries, Arsenal fans charging into the enemy, the enemy scattering, the police taking control. These were ritualistic charges, the violence usually contained in the movement itself rather than in fists and boots (it was this 'running' that caused the Heysel tragedy, rather than any real physical attack). But occasionally, particularly against West Ham, Tottenham, Chelsea or Manchester United, the trouble was just as likely to be at the North Bank end of the ground where the noise comes from: when away fans could amass sufficient numbers they would attempt to seize the home fans' territory as if it were an island of strategic military importance.

Consequently it was very difficult to watch football safely at away grounds. Standing in the section 'reserved' for visitors didn't ensure any protection; in fact, it merely informed the opposition of your identity. Standing at the other end was either dangerous (if the Arsenal fans were intending to invade the home end) or pointless – why bother to travel half the length of the country if you then had to pretend to support the opponents? I settled for a place along the side, if possible, where it was quiet; if not, then in the 'away' end, but towards a corner, as far from the more gung-ho members of the Arsenal touring party as possible. But I never enjoyed away games. I felt constantly nervous, often with good reason: at random points throughout the afternoon, fighting would break out, prefaced by the same kind of roar that greeted a goal; but the fact that the roar might occur when the play was nowhere near either end of the pitch was disorienting in the extreme. I have seen players look around, perplexed that their efforts at a throw-in should meet with such vocal enthusiasm.

The afternoon at Derby was worse than most. There had been trouble before the game and at sporadic intervals during it, and though I was way down the terraces, hidden among younger kids and their fathers, I was scared – so scared that in fact I was ambivalent about an Arsenal victory. A draw would have suited me fine, but I could live with defeat and an exit from the Cup if it meant I could get back to Derby station without anything untoward happening to my head. It is at times like this that the players have more responsibilities than they could ever perceive or understand; in any case, this sort of perception was not one of Charlie George's most obvious qualities.

Charlie George is one of the few seventies icons who has so far managed to avoid being deconstructed, possibly because he appears at first glance to be one of the identikit George Best/ Rodney Marsh/Stan Bowles long-haired, wayward wasters who were two a new pee twenty years ago. It is true that he was as outrageously gifted as the best of the breed, and that these gifts were appallingly underexploited throughout his career (he only played for England on two or three occasions, and towards the end of his time at Arsenal could not even gain a place in the first team); all this and more – his temper, his problems with managers, the fierce devotion he attracted from younger fans and women – was par for the course, commonplace at a time when football was beginning to resemble pop music in both its presentation and its consumption.

Charlie George differed slightly from the rebel norm on two counts. Firstly, he had actually spent his early teenage years on the terraces of the club for which he later played; and though this is not unusual in itself – plenty of Liverpool and Newcastle players supported these clubs when they were young – George is one of the few genius misfits to have jumped straight over the perimeter fence into a club shirt and shorts. Best was Irish, Bowles and Marsh were itinerant . . . not only was George

Arsenal's own, nurtured on the North Bank and in the youth team, but he looked and behaved as if running around on the pitch dressed as a player were the simplest way to avoid ejection from the stadium. Physically, he did not fit the mould: he was powerfully built and over six feet tall, too big to be George Best. On my birthday in 1971, shortly before his goal against Newcastle, one of the frequent red mists that plagued him had descended, and he had grabbed a rugged Newcastle defender by the throat and lifted him from the ground. This was not misfit petulance, this was hard-man menace, and the likely lads on the terraces have never had a more convincing representative.

And secondly, he was not a media rebel. He could not give interviews (his inarticulacy was legendary and genuine); his long, lank hair remained unfeathered and unlayered right up until the time he unwisely decided upon a bubble perm from hell some time in the mid-seventies, and when he first played in the team, at the beginning of the 69/70 season, it looked suspiciously as if he were trying to grow out a number one crop; and he seemed uninterested in womanising – Susan Farge, the fiancée whose name I still remember, is intimidatingly prominent in most of the off-the-pitch photographs. He was a big star, and the media were interested, but they didn't know what to do with him. The Egg Marketing Board tried, but their slogan, 'E for B and Charlie George', was significantly incomprehensible. Somehow, he had made himself unpackageable, media-proof – possibly the very last star of any iconic stature to do so. (For some reason, however, he managed to remain in the otherwise colander-like consciousness of my grandmother for some years after his retirement. 'Charlie George!' she spat disapprovingly and opaquely circa 1983, when I told her that I was off to Highbury to watch a game. What he means to her will, I fear, never properly be understood.)

At Derby he was astonishing on a dreadful, muscle-jellifying winter pitch (Those pitches! The Baseball Ground at Derby,

White Hart Lane, Wembley even . . . was winter grass really an eighties innovation, like the video machine or frozen yoghurt?). He scored twice, two screamers, and to the tune of Andrew Lloyd Webber's then-recent hit, we sang 'Charlie George! Superstar! How many goals have you scored so far?' (to which the Derby fans, like others all over the country had done before them, replied 'Charlie George! Superstar! Walks like a woman and he wears a bra!' It is hard not to laugh when people remember the sixties and seventies as the golden age of terrace wit). Despite Charlie's double, the game finished 2–2 after a late Derby equaliser, and I therefore got the draw I'd been cravenly hoping for, but not the aggro-free walk back to the station that was supposed to be mine as a consequence.

It was Charlie's fault. A goal, for reasons that would require a book in itself to explain, is a provocative gesture, especially when the terraces are already bathed in a sort of half-light of violence, as they were on that afternoon. I understood that Charlie was a professional footballer, and that if an opportunity to score came his way then our tenuous safety should not in itself be a consideration. This much was clear. But whether it was absolutely essential to celebrate by running over to the Derby fans – in whose snarling, southern-poof hating, Cockney baiting, skinheaded, steel-toecapped company we were obliged to spend the remainder of the afternoon, and through whose hostile, alleywayed territory we were obliged to scuttle after the final whistle – and making an unambiguous take-that-you-provincial-fuckers V-sign . . . this was much more opaque. The way I saw it, Charlie's sense of responsibility and duty had momentarily let him down.

He got booed off the pitch and fined by the FA; we got chased all the way on to our train, bottles and cans cascading around our ears. Cheers, Charlie.

SOCIAL HISTORY

ARSENAL v DERBY
29.2.72

The replay finished nil–nil, a game with no merit whatsoever.
But it remains the only first-team game that has taken place at
Highbury on a midweek afternoon during my Arsenal time:
February 1972 was the time of the power workers' strike. For
all of us it meant sporadic electricity, candlelight, occasional
cold suppers, but for third-year football fans it meant visits to
the Electricity Board showroom, where the cut-off rota was
posted, in order to discover which of us were able to offer *The
Big Match* on Sunday afternoons. For Arsenal, the power crisis
meant no floodlights, hence the Tuesday afternoon replay.

I went to the game, despite school, and though I had imagined that the crowd might consist of me, a few other teenage
truants, and a scattering of pensioners, in fact there were more
than sixty-three thousand people there, the biggest crowd of
the season. I was disgusted. No wonder the country was going
to the dogs! My truancy prevented me from sharing my disquiet
with my mother (an irony that escaped me at the time), but
what was going on?

For this thirtysomething, the midweek afternoon Cup-tie
(West Ham played giant-killers Hereford on a Tuesday afternoon as well, and got a forty-two-thousand-plus crowd) now
has that wonderful early seventies sheen, like an episode of *The
Fenn Street Gang* or a packet of Number Six cigarettes; maybe
it was just that everyone at Upton Park and Highbury, all one
hundred and six thousand of us, wanted to walk down one of
the millions of tiny alleys of social history.

ME AND BOB McNAB

STOKE CITY v ARSENAL
(Villa Park) 15.4.72

The 71/72 FA Cup was a cracker, an apparently endless source of wonder and tricky trivia questions. Which two teams took eleven hours to settle their fourth qualifying round tie? Which player scored nine goals in his team's first round 11–0 win over Margate? Who did he play for then? Where was he transferred to later? Who were the two Hereford players who scored in their Southern League side's astonishing 2–1 victory against First Division Newcastle? (A clue: the surnames have special resonance for Arsenal fans.) Oxford City and Alvechurch; Ted Macdougall; Bournemouth; Manchester United; Ronnie Radford and Ricky George: one point for each, seven points and you've won a pair of Malcolm Macdonald sideboards.

And then there were the afternoon Cup replays and Charlie's V-sign, and at Villa Park, in our semi-final against Stoke, our goalkeeper Bob Wilson was carried off in the middle of our 1–1 draw (John Radford had to take over) and I spoke to Bob McNab, the Arsenal left-back, a couple of hours before the kick-off.

I went up to Villa Park with Hislam, a wannabee hooligan from Maidenhead whom I ran into on trains every now and again. I was in awe of him. He wore a white butcher's coat covered in crudely drawn red Arsenal slogans, *de rigueur* for anyone with any terrace pretensions; and on the way home from games he would sit down next to me on the 5.35 from Paddington and ask me the score, explaining that he had been detained in the police cells under the pitch and therefore had no idea of what had been going on above his head. Jenkins, the apparently legendary leader of the North Bank (I'd never heard of him, needless to say), was a personal friend of his.

I was soon to find out, predictably, that this was all rubbish, and that Hislam's relationship with reality was tenuous even on a good day. If there was such a person as Jenkins (the Leader, a scheming hooligan-general responsible for military tactics, probably has its roots in urban, or even suburban, myth) Hislam didn't know him; and even I, desperate to number among my acquaintances a real-life criminal, began to wonder how an ostensibly harmless-looking fourteen-year-old managed to get himself arrested every single Saturday for offences which remained frustratingly vague.

Football culture is so amorphous, so unwieldy, so *big* (when I listened to Hislam talk about incidents in King's Cross and Euston and the back streets of Paddington, the whole of London seemed within the grasp of its tentacles) that it inevitably attracts more than its fair share of fantasists. If you wish to have taken part in a fearsome battle with Tottenham fans, it doesn't have to have happened within the stadium where it could easily be verified. It could have taken place at a station, or on a route to the ground, or in an enemy pub: football rumours of this kind have always been as thick and as impenetrable as smog. Hislam knew this, and was as happy as Larry inventing his gruesome and improbable lies; football was perfectly equipped to feed his ravenous appetite for self-deception, just as it was able to feed mine. For a while, we had a satisfying symbiosis going. He wanted to believe he was a hooligan, and so did I, and for a while he could have told me anything.

Dad had obtained two terrace tickets for the game for me (I hadn't explained to him the full extent of my football solitude) and Hislam had generously agreed to take the spare. When we arrived at Villa Park we had to find the box office to pick them up. It was one-thirty, and a few of the players were there, distributing tickets to wives and family and friends. Bob McNab, the left-back, was one of them; he hadn't played in the first team since January, and I was surprised to see him. I couldn't believe that Bertie Mee was going to give him his first run-out for three months in an FA Cup semi-final. In the end my curiosity overcame my shyness.

'Are you playing, Bob?'

'Yeah.'

Dialogue in works of autobiography is quite naturally viewed with some suspicion. How on earth can the writer remember verbatim conversations that happened fifteen, twenty, fifty years ago? But 'Are you playing, Bob?' is one of only four sentences I have ever uttered to any Arsenal player (for the record the others are 'How's the leg, Bob?' to Bob Wilson, recovering from injury the following season; 'Can I have your autograph, please?' to Charlie George, Pat Rice, Alan Ball and Bertie Mee; and, well, 'How's the leg, Brian?' to Brian Marwood outside the Arsenal club shop when I was old enough to know better) and I can therefore vouch for its absolute authenticity.

I have imagined conversations, of course. Even now I frequently take Alan Smith or David O'Leary to the pub, buy them a low-alcohol lager, sit them down and talk until last-orders and beyond about George Graham's alleged parsimony, Charlie Nicholas's fitness or John Lukic's transfer. But the plain truth is that the club means more to us than it does to them. Where were they twenty years ago? Where will they be in twenty years' time? Where will they be in *two* years' time, a couple of them? (At Villa Park or Old Trafford, bearing down on the Arsenal goal with the ball at their feet, that's where.)

No, I'm happy with things the way they are, thank you very much. They're players and I'm a fan, and I don't want to blur the boundaries. Men laugh at what they see as the grotesque inadequacy of groupies, but a one-night stand with a star is perfectly understandable, and has its own balance and logic. (If I were a nubile twenty-year-old, I'd probably be down at the training ground throwing my panties at David Rocastle, although this kind of confession from a man, however New he is, is regrettably still not acceptable.) Yet many of us have had opportunities to talk to the players, at boot launches or sports shop openings, in nightclubs or restaurants, and most of us have taken them. ('How's the leg, Bob?' 'Thought you were brilliant Saturday, Tony.' 'Hey, make sure you do Tottenham next week, yeah?') And what are these clumsy, embarrassing, fumbling encounters if they are not passes, beery gropes in the dark? We're not young and desirable nymphettes, we're grown-ups with pot-bellies, and we have nothing to offer at all. Professional footballers are as beautiful and unattainable as models, and I don't want to be a middle-aged bottom-pincher.

I hadn't worked all this out then, when I saw Bob McNab in his pre-match suit. And when I got into the ground, and two blokes in front of me started talking about team changes, I told them that McNab was playing, because he'd told me himself, and they looked at me and then looked at each other and shook their heads (although when the changes were read out over the tannoy they looked at me again). Meanwhile Hislam had taken himself off up to the top of Villa's massive Holte End, to be with The Lads, and was busy telling anyone who would listen how he'd bunked into the ground under the turnstiles (he made this claim to someone he may or may not have known as soon as we walked into the ground). Which of us was the fantasist here? I was, obviously. No one talks to the players before the game, but bunking in without paying . . . what would be the point of lying about that if you had a ticket stub in your pocket?

WEMBLEY II – THE NIGHTMARE CONTINUES

LEEDS v ARSENAL
5.5.72

A classic anxiety dream, banal in its obviousness. I am attempting to get to Wembley, and I have a ticket for the Final in

my pocket. I leave home in plenty of time for the game, but every
attempt to travel towards the stadium takes me in the opposite
direction. At first this is just an amusing irritation, but eventually
it induces panic; at two minutes to three I am in central London,
trying to hail a cab and beginning to realise that I'm not going
to get to see the match. I like the dream though, in a funny sort
of way. I have had it six times now, before every Cup Final that
Arsenal have played in since 1972, and so it is a nightmare
inextricably linked with success. I wake up sweating, but the
sweat serves as the first anticipatory moment of the day.

My Cup Final ticket had come directly from the club, rather
than via touts and my dad, and I was ludicrously proud of it.
(Even more eccentric was the joy I took in the compliment slip
that came with it, which I stored away for years afterwards.)
Cup tickets were allocated on the basis of the numbered
vouchers that appeared on the back of the programme. If you
had all the programmes, as I did, you were more or less assured
of a ticket; thus the system was supposed to reward loyal fans,
although in effect it rewarded those with enough energy to
track down the programmes they needed among the *ad hoc*
programme stands outside the ground (a laborious process
which constituted a kind of loyalty in itself). I had been to the
vast majority of the home games and a few of the aways; I had
as much right as any, and probably more right than most, to a
spot on the terraces at Wembley, and so my pride came from
the feeling of belonging I had lacked in the previous year.

(This sense of belonging is crucial to an understanding of
why people travel to the meaningless game in Plymouth on a
Wednesday night, and without it football would fail as a business. But where does it end? Those fans who travel the length
and breadth of the country every week; does the club 'belong'
to them more than it does to me? And the old geezer who only
gets along ten times a season, but has been going to Highbury
since 1938 . . . doesn't the club belong to him too, and he to

the club? Of course. But it took me another few years to discover that; in the meantime, it was no pain, no gain. Unless I had suffered and shivered, wept into my scarf and paid through the nose, it was simply not possible to take pleasure in or credit for the good times.)

The game itself was as dismal as all the other Arsenal–Leeds games had been: the two teams had developed something of a History, and their meetings were usually violent and low-scoring. My friend Bob McNab was booked in the first two minutes, and from that moment there was a procession of free kicks and squabbles, ankle taps and pointing fingers, and snarls. What made it worse was that this was the Centenary Cup Final; I am sure that if the top brass at the FA had had a free hand in choosing who the two finalists would be, Arsenal and Leeds would have come pretty low down on their list. The pre-match anniversary celebrations (I had found my spot on the terraces a good ninety minutes before the kick-off, as was my custom), which consisted of representatives of all the other Cup finalists marching round the pitch behind banners, suddenly appeared almost satirical in its intent. You remember the Matthews Final in '53? Bert Trautmann playing in goal with a broken neck in '56? Tottenham's Double team in '61? Everton's comeback in '66? Osgood's diving header in '70? Now watch Storey and Bremner attempting to gouge lumps out of each other's thighs. The sourness of the game simply exacerbated the tension in my stomach, every bit as debilitating as it had been during the Swindon game three years earlier. If no one was going to bother with any of the niceties of the game (and there were stretches when it appeared that no one was even going to bother with the ball) then winning the Cup became even more important: there wasn't anything else to think about.

At the beginning of the second half, Mick Jones wriggled to the byline and crossed for Allan Clarke to score for Leeds with a ridiculously effortless nod of the head. Inevitably it was the only goal of the game. We hit the post or the bar or something,

and had a shot kicked off the line, but these were token Cup
Final moments, not to be taken seriously; you could see that
the Arsenal players understood the pointlessness of their effort.

As the end of the game approached I braced myself for the
grief that I knew would swallow me whole, as it had done after
the Swindon match. I was fifteen, and the option of tears was
not available as it had been in 1969; when the final whistle went
I can recall my knees buckling slightly. I didn't feel sorry for
the team or for the rest of the fans, but for myself, although
now I realise that all football sorrow takes this form. When our
teams lose at Wembley we think of the colleagues and classmates we have to face on Monday morning, and of the delirium
that has been denied us; it seems inconceivable that we will
allow ourselves to be this vulnerable ever again. I felt that
I didn't have the *courage* to be a football fan. How could I
contemplate going through this again? Was I going to come to
Wembley every three or four years for the rest of my life and
end up feeling like this?

I felt an arm around my shoulders and realised for the first
time that I was standing next to three Leeds fans, an old man,
his son, and his grandson. 'Never mind, lad,' said the old man.
'They'll be back.' For a moment it felt as though he was holding
me upright, until the first and most intense spasm of misery
passed and I regained the strength in my legs. Almost immediately a couple of Arsenal suedeheads with an unmistakable and
ominous fury in their eyes pushed their way through the crowd
towards the four of us. I stepped back, and they removed the
Leeds scarf that was around the little boy's neck. 'Give that
back,' his dad said, but only because he knew it would be a
weak father who said nothing, not in any expectation of success.
There was a brief windmilling of fists and the two older men
staggered backwards; I didn't stay around to find out what kind
of beating they took. I ran for the gangway and went straight
home, frightened and sick. It was the only manner, really, in
which the Centenary Cup Final could have ended.

A NEW FAMILY

ARSENAL v WOLVES
15.8.72

Over the summer of 1972, things changed. Arsenal, the most British (that is to say, the dourest and most aggressive) team you could imagine, went all continental on us, and for half a dozen games at the start of the 72/73 season decided to play Total Football. (This, for the benefit of those with only a sketchy grasp of football tactics, was a Dutch invention which necessitated flexibility from all the players on the pitch. Defenders were required to attack, attackers to play in midfield; it was football's version of post-modernism, and the intellectuals loved it.) That August at Highbury, gentle and appreciative applause was as familiar a sound as sixty thousand shuffling feet had been a couple of years earlier. Imagine Mrs Thatcher coming back from Brussels and lecturing us on the perils of jingoism, and you will have some idea of the improbability of the conversion.

A win at Leicester on the opening Saturday was followed by this destruction of Wolves (5–2, with goals from defenders McNab and Simpson). 'I have never been so excited by an Arsenal performance,' said the man in the *Daily Mail* the next morning. 'They played more good football than in a dozen matches in their Double year.' 'Arsenal have genuinely changed their nature,' said the *Telegraph*. 'The old hardness and obsessive search for the heads of the strikers have disappeared. Instead, as hapless Wolves discovered, there is a new inventiveness and improvisation.'

For the first, but certainly not the last, time, I began to believe that Arsenal's moods and fortunes somehow reflected my own. It wasn't so much that we were both playing brilliantly and winning (although my two recent O-level passes were all the proof I needed that I was a genuine Championship of Life contender); more that during the summer of 1972 my life seemed to me to have become suddenly and bewilderingly exotic, and my team's mysterious adoption of a flamboyant continental style was perfectly and inexplicably analogous. Everything about the Wolves game was disorienting – the five goals, the quality of the passing (Alan Ball was outstanding), the purr of the crowd, the genuine enthusiasm of a normally hostile press. And I watched all this from the Lower East Stand with my father and my stepmother, a woman I had met just a few weeks earlier and whom I had previously always thought of, when I had thought of her at all, simply as The Enemy.

In the four or five years since my parents' separation, I had asked my father almost nothing about his personal life. Part of this was understandable: like most kids I possessed neither the vocabulary nor the nerve to talk about things like this. Another part of it was not quite as easy to explain, and had more to do with the fact that none of us ever referred to what had happened if we could possibly avoid doing so. Even though I was aware that there had been Another Woman when my father left, I never asked him about her; my picture of my father was therefore curiously incomplete. I knew that he worked, and that he lived abroad, but I never attempted to envision any sort of *life* for him: he took me to football, asked me about school and then disappeared for another couple of months into some sort of unimaginable limbo.

It was inevitable that sooner or later I would be made to confront the fact that Dad, like all of us, had another, fuller context. That confrontation eventually occurred in the early summer of 1972, when I discovered that my father and his second wife were the parents of two small children. In July, the amazing news still undigested, I went to visit the undreamed-of family at their home in France. The fact that this set-up had hitherto been concealed from me meant that there had been none of the gradual accumulation of detail that usually occurs in such cases: like Mia Farrow in *The Purple Rose of Cairo*, dragged from the audience through the screen into a film by one of its characters, I was propelled into a world that had been imagined and completed without my participation, entirely alien but still somehow recognisable. My half-brother was small and dark and looked up to and after his little sister, eighteen months younger, blonde and bright and self-confident . . . where had I seen these two before? In our home movies, that's where. But if they were us, Gill and I, why were they speaking half in French and half in English? And what was I supposed to be to them, a brother, or some kind of third parent, or something in between, a trainee intermediary from the adult world? And how come there was a swimming pool and a permanent supply of Coke in the fridge? I loved it and I hated it and I wanted to go home on the next plane and I wanted to stay for the rest of the summer.

When I did get back, I had to invent a *modus vivendi* that would do me for the next few years, a task I thought best accomplished by ensuring that the new world was never ever mentioned in the old, although it wouldn't have achieved much to complain about the absence of a swimming pool in our tiny back garden in any case; thus one huge and important part of my life was kept entirely and pacifically separate from another, an arrangement perfectly designed to produce mendacity, self-delusion and schizophrenia in an already confused teenager.

When my stepmother sat down next to me at Highbury for the Wolves game, it was as if Elsie Tanner had walked into the Crossroads Motel; the appearance of an inhabitant from one world at the centre of the other somehow drained the reality out of both. And then Arsenal started to bang inch-perfect passes along the ground all over the pitch, and our defenders popped up in the opposing penalty area to lob the opposing goalkeeper with Cruyff-like precision and delicacy, and my suspicion that this was a world gone mad was confirmed. I was sitting with the Enemy, Arsenal thought they were Holland, and if I had looked carefully, I would surely have seen pigs floating serenely over the Clock End.

A couple of months later we got thumped 5–0 at Derby and immediately reverted to our old, dogged and reassuring ways; the fact that the experiment had been so brief seemed to reinforce the impression that it had all been a particularly ingenious metaphor, invented for my benefit and abandoned the moment I had understood it.

A MATTER OF LIFE AND DEATH

CRYSTAL PALACE v LIVERPOOL
October 1972

I have learned things from the game. Much of my knowledge of locations in Britain and Europe comes not from school, but from away games or the sports pages, and hooliganism has given me both a taste for sociology and a degree of fieldwork experience. I have learned the value of investing time and emotion in things I cannot control, and of belonging to a community whose aspirations I share completely and uncritically. And on my first visit to Selhurst Park with my friend Frog, I saw a dead body, still my first, and learned a little bit about, well, life itself.

As we walked towards the railway station after the game, we saw the man lying in the road, partially covered by a raincoat, a purple-and-blue Palace scarf around his neck. Another younger man was crouched over him, and the two of us crossed the road and went to have a look.

'Is he all right?' Frog asked.

The man shook his head. 'No. Dead. I was just walking behind him and he keeled over.'

He looked dead. He was grey and, as far as we were concerned, unimaginably motionless. We were impressed.

Frog sensed a story that would interest not only the fourth year but much of the fifth as well. 'Who done him? Scousers?'

At this point the man lost patience. 'No. He's had a heart attack, you little prats. Now fuck off.'

And we did, and that was the end of the incident. But it has never been very far away from me since then, my one and only image of death; it is an image which instructs. The Palace scarf, a banal and homely detail; the timing (after the game, but mid-season), the stranger paying distressed but ultimately detached attention. And, of course, the two idiotic teenagers gawping at a tiny tragedy with unembarrassed fascination, even glee.

It worries me, the prospect of dying in mid-season like that, but of course, in all probability I *will* die sometime between August and May. We have the naive expectation that when we go, we won't be leaving any loose ends lying around: we will have made our peace with our children, left them happy and stable, and we will have achieved more or less everything that we wanted to with our lives. It's all nonsense, of course, and football fans contemplating their own mortality know that it is all nonsense. There will be hundreds of loose ends. Maybe we will die the night before our team appears at Wembley, or the day after a European Cup first-leg match, or in the middle of a promotion campaign or a relegation battle, and there is every prospect, according to many theories about the afterlife, that we will not be able to discover the eventual outcome. The whole *point* about death, metaphorically speaking, is that it is almost bound to occur before the major trophies have been awarded. The man lying on the pavement would not, as Frog observed on the way home, discover whether Palace stayed up or not that season; nor that they would continue to bob up and down between the divisions over the next twenty years, that they would change their colours half a dozen times, that they would eventually reach their first FA Cup Final, or that they would end up running around with the legend 'VIRGIN' plastered all over their shirts. That's life, though.

I do not wish to die in mid-season but, on the other hand, I am one of those who would, I think, be happy to have my ashes scattered over the Highbury pitch (although I understand that there are restrictions: too many widows contact the club, and there are fears that the turf would not respond kindly to the contents of urn after urn). It would be nice to think that I could hang around inside the stadium in some form, and watch the first team one Saturday, the reserves the next; I would like to feel that my children and grandchildren will be Arsenal fans and that I could watch with them. It doesn't seem a bad way to spend eternity, and certainly I'd rather be sprinkled over the East Stand than dumped into the Atlantic or left up some mountain.

I don't want to die immediately after a game, though (like Jock Stein, who died seconds after Scotland beat Wales to qualify for the World Cup, or like a friend's father, who died at a Celtic–Rangers game a few years ago). It seems *excessive*, somehow, as if football were the only fitting context for the death of a football fan. (And I'm not talking about the deaths of Heysel or Hillsborough or Ibrox or Bradford here, of course; those were tragedies of a different order altogether.) I don't want to be remembered with a shake of the head and a fond smile intended to imply that this is the way I would have chosen to go out if I could; give me gravitas over cheap congruence any time.

So let's get this straight. I don't want to peg out in Gillespie Road after a game because I might be remembered as a crank; and yet, crankily, I want to float around Highbury as a ghost watching reserve games for the rest of time. And in a sense these two desires – at first glance incomprehensibly inconsistent, I would imagine, to those without equivalent fixations – characterise obsessives and encapsulate their dilemma. We hate being patronised (there are some people who know me *only* as a monomaniac, and who ask me slowly and patiently, in words of one syllable, about Arsenal results before turning to someone else to talk about life – as if being a football fan precludes the possibility of possessing a family or a job or an opinion on alternative medicine), but our lunacy makes condescension almost inevitable. I know all this, and I *still* want to lumber my son with the names Liam Charles George Michael Thomas. I get what I deserve, I guess.

GRADUATION DAY

ARSENAL v IPSWICH
14.10.72

By the time I was fifteen I was no longer quite so small – indeed, there were now a number of boys in my year smaller than me. This was a relief in most ways, but brought with it a problem that gnawed at me constantly for some weeks: I could no longer, if I was to maintain any self-respect, postpone my transfer from the Schoolboys' Enclosure to the North Bank, the covered terrace behind one of the goals where Arsenal's most vocal supporters stood.

I had plotted my début with great care. For much of that season I'd spent more time staring at the alarming lump of noisy humanity to my right than straight ahead at the pitch; I was trying to work out exactly where I would make for and what parts I should avoid. The Ipswich game looked like my ideal opportunity: Ipswich fans were hardly likely to attempt to 'take' the North Bank, and the crowd wouldn't be much more than thirty thousand, about half the capacity. I was ready to leave the Schoolboys behind.

It is difficult to recall now exactly what concerned me. After all, when I travelled up to Derby or Villa I usually stood in the away end, which was simply a displaced North Bank, so it couldn't have been the prospect of trouble (always more likely at away games or at the other end of Arsenal's ground), or fear of the type of people I would be standing with. I rather suspect that I was frightened of being revealed, as I had been at Reading earlier on that year. Supposing the people around me found out I wasn't from Islington? Supposing I was exposed as a suburban interloper who went to a grammar school and was studying for Latin O-level? In the end I had to take the risk. If, as seemed probable, I provoked the entire terrace into a deafening chant of 'HORNBY IS A WANKER' or 'WE ALL HATE SWOTS, HATE SWOTS, HATE SWOTS' to the tune of the 'Dambusters' March', then so be it; at least I would have tried.

I arrived on the terrace shortly after two o'clock. It seemed enormous, bigger even than it had looked from my usual position: a vast expanse of steep grey steps over which had been sprinkled a complex even pattern of metal crush barriers. The position I had decided on – dead centre, half-way down – indicated both a certain amount of gung-ho (the noise at most football grounds begins in the centre of the home terrace and radiates outwards; the sides and the seats only join in at moments of high excitement) and a degree of caution (centre back was not a place for the faint-hearted débutant).

Rites of passage are more commonly found in literary novels, or mainstream Hollywood films with pretensions, than they are in real life, particularly in real suburban life. All the things that were supposed to change me – first kiss, loss of virginity, first fight, first drink, first drugs – just seemed to *happen*; there was no will involved, and certainly no painful decision-making process (peer-group pressure, bad temper and the comparative sexual precocity of the female teenager made all the decisions for me), and perhaps as a consequence I emerged from all these formative experiences completely unformed. Walking through the North Bank turnstile was the only time I can remember consciously grasping a nettle until I was in my mid-twenties (really – this is not the place to go through all the nettles I should have grasped by then, but I know I didn't bother): I wanted to do it, but at the same time I was, pathetically, a little afraid. My only rite of passage, then, involved standing on one piece of concrete as opposed to another; but the fact that I had made myself do something that I only half-wanted to do, and that it all turned out OK . . . this was important to me.

An hour before the kick-off the view from my spot was spectacular. No corner of the pitch was obscured, and even the far goal, which I had imagined would look tiny, was quite clear. By three o'clock, however, I could see a little strip of the pitch, a narrow grass tunnel running from the near penalty area to the touchline at the far end. The corner flags had disappeared entirely, and the goal beneath me was visible only if I jumped at the crucial moment. Whenever there was a near-miss at our end, the crowd tumbled forward; I was forced seven or eight steps down the terracing and, when I looked round, the carrier bag containing my programme and my *Daily Express* that I had placed at my feet seemed miles away, like a towel on the beach when you're in a rough sea. I did see the one goal of the game, a George Graham volley from about twenty-five yards, but only because it was scored at the Clock End.

I loved it there, of course. I loved the different *categories* of noise: the formal, ritual noise when the players emerged (each player's name called in turn, starting with the favourite, until he responded with a wave); the spontaneous shapeless roar when something exciting was happening on the pitch; the renewed vigour of the chanting after a goal or a sustained period of attacking. (And even here, among younger, less alien-ated men, that football grumble when things were going badly.) After my initial alarm I grew to love the movement, the way I was thrown towards the pitch and sucked back again. And I loved the anonymity: I was not, after all, going to be found out. I stayed for the next seventeen years.

There is no North Bank now. The Taylor Report recommended that, post-Hillsborough, football stadia should become all-seater, and the football clubs have all decided to act on that recommendation. In March 1973, I was among a crowd of sixty-three thousand at Highbury for an FA Cup replay against Chelsea; crowds of that size are no longer possible, at Highbury or in any other English stadium apart from Wembley. Even in 1988, the year before Hillsborough, Arsenal had two crowds of fifty-five thousand in the same week, and the second of them, the Littlewoods Cup semi-final against Everton, now looks like the last of the sort of game that comes to represent the football experience in the memory: floodlights, driving rain and an enormous, rolling roar throughout the match. So, yes, of course it is sad; football crowds may yet be able to create a new environment that electrifies, but they will never be able to recreate the old one which required vast numbers and a context in which those numbers could form themselves into one huge reactive body.

Even sadder, though, is the way that Arsenal have chosen to redevelop the stadium. It cost me 25p to watch the Ipswich match; the Arsenal Bond scheme means that from September 1993 entry to the North Bank will cost a minimum £1100 *plus the price of a ticket*, and, even allowing for inflation, that sounds a bit steep to me. A debenture plan makes sound financial sense for the club, but it is inconceivable that football at Highbury will ever be the same again.

The big clubs seem to have tired of their fan-base, and in a way who can blame them? Young working-class and lower-middle-class males bring with them a complicated and occasionally distressing set of problems; directors and chairmen might argue that they had their chance and blew it, and that middle-class families – the new target audience – will not only behave themselves, but pay much more to do so.

This argument ignores central questions about responsibility, fairness, and whether football clubs have a role to play in the local community. But even without these problems, it seems to me that there is a fatal flaw in the reasoning. Part of the pleasure to be had in large football stadia is a mixture of the vicarious and the parasitical, because unless one stands on the North Bank, or the Kop, or the Stretford End, then one is relying on others to provide the atmosphere; and atmosphere is one of the crucial ingredients of the football experience. These huge ends are as vital to the clubs as their players, not only because their inhabitants are vocal in their support, not just because they provide clubs with large sums of money (although these are not unimportant factors) *but because without them nobody else would bother coming*.

Arsenal and Manchester United and the rest are under the impression that people pay to watch Paul Merson and Ryan Giggs, and of course they do. But many of them – the people in the twenty pound seats, and the guys in the executive boxes – also pay to watch people watching Paul Merson (or to listen to people shouting at him). Who would buy an executive box if the stadium were filled with executives? The club sold the boxes on the understanding that the atmosphere came free, and so the North Bank generated as much income as any of the players ever did. Who'll make the noise now? Will the suburban middle-class kids and their mums and dads still come if they have to generate it themselves? Or will they feel that they have been conned? Because in effect the clubs have sold them tickets to a show in which the principal attraction has been moved to make room for them.

One more thing about the kind of audience that football has decided it wants: the clubs have got to make sure that they're good, that there aren't any lean years, because the new crowd won't tolerate failure. These are not the sort of people who will come to watch you play Wimbledon in March when you're eleventh in the First Division and out of all the Cup competitions. Why should they? They've got plenty of other things to do. So, Arsenal . . . no more seventeen-year losing streaks, like the one between 1953 and 1970, right? No flirting with relegation, like in 1975 and 1976, or the odd half-decade where you don't even get to a final, like we had between 1981 and 1987. We mug punters put up with that, and at least twenty thousand of us would turn up no matter how bad you were (and sometimes you were very, very bad indeed); but this new lot . . . I'm not so sure.

THE WHOLE PACKAGE

ARSENAL v COVENTRY
4.11.72

The only trouble with the North Bank was that I bought the whole package. In the second half of my third game there (the middle one against Manchester City was memorable only because our new signing Jeff Blockley, an incompetent to rival Ian Ure, pushed a City corner against the underside of the bar with his hands, the ball bounced down behind the line and the referee wouldn't give them the penalty or the goal – how we laughed!), Coventry City's Tommy Hutchison scored a stunning solo goal. He picked the ball up about forty yards out on the left wing, left a trail of Arsenal defenders in his wake, and curled the ball round Geoff Barnett as he came out right into the far corner. On the North Bank there was a split second of silence as we watched the Coventry fans cavorting around on the Clock End like dolphins, and then came the fierce, unanimous and heartfelt chant, 'You're going to get your fucking heads kicked in.'

I had heard it before, obviously. For a good fifteen years it was the formal response to any goal scored by any away team at any football ground in the country (variations at Highbury were 'You're going home in a London ambulance.' 'We'll see you all outside.' and 'Clock End, do your job.' (the Arsenal supporters at the Clock End being nearer to the opposing fans, and thus charged with the responsibility of vengeance). The only difference on this occasion was that I roared along with the imprecation for the first time. I was as outraged by the goal, as offended and as stricken, as anyone on the terrace; it was fortunate that there was an entire football pitch between me and the Coventry fans, or, or . . . or I would have done such things, I knew not what they were, but they would have been the terror of N5.

In many ways, of course, this was funny, in the way that the vast majority of teenage hooligan pretensions are funny, and yet even now I find it difficult to laugh at myself: half my life ago, and I'm still embarrassed. I like to think that there was none of me, the adult man, in that furious fifteen-year-old, but I suspect that this is over-optimistic. A lot of the fifteen-year-old remains, inevitably (as it does in millions of men), which accounts for some of the embarrassment; the rest of it stems from the recognition of the adult in the boy. Either way, it's bad news.

I did learn, in the end. I learned that my threatening anybody was preposterous – I might just as well have promised the Coventry fans to bear their children – and that in any case violence and its attendant culture is uncool (none of the women I have ever wanted to sleep with would have been particularly impressed with me that afternoon). The big lesson, though, the one that tells you football is only a game and that if your team loses there's no need to go berserk . . . I like to think I've learned that one. But I can still feel it in me, sometimes, at away games when we're surrounded by opposing fans and the referee's giving us nothing and we're hanging on and hanging on and then Adams slips and their centre-forward's in and then there's this terrible needling bellow from all around you . . . Then I'm back to remembering just two of the three lessons, which is enough in some ways but not enough in others.

Masculinity has somehow acquired a more specific, less abstract meaning than femininity. Many people seem to regard femininity as a quality; but according to a large number of both men and women, masculinity is a shared set of assumptions and values that men can either accept or reject. You like football? Then you also like soul music, beer, thumping people, grabbing ladies' breasts, and money. You're a rugby or a cricket man? You like Dire Straits or Mozart, wine, pinching ladies' bottoms and money. You don't fit into either camp? *Macho, nein danke?* In which case it must follow that you're a pacifist vegetarian, studiously oblivious to the charms of Michelle Pfeiffer, who thinks that only leering wideboys listen to Luther Vandross.

It's easy to forget that we can pick and choose. Theoretically it is possible to like football, soul music and beer, for example, but to abhor breast-grabbing and bottom-pinching (or, one has to concede, vice versa); one can admire Muriel Spark *and* Bryan Robson. Interestingly it is men who seem to be more aware than women of the opportunities for mix 'n' match: a feminist colleague of mine literally refused to believe that I watched Arsenal, a disbelief that apparently had its roots in the fact that we had once had a conversation about a feminist novel. How could I possibly have read the book *and* have been to Highbury? Tell a thinking woman that you like football and you're in for a pretty sobering glimpse of the female conception of the male.

And yet I have to accept that my spiteful fury during the Coventry game was the logical conclusion to what had begun four years before. At fifteen I was not capable of picking and choosing, nor of recognising that this culture was not necessarily discrete. If I wanted to spend Saturdays at Highbury watching football, then I also had to wave a spear with as much venom as I could muster. If, as seems probable given my sporadically fatherless state, part of my obsession with Arsenal was that it gave me a quick way to fill a previously empty trolley in the Masculinity Supermarket, then it is perhaps understandable if I didn't sort out until later on what was rubbish and what was worth keeping. I just threw in everything I saw, and stupid, blind, violent rage was certainly in my field of vision.

I was lucky (and it *was* luck, I can take no credit for it) that I nauseated myself pretty quickly; lucky most of all that the women I fancied, and the men I wanted to befriend (at this stage those verbs belonged exactly where I have placed them), would have had nothing to do with me if I hadn't. If I'd met the kind of girl who accepted or even encouraged masculine belligerence then I might not have had to bother. (What was that anti-Vietnam slogan? 'Women say yes to men who say no'?) But there are football fans, thousands of them, who have neither the need nor the desire to get a perspective on their own aggression. I worry for them and I despise them and I'm frightened of them; and some of them, grown men in their mid-thirties with kids, are too old now to go around threatening to kick heads, but they do anyway.

CAROL BLACKBURN

ARSENAL v DERBY
31.3.73

At this point I feel that I have to defend the accuracy of my memory, and perhaps that of all football fans. I have never kept a football diary, and I have forgotten hundreds and hundreds of games entirely; but I have measured out my life in Arsenal fixtures, and any event of any significance has a footballing shadow. The first time I was best man at a wedding? We lost 1–0 to Spurs in the FA Cup third round, and I listened to the account of Pat Jennings' tragic mistake in a windy Cornish car park. When did my first real love affair end? The day after a disappointing 2–2 draw with Coventry in 1981. That these events are commemorated is perhaps understandable, but what I cannot explain is why I remember some of the other stuff.

My sister, for example, recalls coming to Highbury twice, but knows no more than that; I know that she saw a 1–0 win against Birmingham in 1973 (a Ray Kennedy goal, on the afternoon that Liam Brady made his début) and a 2–0 win against Stoke in 1980 (Hollins and Sansom). My half-brother first came in January 1973 to see a 2–2 cup-tie against Leicester, but how come it is I rather than he who knows this? Why, when somebody tells me that he or she came to Highbury in 1976 to see a 5–2 game against Newcastle, do I feel compelled to tell them that the score was actually 5–3? Why can't I smile politely and agree that, yes, that was a great game?

I know how annoying we are, how cranky we must seem, but there is nothing much we can do about it now. (My father is much the same about Bournemouth football and Hampshire cricket in the 1940s.) These scores and scorers and occasions are of a piece: Pat's slip against Tottenham was not, of course, as important as Steve's wedding, but to me the two events have now become intrinsic and complementary parts of some new and different whole. An obsessive's memory is therefore, perhaps, more *creative* than that of an ordinary person; not in the sense that we make things up, but in the sense that we have baroque cinematic recall, full of jump-cuts and split-screen innovation. Who else but a football fan would use a fumble on a muddy field three hundred miles away to recall a wedding? Obsession requires a commendable mental agility.

It is this agility that allows me to date the arrival of my adolescence quite precisely: it arrived on Thursday, 30th November 1972, when Dad took me to London to buy some new clothes. I chose a pair of Oxford bags, a black polo-neck jumper, a black raincoat and a pair of black stack-heeled shoes; I remember the date because on the Saturday, when Arsenal played Leeds United at Highbury and beat them 2–1, I was wearing the entire outfit and feeling better inside myself than I had ever felt. I developed a new hairstyle (supposed to resemble Rod Stewart's, but I never found the courage for the spikes) to go with the clobber; and I developed an interest in girls to go with the haircut. One of these three innovations changed everything.

The Derby game was a really big one. After the indifferent spell that had brought about the end of the Total Football experiment, Arsenal had clawed their way back into the Championship race simply by being what they had always been – mean, fierce, competitive, hard to beat. If they won this game (against the reigning champions), then they stood a chance of going top of the First Division for the first time since the Double year; they were level on points with Liverpool, who were at home to Tottenham that afternoon. And looking at the programme for the Derby game, one is reminded of how extraordinarily balanced football fortunes are. If we had beaten Derby, there would have been every prospect of winning the Championship again; in fact, we lost it by three points, the very gap we allowed to open up that afternoon. The following Saturday we were playing Second Division Sunderland in the FA Cup semi-final, and we lost that too. The two defeats prompted Bertie Mee to break the whole team up, but he never got a new one together again, and three years later he was gone. If we'd won either of the games – and we should and could have won both – then the modern history of the club might have been entirely different.

So the course of the next decade was to be mapped out for Arsenal that afternoon, but I didn't care. The previous evening Carol Blackburn, my girlfriend of some three or four weeks (I can remember watching the TV highlights of the Chelsea–Arsenal FA Cup quarter-final at Stamford Bridge with her – she was a Chelsea fan – at a friend's house a fortnight before) had packed me in. She was, I thought, beautiful, with the long, straight, centre-parted hair and the melting doe eyes of Olivia Newton-John; her beauty had reduced me to nervous and miserable silence for much of the duration of our relationship, and it was no real surprise when she moved on to a boy called Daz, a year older than me and already, incredibly, at work.

I was unhappy during the game (I watched it from the Clock End, although I don't know why; perhaps I felt that the focused energy of the North Bank would be inappropriate), but not because of what was going on in front of me: for the first time in nearly five years of watching Arsenal events on the pitch seemed meaningless, and it hardly registered that we lost 1–0 and blew the chance to go top. I knew instinctively, as Arsenal searched for an equaliser in the later stages of the game, that we would not score, that even if the Derby centre-half caught the ball and threw it at the referee we would miss the resultant penalty. How could we possibly win or draw, with me feeling like this? Football as metaphor, again.

I regretted our defeat against Derby, of course, although not as much as I regretted being dumped by Carol Blackburn. But what I regretted most of all – and this regret came to me much, much later on – was the wedge that had been driven between me and the club. Between 1968 and 1973, Saturdays were the whole point of my entire week, and whatever happened at school or at home was just so much fluff, the adverts in between the two halves of the Big Match. In that time football *was* life, and I am not speaking metaphorically: I experienced the big things – the pain of loss (Wembley '68 and '72), joy (the Double year), thwarted ambition (the European Cup quarter-final against Ajax), love (Charlie George) and ennui (most Saturdays, really) – only at Highbury. I even made new friends, through the youth team or the transfer market. What Carol Blackburn did was to give me another sort of life, the real, untransposed kind in which things happened to me rather than to the club, and as we all know, that is a rum sort of a gift.

GOODBYE TO ALL THAT

ARSENAL v MANCHESTER CITY
4.10.75

I have a few programmes for the 73/74 season, so I must have
been to some of the games that year, but I can't remember any
of them. I know that the following season I didn't go at all, and
that the season after that, 75/76, I only went the once, with my
Uncle Brian and my young cousin Michael.

I stopped partly because Arsenal were dire: George, McLintock and Kennedy had gone, and were never properly replaced,
Radford and Armstrong were way past their best, Ball couldn't
be bothered, a couple of the young players (Brady, Stapleton
and O'Leary were all playing) were having understandable
difficulties settling in to a struggling side, and some of the new
purchases simply weren't up to the mark. (Terry Mancini,
for example, a bald, cheerful and uncomplicated centre-half,
seemed to have been bought for the Second Division promotion
campaign that was beginning to look inevitable.) In seven years
Highbury had once again become the unhappy home of a mori-
bund football team, just as it had been when I first fell in love
with it.

This time around, though, I didn't want to know (and neither
did a good ten thousand others). I'd seen it all before. What I
hadn't seen before were the high school and convent girls who
worked in the Maidenhead High Street branch of Boots at
weekends; and thus it was that some time in 1974, my after-
school clearing-up and restocking job (which I had taken on
only because I needed to find some football money) became an
after-school and Saturday job.

I was still at school in 1975, but only just. I took my A-levels
that summer, and scraped by in two of the three subjects; then,
with breathtaking cheek, I decided to stay on for an extra term
to study for the Cambridge entrance examinations – not, I
think, because I wanted to go to Cambridge, but because I

didn't want to go to university immediately, and yet neither did I want to travel around the world, or teach handicapped children, or work on a kibbutz, or do anything at all that might make me a more interesting person. So I worked a couple of days a week at Boots, went into school now and again, and hung out with the few people I knew who hadn't yet gone on to college.

I didn't miss football too much. I had swapped one group of friends for another during the sixth form: the football crowd who had got me through the first five years of secondary school, Frog, Larry aka Caz and the rest, had started to seem less interesting than the depressive and exquisitely laconic young men in my English set, and suddenly life was all drink and soft drugs and European literature and Van Morrison. My new group revolved around Henry, a newcomer to the school, who stood as a Raving Maoist in the school election (and won), took all his clothes off in pubs, and eventually ended up in some kind of asylum after stealing mailbags from the local railway station and throwing them up a tree. Kevin Keegan and his astonishing workrate seemed dull, perhaps understandably, by comparison. I watched football on TV, and two or three times went to see QPR in the season they nearly won the Championship with Stan Bowles, Gerry Francis, and the kind of swaggering football that had never really interested Arsenal. I was an intellectual now, and Brian Glanville's pieces in the *Sunday Times* had taught me that intellectuals were obliged to watch football for its art rather than its soul.

My mother has no brothers and sisters – all my relatives come from my father's side – and my parents' divorce isolated my mother and sister and me from the leafier branch of the family, partly through our own choice, partly through our geographical distance. It has been suggested to me that Arsenal substituted for an extended family during my teens, and though this is the kind of excuse I would like to make for myself, it is difficult even for me to explain how football could have performed the same function in my life as boisterous cousins, kindly aunts and avuncular uncles. There was a certain sort of symmetry, then, when my Uncle Brian rang to say that he was taking his Arsenal-loving thirteen-year-old to Highbury and to ask whether I would accompany them: maybe as football was ceasing to be a potent force in my life, the joys of extended family life were about to be revealed to me.

It was strange watching Michael, a younger version of myself, agonising for his team as they went 3–0 down and huffed their way back into the game (Arsenal lost 3–2 without ever really suggesting that they would get so much as a point). I could see the distraction in his face, and began to understand how football could mean so much to boys of that age: what else can we lose ourselves in, when books have started to become hard work and before girls have revealed themselves to be the focus that I had now discovered they were? As I sat there, I knew it was all over for me, the Highbury scene. I didn't need it any more. And of course it was sad, because these six or seven years had been very important to me, had saved my life in several ways; but it was time to move on, to fulfil my academic and romantic potential, to leave football to those with less sophisticated or less developed tastes. Maybe Michael would take over for a few years, before passing it all on to someone else. It was nice to think that it wouldn't disappear from the family altogether, and maybe one day I would come back, with my own boy.

I didn't mention it to my uncle or to Michael – I didn't want to patronise him by suggesting in any way that football fever was an illness that only afflicted children – but when we were making our way out of the ground I bade it a private and sentimental farewell. I'd read enough poetry to recognise a heightened moment when I saw one. My childhood was dying, cleanly and decently, and if you can't mourn a loss of that resonance properly, then what can you mourn? At eighteen, I had at last grown up. Adulthood could not accommodate the kind of obsession I had been living with, and if I had to sacrifice Terry Mancini and Peter Simpson so that I could understand Camus properly and sleep with lots of nervy, neurotic and rapacious art students, then so be it. Life was about to begin, so Arsenal had to go.

1976–1986

MY SECOND CHILDHOOD

ARSENAL v BRISTOL CITY
21.8.76

As it turned out, my coolness towards all things Arsenal had had nothing to do with rites of passage, or girls, or Jean-Paul Sartre, or Van Morrison, and quite a lot to do with the ineptitude of the Kidd/Stapleton strikeforce. When Bertie Mee resigned in 1976, and his replacement Terry Neill bought Malcolm Macdonald for £333,333 from Newcastle, my devotion mysteriously resurrected itself, and I was back at Highbury for the start of the new season, as stupidly optimistic for the club and as hungry to see a game as I had ever been in the early seventies, when my obsession had been at fever pitch. If I had been correct in assuming previously that my indifference marked the onset of maturity, then that maturity had lasted just ten months, and by the age of nineteen I was already into my second childhood.

Terry Neill was nobody's idea of a saviour, really. He had come directly from Tottenham, which didn't endear him to some of the Arsenal crowd, and it wasn't even as if he had done a great job there: he had only just avoided taking them into the Second Division (although they were destined for the drop anyway). But he was a new broom, at least, and there were some pretty cobwebbed corners in our team; judging from the size of the crowd for his first game in charge, I was not the only one who had been lured back by the promise of a new dawn.

In fact, Macdonald and Neill and a new era were only partly

responsible for my return to the fold. Over the previous few months I had managed to turn myself into a schoolboy again, and I had done it, paradoxically, by leaving school and getting a job. After my university entrance exams I went to work for a huge insurance company in the City; the idea, I think, was to take my fascination with London to some kind of conclusion by becoming a part of the place, but this proved harder to do than I had imagined. I couldn't afford to live there, so I commuted from home (my salary went on the train fares and drinks after work), and I didn't even get to meet that many Londoners (although as I was fixed on the notion that *real* Londoners were people who lived in Gillespie Road, Avenell Road or Highbury Hill, N5, they were always going to be elusive). My workmates were for the most part like me, young commuters from the Home Counties.

So instead of turning myself into a metropolitan adult, I ended up recreating my suburban adolescence. I was bored witless most of the time, just as I had been at school (the company was about to relocate to Bristol, and we were all woefully underemployed); we sat, scores of us, in rows of desks trying to look busy, while embittered supervisors, denied even the minor dignity of the tiny cubicles in which their bosses worked, watched us like hawks and reprimanded us when our timewasting became too conspicuous or noisy. It is in climates like this that football flourishes: I spent most of the long and lethally hot summer of 1976 talking about Charlie and the Double and Bobby Gould to a colleague, a dedicated and therefore somewhat wry fellow fan who was about to become a policeman just as I was about to become an undergraduate. Before very long I could feel some of my old enthusiasm beginning to re-exert its fierce grip.

Serious fans of the same club always see each other again somewhere – in a queue, or a chip shop, or a motorway service station toilet – and so it was inevitable that I would meet up with Kieran again. I saw him two years later, after the '78 Cup

Final: he was sitting on a wall outside Wembley waiting for some friends, his banner drooping miserably in the post-match gloom, and it wasn't the right time to tell him that if it hadn't been for our office conversations that summer, I probably wouldn't even have been there that afternoon, feeling as miserable as he looked.

But that's another story. After my first game back, against Bristol City, I went home feeling as though I'd been tricked. Despite the introduction of Malcolm Macdonald, whose imperious wave to the crowd before the game led one to suspect the worst, Arsenal seemed no better than they had been for the last couple of years; in fact, given that they lost 1–0 at home to a Bristol City side which had crept up from the Second Division to struggle for four years in the First, it could well be argued that they were a good deal worse. I sweated in the August sunshine, and I cursed, and I felt the old screaming frustration that I had been happily living without. Like alcoholics who feel strong enough to pour themselves just one small one, I had made a fatal mistake.

SUPERMAC

ARSENAL v EVERTON
18.9.76

On one of my videos (*George Graham's Greatest Ever Arsenal Team*, if anyone is interested), there is a perfect Malcolm Macdonald moment. Trevor Ross gets hold of the ball on the right, crosses before the Manchester United left-back can put a challenge in, Frank Stapleton leaps, nods and the ball trundles over the line and into the net. Why is this so quintessentially Supermac, given his lack of involvement in any part of the goal? Because there he is, making a desperate lunge for the ball before it crosses the line, apparently failing to make contact, and charging away to the right of the picture with his arms aloft, not to congratulate the goalscorer *but because he is staking a claim to the goal.* (There is an anxious little glance back over his shoulder when he realises that his team-mates seem un-interested in mobbing him.)

That Manchester United match is not the only example of his embarrassing penchant for claiming anything that came any-where near him. In the FA Cup semi-final against Orient the following season, the record books show that he scored twice. In fact, both shots would have gone off for throw-ins – that is to say, they were not travelling even roughly in the direction of the goal – had they not hit an Orient defender (the same one each time) and looped in a ridiculous arc over the goalkeeper and into the net. Such considerations were beneath Malcolm, however, who celebrated both goals as if he had run the length of the field and beaten every defender before thumping the ball into the bottom left-hand corner. He wasn't much of a one for self-irony.

During this game against Everton, which we won 3–1 (a result which led us all to believe, once more, that a corner had been turned and that Terry Neill was building a team capable of winning the League again), there was another gem. Mac-donald is in a chase with the centre-half, who gets a foot in, and lifts the ball agonisingly over his own advancing goalkeeper; but immediately Macdonald's arms are in the air, he is pounding towards us on the North Bank, he turns to acknowledge the joy of the rest of the team. Defenders are famously quick to disclaim an own goal if it is possible, but the Everton centre-half, staggered by his opponent's cheek, told the newspapers that our number nine hadn't got anywhere near the ball. Even so, Macdonald got the credit for it.

In truth, he didn't have much of a career at Arsenal. He retired with a serious knee injury after just three seasons with us, but in that last season he only played four times. He still managed to turn himself into a legend, though. He was a magnificent player, on his day, but there weren't too many of those at Highbury; his best spell was at Newcastle, a habitually poor team, but such was his ambition that he seems to have succeeded in muscling his way into the Arsenal Hall of Fame. (*Arsenal 1886–1986*, by Phil Soar and Martin Tyler, the definitive history of the club, features him prominently on the cover, whereas Wilson and Brady, Drake and James are nowhere to be seen.)

So why have we let him take over in this way? Why is a player who played less than a hundred games for Arsenal associated with the club more readily than others who played six or seven times that number? Macdonald was, if nothing else, a *glamorous* player, and we have never been a glamorous team; so at Highbury we pretend that he was more important than he really was, and we hope that when we put him on the cover of our glossy books, nobody will remember that he only played for us for two years, and that therefore we will be mistaken for Manchester United, or Tottenham, or Liverpool. Despite Arsenal's wealth and fame, we've never been in that mould – we have always been too grey, too suspicious of anyone with an ego – but we don't like to admit it. The Supermac myth is a confidence trick that the club plays on itself, and we are happy to indulge it.

A FOURTH DIVISION TOWN

CAMBRIDGE UNITED v DARLINGTON
29.1.77

I applied to Cambridge from the right place, at the right time. The university was actively looking for students who had been educated through the state system, and even my poor A-level results, my half-baked answers to the entrance examination and my hopelessly tongue-tied interview did not prevent me from being granted admission. At last my studiously dropped aitches were paying dividends, although not in the way that I had at one stage anticipated. They had not resulted in my acceptance on the North Bank, but they had resulted in my acceptance at Jesus College, Cambridge. It is surely only in our older universities that a Home Counties grammar school education carries with it some kind of street-cred.

It is true that most football fans do not have an Oxbridge degree (football fans are people, whatever the media would have us believe, and most people do not have an Oxbridge degree, either); but then, most football fans do not have a criminal record, or carry knives, or urinate in pockets, or get up to any of the things that they are all supposed to. In a book about football, the temptation to apologise (for Cambridge, and for not having left school at sixteen and gone on the dole, or down the pits, or into a detention centre) is overwhelming, but it would be entirely wrong to do so.

Whose game is it anyway? Some random phrases from Martin Amis's review of *Among the Thugs*, by Bill Buford: 'a love of ugliness'; 'pitbull eyes'; 'the complexion and body scent of a cheese-and-onion crisp'. These phrases are intended to build up a composite picture of the typical fan, and typical fans know this picture is wrong. I am aware that as far as my education and interests and occupation are concerned, I am hardly representative of a good many people on the terraces; but when it comes to my love for and knowledge of the game, the way I can and do talk about it whenever the opportunity presents itself, and my commitment to my team, I'm nothing out of the ordinary.

Football, famously, is the people's game, and as such is prey to all sorts of people who aren't, as it were, the people. Some like it because they are sentimental socialists; some because they went to public school, and regret doing so; some because their occupation – writer or broadcaster or advertising executive – has removed them far away from where they feel they belong, or where they have come from, and football seems to them a quick and painless way of getting back there. It is these people who seem to have the most need to portray football grounds as a bolt-hole for a festering, vicious underclass: after all, it is not in their best interests to tell the truth – that 'pitbull eyes' are few and far between, and often hidden behind specs, and that the stands are full of actors and publicity girls and teachers and accountants and doctors and nurses, as well as salt-of-the-earth working-class men in caps and loud-mouthed thugs. Without football's myriad demonologies, how are those who have been distanced from the modern world supposed to prove that they understand it?

'I would suggest that casting football supporters as "belching sub-humanity" makes it easier for us to be treated as such, and therefore easier for tragedies like Hillsborough to occur,' a wise man called Ed Horton wrote in the fanzine *When Saturday Comes* after reading Amis's review. 'Writers are welcome at football – the game does not have the literature it deserves. But snobs slumming it with "the lads" – there is nothing we need less.' Precisely. So the worst thing I can do for the game is offer atonement for, or deny, or excuse my education; Arsenal came long before Cambridge, and has stayed with me long after, and those three years make no difference to anything, as far as I can see.

In any case, when I arrived at college, it became clear that I was not alone: there were scores of us, boys from Nottingham and Newcastle and Essex, many of whom had been educated through the state system and welcomed by a college anxious to modulate its élitist image; and we all played football, and supported football teams, and within days we had all found each other, and it was like starting at grammar school all over again, except without the Soccer Star stickers.

I went up to Highbury from Maidenhead in the holidays, and travelled down from Cambridge for the big games, but I couldn't afford to do it very often – which is how I fell in love all over again, with Cambridge United. I hadn't intended to – the Us were only supposed to scratch the Saturday-afternoon itch, but they ended up competing for attention in a way that nobody else had managed before.

I was not being unfaithful to Arsenal, because the two teams did not inhabit the same universe. If the two objects of my adoration had ever run up against each other at a party, or a wedding, or another of those awkward social situations one tries to avoid whenever possible, they would have been confused: if he loves *us*, whatever does he see in *them*? Arsenal had Highbury and big stars and huge crowds and the whole weight of history on their back; Cambridge had a tiny, ramshackle little ground, the Abbey Stadium (their equivalent of the Clock End was the Allotments End, and occasionally, naughty visiting fans would nip round the back of it and hurl pensioners' cabbages over the wall), less than four thousand watching at most games, and no history at all – they had only been in the Football League for six years. And when they won a game, the tannoy would blast out 'I've Got a Lovely Bunch of Coconuts', an eccentric touch that nobody seemed to be able to explain. It was impossible not to feel a warm, protective fondness for them.

It only took a couple of games before their results started to matter to me a great deal. It helped that they were a first-class Fourth Division team – manager Ron Atkinson had them playing stylish, fast, ball-to-feet football which usually brought them three or four goals at home (they beat Darlington 4–0 on my first visit), and it helped that in goalkeeper Webster and full-back Batson there was an Arsenal connection. I'd seen Webster throw in two goals (from George Best) during one of his few games for Arsenal back in 1970; and Batson, one of the first black players in the Football League in the early seventies, had been converted from a poor midfield player to a classy full-back since his move from Highbury.

What I enjoyed most of all, however, was the way the players revealed themselves, their characters and their flaws, almost immediately. The modern First Division player is for the most part an anonymous young man: he and his colleagues have interchangeable physiques, similar skills, similar pace, similar temperaments. Life in the Fourth Division was different. Cambridge had fat players and thin players, young players and old players, fast players and slow players, players who were on their way out and players who were on their way up. Jim Hall, the centre-forward, looked and moved like a 45-year-old; his striking partner Alan Biley, who later played for Everton and Derby, had an absurd Rod Stewart haircut and a greyhound's pace; Steve Spriggs, the midfield dynamo, was small and squat, with little stubby legs. (To my horror I was repeatedly mistaken for him during my time in the city. Once a man pointed me out to his young son as I was leaning against a wall, smoking a Rothmans and eating a meat pie, some ten minutes before a game in which Spriggs was appearing – a misapprehension which says much for the expectations the people of Cambridge had for their team; and once, in a men's toilet in a local pub, I got into an absurd argument with someone who simply refused to accept that I was not who I said I wasn't.) Most memorable of all was Tom Finney, a sly, bellicose winger who, incredibly, was to go on to the 1982 World Cup finals with Northern Ireland, although he only ever sat on the bench, and whose dives and fouls were often followed by outrageous winks to the crowd.

I used to believe, although I don't now, that growing and growing up are analogous, that both are inevitable and uncontrollable processes. Now it seems to me that growing up is governed by the will, that one can *choose* to become an adult, but only at given moments. These moments come along fairly infrequently – during crises in relationships, for example, or when one has been given the chance to start afresh somewhere – and one can ignore them or seize them. At Cambridge I could have reinvented myself if I had been smart enough; I could have shed the little boy whose Arsenal fixation had helped him through a tricky patch in his childhood and early teens, and become somebody else completely, a swaggeringly confident and ambitious young man sure of his route through the world. But I didn't. For some reason, I hung on to my boyhood self for dear life, and I let him guide me through my undergraduate years; and thus football, not for the first or last time, and through no fault of its own, served both as a backbone and as a retardant.

And that was university, really. No Footlights, no writing for *Broadsheet* or *Stop Press*, no Blue, no Presidency of the Union, no student politics, no dining clubs, no scholarships or exhibitions, no nothing. I watched a couple of films a week, I stayed up late and drank beer, I met a lot of nice people whom I still see regularly, I bought and borrowed records by Graham Parker and Television and Patti Smith and Bruce Springsteen and the Clash, I attended one lecture in my entire first year, I played twice a week for the college second or third teams . . . and I waited for home games at the Abbey or cup-ties at Highbury. I managed, in fact, to ensure that any of the privileges a Cambridge education can confer on its beneficiaries would bypass me completely. In truth I was scared of the place, and football, my childhood comforter, my security blanket, was a way of coping with it all.

BOYS AND GIRLS

ARSENAL v LEICESTER CITY
2.4.77

I did something else in that year, apart from watch football, talk and listen to music: I fell stomach-clenchingly for a smart, pretty and vivacious girl from the teacher-training college. We cleared our desks (she had already attracted the attention of several other suitors in the first few weeks, and I had a girlfriend at home) and spent much of the next three or four years in each other's company.

She is a part of this story, I think, in several ways. For a start, she was the first girlfriend who ever came to Highbury (in the Easter holidays at the end of our second term). The early-season new-broom promise had long since disappeared; in fact, Arsenal had just beaten the club record for the longest losing streak in their history – they had managed to lose, in consecutive games, to Manchester City, Middlesbrough, West Ham, Everton, Ipswich, West Brom and QPR. She charmed the team, however, much as she had charmed me, and we scored three times in the first quarter of the game. Graham Rix got the first on his début and David O'Leary, who went on to score maybe another half a dozen times in the next decade, got two in the space of ten minutes. Once again Arsenal were thoughtful enough to behave so oddly that the match, and not just the occasion, would be memorable for me.

It was strange having her there. In a misguided notion of gallantry – I'm sure she would rather have stood – I insisted that we bought seats in the Lower West Stand; all I remember now is how she responded each time Arsenal scored. Everyone in the row stood up apart from her (in the seats, standing up to acclaim a goal is an involuntary action, like sneezing); three times I looked down to see her shaking with laughter. 'It's so *funny*,' she said by way of explanation, and I could see her point. It had really never occurred to me before that football was, indeed, a funny game, and that like most things which only work if one *believes*, the back view (and because she remained seated she had a back view, right down a line of mostly misshapen male bottoms) is preposterous, like the rear of a Hollywood film set.

*

Our relationship – the first serious, long-term, stay-the-night, meet-the-family, what-about-kids-one-day sort of thing for either of us – was in part all about discovering for the first time the mysteries of our *counterparts* in the opposite sex. I had had girlfriends before, of course; but she and I had similar backgrounds and similar pretensions, similar interests and attitudes. Our differences, which were enormous, arose mostly because of our genders; if I had been born a girl, she was the sort of girl, I realised and hoped, that I would have been. It was probably for this reason that I was so intrigued by her tastes and whims and fancies, and her belongings induced in me a fascination for girls' rooms that continued for as long as girls had rooms. (Now I am in my thirties they don't have rooms any more – they have flats or houses, and they are often shared with a man anyway. It is a sad loss.)

Her room helped me to understand that girls were much quirkier than boys, a realisation that stung me. She had a collection of Yevtushenko's poems (who the hell was Yevtushenko?) and unfathomable obsessions with Anne Boleyn and the Brontës; she liked all the sensitive singer/songwriters, and was familiar with the ideas of Germaine Greer; she knew a little about paintings and classical music, knowledge gleaned from somewhere outside the A-level syllabus. How had that happened? How come I had to rely on a couple of Chandler paperbacks and the first Ramones album to provide me with some kind of identity? Girls' rooms provided countless clues to their character and background and tastes; boys, by contrast, were as interchangeable and unformed as foetuses, and their rooms, apart from the odd Athena poster here and there (I had a Rod Stewart poster on my wall, which I liked to think was aggressively, authentically and self-consciously down-market) were as blank as the womb.

It is true to say that most of us were defined only by the number and extent of our interests. Some boys had more records than others, and some knew more about football; some were interested in cars, or rugby. We had passions instead of personalities, predictable and uninteresting passions at that, passions which could not reflect and illuminate us in the way that my girlfriend's did . . . and this is one of the most inexplicable differences between men and women.

I have met women who have loved football, and go to watch a number of games a season, but I have not yet met one who would make that Wednesday night trip to Plymouth. And I have met women who love music, and can tell their Mavis Staples from their Shirley Browns, but I have never met a woman with a huge and ever-expanding and neurotically alphabeticised record collection. They always seem to have lost their records, or to have relied on somebody else in the house – a boyfriend, a brother, a flatmate, usually a male – to have provided the physical details of their interests. Men cannot allow that to happen. (I am aware, sometimes, in my group of Arsenal-supporting friends, of an understated but noticeable jockeying: none of us likes to be told something about the club that we didn't know – an injury to one of the reserves, say, or an impending alteration to the shirt design, something crucial like that – by any of the others.) I am not saying that the anally retentive woman does not exist, but she is vastly outnumbered by her masculine equivalent; and while there are women with obsessions, they are usually, I think, obsessive about people, or the focus for their obsession changes frequently.

Remembering my late teens at college, when many of the boys were as colourless as tap water, it is tempting to believe that it all starts around that time, that men have had to develop their facility to store facts and records and football programmes to compensate for their lack of distinguishing wrinkles; but that doesn't explain how it is that one ordinary, bright teenager has already become more interesting than another ordinary, bright teenager, simply by virtue of her sex.

It is perhaps no wonder that my girlfriend wanted to come to Highbury: there wasn't really very much else of me (she'd listened to my Ramones album), or at least nothing that I had yet discovered and extracted. I did have things that were mine – my friends, my relationships with my mum and my dad and my sister, my music, my love for cinema, my sense of humour – but I couldn't see that they amounted to very much that was individual, not in the way that her things were individual; but my solitary and intense devotion to Arsenal, and its attendant necessities (my vowel-mangling was by now at a point of almost inoperable crisis) . . . well, at least it had an edge to it, and gave me a couple of features other than a nose, two eyes and a mouth.

JUST LIKE A WOMAN

CAMBRIDGE UNITED v EXETER CITY
29.4.78

My arrival in Cambridge provoked the two best seasons in United's short history. In my first year they won the Fourth Division by a mile; in my second, they found life a bit tougher in the Third, and had to wait until the final week of the season before clinching promotion. They had two games in a week at the Abbey: one on the Tuesday night against Wrexham, the best team in the division, which they won 1–0, and one on the Saturday against Exeter, which they needed to win to be sure of going up.

With twenty minutes to go, Exeter went into the lead, and my girlfriend (who together with her girlfriend and her girlfriend's boyfriend had wanted to experience at first hand the dizzy glory of promotion) promptly did what I had always presumed women were apt to do at moments of crisis: she fainted. Her girlfriend took her off to see the St John's Ambulancemen; I, meanwhile, did nothing, apart from pray for an equaliser, which came, followed minutes later by a winner. It was only after the players had popped the last champagne cork at the jubilant crowd that I started to feel bad about my earlier indifference.

I had recently read *The Female Eunuch*, a book which made a deep and lasting impression on me. And yet how was I supposed to get excited about the oppression of females if they couldn't be trusted to stay upright during the final minutes of a desperately close promotion campaign? And what was to be done about a male who was more concerned about being a goal down to Exeter City of the Third Division than he was about somebody he loved very much? It all looked hopeless.

Thirteen years later I am still ashamed of my unwillingness, my *inability*, to help, and the reason I feel ashamed is partly to do with the awareness that I haven't changed a bit. I don't want to look after anybody when I'm at a match; I am not *capable* of looking after anybody at a match. I am writing some nine hours before Arsenal play Benfica in the European Cup, the most important match at Highbury for years, and my partner will be with me: what happens if *she* keels over? Would I have the decency, the maturity, the common sense, to make sure that she was properly looked after? Or would I shove her limp body to one side, carry on screaming at the linesman, and hope that she is still breathing at the end of ninety minutes, always presuming, of course, that extra time and penalties are not required?

I know that these worries are prompted by the little boy in me, who is allowed to run riot when it comes to football: this little boy feels that women are *always* going to faint at football matches, that they are weak, that their presence at games will inevitably result in distraction and disaster, even though my present partner has been to Highbury probably forty or fifty times and has shown no signs of fainting whatsoever. (In fact it is I who have come closest to fainting on occasions, when the tension of the last five minutes of a cup-tie constricts my chest and forces all the blood out of my head, if that is biologically possible; and sometimes, when Arsenal score, I see stars, literally – well, little splodges of light, literally – which cannot be a sign of great physical robustness.) But then, that is what football has done to me. It has turned me into someone who would not help if my girlfriend went into labour at an impossible moment (I have often wondered about what would happen if I was due to become a father on an Arsenal Cup Final day); and for the duration of the games I am an eleven-year-old. When I described football as a retardant, I meant it.

WEMBLEY III – THE HORROR RETURNS

ARSENAL v IPSWICH
(at Wembley) 6.5.78

It is a truth universally acknowledged that ticket distribution for Cup Finals is a farce: the two clubs involved, as all supporters know, get less than half the tickets, which means that thirty or forty thousand people with no direct interest in the game get the other half. The Football Association's rationale is that the Cup Final is for everybody involved with football, not just the fans, and it's not a bad one: it is, I think, quite reasonable to invite referees and linesmen and amateur players and local league secretaries to the biggest day in football's year. There is more than one way to watch a game, after all, and on this sort of occasion enthusiastic neutrals have their place.

The only flaw in the system is that these enthusiastic neutrals, these unimpeachable servants of the game, invariably decide that their endeavours are best recompensed not by a trip to London to see the big game, but by a phone call to their local tout: a good 90 per cent of them just flog the tickets they are given, and these tickets eventually end up in the hands of the fans who were denied them in the first place. It is a ludicrous process, a typically scandalous slice of Football Association idiocy: everybody knows what is going to happen, and nobody does anything about it.

Dad got me a ticket for the Ipswich final via work contacts, but there were others available, even at university, because the Blues are customarily sent half a dozen. (The following year, when Arsenal were again in the Final, I ended up with two tickets. One was from my next-door-neighbour, who had associations with a very big club in the north-west of England, a club that has been in trouble before with the FA for its cavalier distribution of Cup Final tickets: he simply wrote to them and asked for one, and they sent it to him.) There were, no doubt, many more deserving recipients of a seat than I, people who had spent the season travelling the length of the country watching Arsenal rather than messing around at college, but I was a genuine fan of one of the Cup Final teams, at least, and as such more entitled than many who were there.

My companions for the afternoon were affable, welcoming middle-aged men in their late thirties and early forties who simply had no conception of the import of the afternoon for the rest of us. To them it was an afternoon out, a fun thing to do on a Saturday afternoon; if I were to meet them again, they would, I think, be unable to recall the score that afternoon, or the scorer (at half-time they talked office politics), and in a way I envied them their indifference. Perhaps there is an argument which says that Cup Final tickets are wasted on the fans, in the way that youth is wasted on the young; these men, who knew just enough about football to get them through the afternoon, actively enjoyed the occasion, its drama and its noise and its momentum, whereas I hated every minute of it, as I had hated every Cup Final involving Arsenal.

I had now been an Arsenal supporter for ten seasons – just under half my life. In only two of those ten seasons had Arsenal won trophies; they had reached finals, and failed horribly, in another two. But these triumphs and failures had all occurred in my first four years, and I had gone from the age of fifteen, when I was living one life, to the age of twenty-one, when

I was living a completely different one. Like gas lamps and horse-drawn carriages – or perhaps like Spirographs and Sekidens – Wembley and championships were beginning to seem as though they belonged to a previous world.

When we reached, and then won, the FA Cup semi-final in 1978, it felt as though the sun had come out after several years of November afternoons. Arsenal-haters will have forgotten, or will simply refuse to believe, that this Arsenal team was capable of playing delightful, even enthralling football: Rix and Brady, Stapleton and Macdonald, Sunderland and, best of all, for one season only, Alan Hudson . . . for three or four months it looked as if this was a team that could make us happy in all the ways in which it is possible to be made happy at football.

If I were writing a novel, Arsenal would win the '78 Cup Final. A win makes more sense rhythmically and thematically; another Wembley defeat at this point would stretch the reader's patience and sense of justice. The only excuses I can offer for my poor plotting are that Brady was patently unfit and should never have played, and Supermac, who had made some typical and unwise remarks in the press about what he was going to do to the Ipswich back four, was worse than useless. (He had made the same compound error, of boasting loudly and then failing to deliver, four years earlier, when he was playing for New-castle; some time after the Ipswich fiasco the *Guardian* printed a Cup trivia question: 'What is taken to the Cup Final every year but never used?' The answer they wanted was the ribbons for the losing team, which are never tied on to the handle of the Cup, but some smartass wrote in and suggested Malcolm Macdonald.) It was an overwhelmingly one-sided final, even though Ipswich didn't score until the second half; we never looked like getting the goal back, and lost 1–0.

So I had now lost three out of three at Wembley, and was convinced that I would never, ever see Arsenal running around Wembley with anything at all. Yet '78 is perhaps the least painful of the defeats, because I was with people who were not pained by it at all, not even the man with the red-and-white scarf (suspiciously clean, as if he had bought it outside the stadium). It is a strange paradox that while the grief of football fans (and it is real grief) is private – we each have an individual relationship with our clubs, and I think that we are secretly convinced that none of the other fans understands quite why we have been harder hit than anyone else – we are forced to mourn in public, surrounded by people whose hurt is expressed in forms different from our own.

Many fans express anger, against their own team or the supporters of the opponents – real, foul-mouthed fury that upsets and saddens me. I have never felt the desire to do that; I just want to be on my own to think, to wallow for a little while, and to recover the strength necessary to go back and start all over again. These men, the business types, were sympathetic but unconcerned. They offered me a drink and I declined, so they shook my hand and offered commiserations and I disappeared; to them, it really was only a game, and it probably did me good to spend time with people who behaved for all the world as if football were a diverting entertainment, like rugby or golf or cricket. It's not like that at all, of course, but just for an afternoon it was interesting and instructive to meet people who believed that it was.

SUGAR MICE AND BUZZCOCKS ALBUMS

CAMBRIDGE UNITED v ORIENT
4.11.78

What happened was, Chris Roberts bought a sugar mouse from Jack Reynolds ('The Rock King'), bit its head off, dropped it in the Newmarket Road before he could get started on the body, and it got run over by a car. And that afternoon Cambridge United, who had hitherto been finding life difficult in the Second Division (two wins all season, one home, one away), beat Orient 3–1, and a ritual was born. Before each home game we all of us trooped into the sweet shop, purchased our mice, walked outside, bit the head off as though we were removing the pin from a grenade, and tossed the torsos under the wheels of oncoming cars; Jack Reynolds would stand in the doorway watching us, shaking his head sorrowfully. United, thus protected, remained unbeaten at the Abbey for months.

I know that I am particularly stupid about rituals, and have been ever since I started going to football matches, and I know also that I am not alone. I can remember when I was young having to take with me to Highbury a piece of putty, or blu-tack, or some stupid thing, which I pulled on nervously all afternoon (I was a smoker even before I was old enough to smoke); I can also remember having to buy a programme from the same programme seller, and having to enter the stadium through the same turnstile.

There have been hundreds of similar bits of nonsense, all designed to guarantee victories for one or other of my two teams. During Arsenal's protracted and nerve-racking semi-final campaign against Liverpool in 1980, I turned the radio off half-way through the second half of the last game; Arsenal were winning 1–0, and as Liverpool had equalised in the last seconds of the previous game, I couldn't bear to hear it through to the end. I played a Buzzcocks album instead (the *Singles – Going Steady* compilation album), knowing that side one would take me through to the final whistle. We won the match, and I insisted that my flatmate, who worked in a record store, should play the album at twenty past four on Cup Final afternoon, although it did no good. (I have my suspicions that he might have forgotten.)

I have tried 'smoking' goals in (Arsenal once scored as three of us were lighting cigarettes), and eating cheese-and-onion crisps at a certain point in the first half; I have tried not setting the video for live games (the team seems to have suffered badly in the past when I have taped the matches in order to study the performance when I get home); I have tried lucky socks, and lucky shirts, and lucky hats, and lucky friends, and have attempted to exclude others who I feel bring with them nothing but trouble for the team.

Nothing (apart from the sugar mice) has ever been any good. But what else can we do when we're so *weak*? We invest hours each day, months each year, years each lifetime in something over which we have no control; is it any wonder then, that we are reduced to creating ingenious but bizarre liturgies designed to give us the illusion that we are powerful after all, just as every other primitive community has done when faced with a deep and apparently impenetrable mystery?

WEMBLEY IV – THE CATHARSIS

ARSENAL v MANCHESTER UNITED
(at Wembley) 12.5.79

I had no ambitions for myself whatsoever before I was twenty-six or twenty-seven, when I decided that I could and would write for a living, packed my job in and waited around for publishers and/or Hollywood producers to call me up and ask me to do something for them sight unseen. Friends at college must have asked me what I intended to do with my life, particularly because by now I was in my final term; but the future still seemed to me as unimaginable and as uninteresting as it had when I was four or five, so I have no idea what I might have answered. I probably mumbled something about journalism or publishing (the aimless arts undergraduate's exact equivalent of train driving or astronautics), but privately I was beginning to suspect that as I had spent my three years unwisely, these careers would not be possible. I knew people who had spent their entire undergraduate lives writing for university newspapers who were not being offered jobs, so what chance did I stand? I decided that it would be better not to know, and therefore applied for nothing at all.

I may have had no ideas for myself, but I had big ideas for my football teams. Two of these dreams – Cambridge United's promotion from the Fourth to the Third, and then from the Third to the Second – had been realised already. But the third and most burning ambition, to see Arsenal win the FA Cup at Wembley (and maybe this was, after all, a personal ambition, in that my presence was an essential part of it), still remained unfulfilled.

The team had done remarkably well to return to the Cup Final for a second consecutive season. It took them five games to get past Third Division Sheffield Wednesday (the police have recently decided, in their community-serving way, that the beautiful and strange FA Cup tradition of the multi-game marathon should not be allowed to continue); they then had a tough away draw at Nottingham Forest, the European champions, and another tricky game at Southampton, won after a replay by two brilliant Alan Sunderland goals. The semi-final against Wolves was comparatively straightforward, despite Brady's absence through injury: two second-half goals, from Sunderland and Stapleton, and they were back at Wembley.

Exactly a decade after the Manchester United Cup Final, in May 1989, I was waiting to hear news about a script I had written at the same time as Arsenal's best chance of winning the Championship for eighteen years seemed to be disappearing fast. The script, a pilot for a projected sitcom, had got further than usual; there had been meetings with people from Channel 4, and great enthusiasm, and things looked good. But in despair after a bad result, a home defeat by Derby on the final Saturday of the season, I offered up my work (the acceptance of which would have rescued a career and a self-regard heading for oblivion) on some kind of personal sacrificial altar: if we win the

League, I won't mind the rejection slip. The rejection slip duly came, and hurt like hell for months; but the Championship came too, and now, two years later, when the disappointment has long gone but the thrill of Michael Thomas's goal still gives me goose pimples when I think about it, I know that the bargain I made was the right one.

In May 1979 the potential for trade-offs was extensive and complicated. On the Thursday before the Cup Final, Mrs Thatcher was attempting to win her first General Election; on the Thursday after, my finals began. Of the three events, the Cup Final, obviously, was the one that concerned me most, although I was also perturbed, just as obviously, by the prospect of Mrs Thatcher becoming Prime Minister. (Maybe in another, quieter week I would have found time and energy to fret about my examinations, but a mediocre degree was now an inevitability, and in any case at British universities it is as easy to graduate as it is to have a birthday: just hang around for a while and it will happen.) Yet the terrible truth is that I was willing to accept a Conservative government if it guaranteed an Arsenal Cup Final win; I could hardly have been expected to anticipate that Mrs Thatcher would go on to become the longest serving Prime Minister this century. (Would I have made the same bargain if I had known? Eleven years of Thatcherism for the FA Cup? Of course not. I wouldn't have settled for anything less than another Double.)

The fact that the Tories won comfortably on the Thursday didn't mean that I expected us to win comfortably on the Saturday. I knew that making bargains, like squeezing putty and wearing certain shirts, didn't guarantee success, and in any case the other finalists, Manchester United, were a proper team, not a roll-over-and-die, only-here-for-the-beer shower, like, well, like Ipswich, say, or Swindon. Manchester United were the kind of team who might well unsportingly ignore General Election deals simply by scoring loads of goals and thrashing us.

For most of the game, however, United played as if they knew what my deal had been and were more than happy to fulfil their side of it. Arsenal scored twice in the first half, the opening goal after twelve minutes (the first time in four games I had seen Arsenal take the lead at Wembley), the second goal right before half-time; the interval was a blissfully relaxed fifteen minutes of raucous celebration. Most of the second half passed by in the same way, until with five minutes to go Manchester United scored . . . and with two minutes to go, in traumatising and muddled slow motion, they scored again. We had thrown the game away, players and fans all knew that, and as I watched the United players cavort on the touchline at the far end I was left with the terrible feeling that I'd had as a child – that I hated Arsenal, that the club was a burden I could no longer carry but one that I would never, ever be able to throw off.

I was high up on the terraces with the other Arsenal fans, right behind the goal that Manchester United were defending; I sat down, too dizzy with pain and anger and frustration and self-pity to remain on my feet any longer. There were others who did the same, and behind me a pair of teenage girls were weeping silently, not in the hammy fashion of teenage girls at Bay City Rollers concerts, but in a way that suggested a deep and personal grief.

I was looking after a young American lad for the afternoon, a friend of the family, and his mild sympathy but obvious bafflement threw my distress into embarrassing relief: I *knew* that it was only a game, that worse things happened at sea, that people were starving in Africa, that there might be a nuclear holocaust within the next few months; I knew that the score was still 2–2, for heaven's sake, and that there was a chance that Arsenal could somehow find a way out of the mire (although I also knew that the tide had turned, and that the players were too demoralised to be able to win the game in extra time). But none of this knowledge could help me. I had been but five minutes away from fulfilling the only fully formed ambition I had ever consciously held since the age of eleven; and if people are allowed to grieve when they are passed over for promotion, or when they fail to win an Oscar, or when their novel is rejected by every publisher in London – and our culture allows them to do so, even though these people may only have dreamed these dreams for a couple of years, rather than the decade, the *half-lifetime*, that I had been dreaming mine – then I was bloody well entitled to sit down on a lump of concrete for two minutes and try to blink back tears.

And it really was for only two minutes. When the game restarted, Liam Brady took the ball deep into the United half (afterwards he said that he was knackered, and was only trying to prevent the loss of a third goal) and pushed it out wide to Rix. I was watching this, but not *seeing* it; even when Rix's cross came over and United's goalkeeper Gary Bailey missed it I wasn't paying much attention. But then Alan Sunderland got his foot to the ball, poked it in, right into the goal in front of us, and I was shouting not 'Yes' or 'Goal' or any of the other noises that customarily come to my throat at these times but just a noise, 'AAAARRRRGGGGHHHH', a noise born of utter joy and stunned disbelief, and suddenly there were people on the concrete terraces again, but they were rolling around on top of each other, bug-eyed and berserk. Brian, the American kid, looked at me, smiled politely and tried to find his hands amidst the mayhem below him so that he could raise them and clap with an enthusiasm I suspected he did not feel.

I floated through my finals as if I had been anaesthetised with a benign, idiocy-inducing drug. Some of my fellow-students, grey with sleeplessness and concern, were perplexed by my mood; others, the football fans, understood and were envious. (At college, just as at school, there were no other Arsenal fans.) I got my mediocre degree without any undue alarm; and some two months later, when I had come down from the Cup

Final win and the end-of-year celebrations, I began to face up to the fact that on the afternoon of 12th May I had achieved most of what I had ever wanted to achieve in my life, and that I had no idea what to do with the rest of it. I was twenty-two, and the future suddenly looked blank and scary.

FILLING A HOLE

ARSENAL v LIVERPOOL
1.5.80

It is hard for me, and for many of us, to think of years as being self-contained, with a beginning on 1st January and an ending 365 days later. I was going to say that 1980 was a torpid, blank, directionless year for me but that would be wrong; it was *79/80* that was these things. Football fans talk like that: our years, our units of time, run from August to May (June and July don't really happen, especially in years which end with an odd number and which therefore contain no World Cup or European Championship). Ask us for the best or the worst period in our lives and we will often answer with four figures – 66/67 for Manchester United fans, 67/68 for Manchester City fans, 69/70 for Everton fans, and so on – a silent slash in the middle of them the only concession to the calendar used elsewhere in the western world. We get drunk on New Year's Eve, just as everyone else does, but really it is after the Cup Final in May that our mental clock is wound back, and we indulge in all the vows and regrets and renewals that ordinary people allow themselves at the end of the conventional year.

Perhaps we should be given a day off work on Cup Final Eve, so that we can gather together and celebrate. We are, after all, a community within a community; and just as the Chinese have their New Year, when in London the streets around Leicester Square are closed off and the London Chinese

have a procession and eat traditional food, and the tourists
come to watch them, maybe there is a way in which we can
mark the passing of another season of dismal failure, dodgy
refereeing decisions, bad back-passes and terrible transfer deal-
ing. We could dress up in our horrible new away shirts, and
chant and sing; we could eat Wagon Wheels – the marshmallow
biscuit that only football fans eat, because it is only sold at
football grounds – and gangrenous hamburgers, and drink
warm and luridly orange fizz from a plastic bottle, a refreshment
manufactured especially for the occasion by a company called
something like Stavros of Edmonton. And we could get the
police to keep us standing in . . . oh, forget it. This terrible
litany has made me realise just how awful our lives are for these
nine months, and that when they are over I want to live every
day of the twelve short weeks available to me as if I were a
human being.

For me, 79/80 was a season when football – always hitherto
the backbone of life – provided the entire skeleton. For the
whole season I did nothing else apart from go to the pub,
work (in a garage outside Cambridge, because I could think of
nothing better to do), hang out with my girlfriend, whose course
lasted a year longer than mine, and wait for Saturdays and
Wednesdays. The extraordinary thing was that Arsenal in particular seemed to respond to my need for as much football as
possible: they played seventy games that season, twenty-eight
of them cup-ties of one kind or another. Every time I gave any
indication of becoming more listless than was good for me,
Arsenal obliged by providing another match.

By April 1980 I was sick to death of my job, and my inde-
cision, and myself. But just when it began to seem as though
the holes in my life were too big to be plugged, even by football,
Arsenal's anxiety to distract me became frenzied: between 9th
April and 1st May they played six semi-final games, four against
Liverpool in the FA Cup and two against Juventus in the Cup-
Winners Cup. Only one of these – the first leg of the Juventus

tie – was in London, and so everything revolved around the radio. All I can recall about that entire month is that I worked, and slept, and listened to Peter Jones and Bryon Butler live from Villa Park or Hillsborough or Highfield Road.

I'm not a good radio listener, but then very few fans are. The crowd are much quicker than the commentators – the roars and groans precede the descriptions of the action by several seconds – and my inability to see the pitch makes me much more nervous than I would be if I were at the game, or watching on TV. On the radio, every shot at your goal is heading for the top corner, every cross creates panic, every opposition free kick is right on the edge of the area; in those days before televised live games, when Radio 2 was my only link with Arsenal's distant cup exploits, I used to sit playing with the dial, switching between one station and another, desperate to know what was going on, but equally desperate not to have to hear. Radio football is football reduced to its lowest common denominator. Shorn of the game's aesthetic pleasures, or the comfort of a crowd that feels the same way as you, or the sense of security that you get when you see that your defenders and goalkeeper are more or less where they should be, all that is left is naked fear. The bleak, ghostly howl that used to afflict Radio 2 in the evenings was entirely apposite.

The last two of those four semi-finals against Liverpool nearly killed me. In the third match, Arsenal took the lead in the first minute and hung on to it for the next eighty-nine; I sat and stood and smoked and wandered around for the entirety of the second half, unable to read or talk or think, until Liverpool equalised in injury time. The equaliser was like the shot from a gun that had been aimed at my head for an hour, the sickening difference being that it didn't put an end to it all like a bullet would have done – on the contrary, it forced me to go through the whole thing again. In the fourth game, three days later, Arsenal took the lead once more, which was when I became so fearful that I had to turn the radio off and discovered the talismanic properties of the Buzzcocks. This time, Liverpool didn't come back, and Arsenal reached their third FA Cup Final in three years; the trouble was that I was almost too wrung-out and jumpy and nicotine-poisoned to care.

LIAM BRADY

ARSENAL v NOTTINGHAM FOREST
5.5.80

For a year I had lived with the possibility of Liam Brady's transfer to another club in the same way that, in the late fifties and early sixties, American teenagers had lived with the possibility of the impending Apocalypse. I knew it would happen, yet, even so, I allowed myself to hope; I fretted about it daily, read all the papers scrupulously for hints that he might sign a new contract, studied his onfield relationship with the other players at the club carefully in case it revealed signs of bonds too strong to be broken. I had never felt so intensely about an Arsenal player: for five years he was the focus of the team, and therefore the centre of a very important part of myself, and the consciousness of his rumoured desire to leave Arsenal was always with me, a small shadow on any X-ray of my well-being.

Most of this fixation was easy to explain. Brady was a midfield player, a passer, and Arsenal haven't really had one since he left. It might surprise those who have a rudimentary grasp of the rules of the game to learn that a First Division football team can try to play football without a player who can pass the ball, but it no longer surprises the rest of us: passing went out of fashion just after silk scarves and just before inflatable bananas. Managers, coaches and therefore players now favour alternative methods of moving the ball from one part of the field to another, the chief of which is a sort of wall of muscle strung across the half-way line in order to deflect the ball in the general direction of the forwards. Most, indeed all, football fans regret this. I think I can speak for all of us when I say that we used to *like* passing, that we felt that on the whole it was a good thing. It was nice to watch, football's prettiest accessory (a good player could pass to a team-mate we hadn't seen, or find an angle we wouldn't have thought of, so there was a pleasing geometry to it), but managers seemed to feel that it was a lot of trouble, and therefore stopped bothering to produce any players who could do it. There are still a couple of passers in England, but then, there are still a number of blacksmiths.

We overrate the seventies, most of us in our thirties. We look back on it as a golden age, and buy the old shirts, and watch old videos, and talk with awe and regret of Keegan and Toshack, Bell and Summerbee, Hector and Todd. We forget that the England team didn't even qualify for two World Cups, and we overlook the fact that most First Division teams contained at least one player – Storey at Arsenal, Smith at Liverpool, Harris at Chelsea – who simply wasn't very good at football at all. Commentators and journalists complain about the behaviour of today's professionals – Gazza's petulance, Fashanu's elbows, Arsenal's brawling – but they chuckle indulgently when they remember Lee and Hunter scrapping all the way back to the dressing rooms after they had been sent off, or Bremner and Keegan being banished for fighting in a *Charity Shield* game. Players in the seventies weren't as fast or as fit, and probably most of them weren't even as skilful; but every single side had someone who could pass the ball.

Liam Brady was one of the best two or three passers of the last twenty years, and this in itself was why he was revered by every single Arsenal fan, but for me there was more to it than that. I worshipped him because he was great, and I worshipped him because, in the parlance, if you cut him he would bleed

Arsenal (like Charlie George he was a product of the youth team); but there was a third thing, too. *He was intelligent.* This intelligence manifested itself primarily in his passing, which was incisive and imaginative and constantly surprising. But it showed off the pitch too: he was articulate, and drily funny, and engaged ('Come on David, put it away' he cried from the commentary box when his friend and old Arsenal colleague David O'Leary was about to take the decisive penalty for Ireland in the 1990 World Cup-tie against Romania); as I progressed through the academic strata, and more and more people seemed to make a distinction between football on the one hand and the life of the mind on the other, Brady seemed to provide a bridge between the two.

Of course, intelligence in a footballer is no bad thing, particularly in a midfield player, a playmaker, although this intelligence is not the same intelligence as that required to enjoy, say, a 'difficult' European novel. Paul Gascoigne has the footballing intelligence by the bucketload (and it is a dazzling intelligence, involving, among other skills, astonishing co-ordination and a lightning-fast exploitation of a situation that will change within a couple of seconds), yet his lack of even the most basic common sense is obvious and legendary. All the best footballers have some kind of wit about them: Lineker's anticipation, Shilton's positioning, Beckenbauer's understanding, are products of their brain rather than functions of simple athleticism. Yet it is the classical midfielder whose cerebral attributes receive the most attention, particularly from the sports writers on the quality papers and from the middle-class football fans.

This is not only because the sort of intelligence that Brady and his ilk possess is the most visible, in footballing terms, but because it is analogous to the sort of intelligence that is prized in middle-class culture. Look at the adjectives used to describe playmakers: *elegant, aware, subtle, sophisticated, cunning, visionary* . . . these are words that could equally well describe a poet, or a film-maker, or a painter. It is as if the truly gifted footballer is too good for his milieu, and must be placed on a different, higher plane.

Certainly there was an element of this attitude in my deification of Brady. Charlie George, the previous idol of the Arsenal North Bank, had never been *mine* in the way Liam was. Brady was different (although of course he wasn't, really – his background was pretty much the same as that of most footballers) because he was languid and mysterious, and though I possessed neither of these qualities, I felt that my education had equipped me to recognise them in others. 'A poet of the left foot,' my sister used to remark drily whenever I mentioned his name, which was often, but there was a truth behind her irony: for a time I wanted footballers to be as unlike themselves as possible and, though this was stupid, other people do it still. Pat Nevin, particularly in his Chelsea days, became a much better player when it was discovered that he knew about art and books and politics.

The Nottingham Forest game, a sleepy nil–nil draw on a sleepy, grey, Bank Holiday Monday, was Brady's last at Highbury; he had decided that his future lay abroad, in Italy, and he was gone for several years. I was there to see him off, and he did a slow, sad lap of honour with the rest of the team. Deep down I think I still hoped that he would change his mind, or that the club would eventually become aware of the irreparable damage it would do to itself if it allowed him to leave. Some said that money was at the heart of it, and that if Arsenal had stumped up more he would have stayed, but I preferred not to believe them. I preferred to believe that it was the promise of Italy itself, its culture and style, that had lured him away, and that the parochial pleasures of Hertfordshire or Essex or wherever he lived had inevitably begun to fill him with an existential ennui. What I knew most of all was that he didn't want to leave us all, that he was torn, that he loved us as much as we loved him and that one day he would come back.

*

Just seven months after losing Liam to Inter Milan I lost my girlfriend to another man, slap-bang in the middle of the first dismal post-Brady season. And though I knew which loss hurt the most – Liam's transfer induced regret and sadness, but not, thankfully, the insomnia and nausea and impossible, inconsolable bitterness of a twenty-three-year-old broken heart – I think that in some strange way she and Liam got muddled up in my mind. The two of them, Brady and the Lost Girl, haunted me for a long time, five or six years, maybe, so in a way it was predictable that one ghost should melt into the other. After Brady had gone Arsenal tried out a string of midfield players, some of them competent, some not, all of them doomed by the fact that they weren't the person they were trying to replace: between 1980 and 1986 Talbot, Rix, Hollins, Price, Gatting, Peter Nicholas, Robson, Petrovic, Charlie Nicholas, Davis, Williams and even centre-forward Paul Mariner all played in central midfield.

And I had a string of relationships over the next four or five years, some serious, some not . . . the parallels were endless. Brady's often-rumoured return (he played for four different clubs in his eight years in Italy, and before each transfer the English tabloids were full of unforgivably cruel stories about how Arsenal were on the verge of re-signing him) began to take on a shamanistic quality. I knew, of course, that the bouts of vicious, exhausting depression that afflicted me in the early-to-mid eighties were not caused either by Brady or the Lost Girl. They were to do with something else, something much more difficult to comprehend, and something that must have been in me for much longer than either of these two blameless people. But during these terrifying downs, I would think back to times when I had last felt happy, fulfilled, energetic, optimistic; and she and Brady were a part of those times. They weren't entirely responsible for them, but they were very much there during them, and that was enough to turn these two love affairs into the twin supporting pillars of a different, enchanted age.

Some five or six years after he had gone, Brady did come home, to play for Arsenal in Pat Jennings's testimonial game. It was a strange night. We were in even more need of him than ever (a graph of Arsenal's fortunes in the eighties would resemble a U-bend), and before the game I felt nervous, but not in the way that I usually felt nervous before big games – these were the nerves of a former suitor about to embark on an unavoidably painful but long-anticipated reunion. I hoped, I suppose, that an ecstatic and tearful reception would trigger something off in Brady, that he would realise that his absence made him, as well as us, less than whole somehow. But nothing of the kind happened. He played the game, waved at us and flew back to Italy the next morning, and the next time we saw him he was wearing a West Ham shirt and smashing the ball past our goalkeeper John Lukic from the edge of the area.

We never did replace him satisfactorily, but we found different people, with different qualities; it took me a long time to realise that this is as good a way of coping with loss as any.

ARSENALESQUE

WEST HAM v ARSENAL
10.5.80

Everyone knows the song that Millwall fans sing, to the tune of 'Sailing': 'No one likes us/No one likes us/No one likes us/We don't care.' In fact I have always felt that the song is a little melodramatic, and that if anyone should sing it, it is Arsenal.

Every Arsenal fan, the youngest and the oldest, is aware that no one likes us, and every day we hear that dislike reiterated. The average media-attuned football fan – someone who reads a sports page most days, watches TV whenever it is on, reads a fanzine or a football magazine – will come across a slighting reference to Arsenal maybe two or three times a week (about as often as he or she will hear a Lennon and McCartney song, I would guess). I have just finished watching *Saint and Greavsie*, during the course of which Jimmy Greaves thanked the Wrexham manager for 'delighting millions' with the Fourth Division team's victory over us in the FA Cup; the cover of a football magazine kicking around in the flat promises an article entitled 'Why does everyone hate Arsenal?' Last week there was an article in a national newspaper attacking our players for their lack of artistry; one of the players thus abused was eighteen years old and hadn't even played for the first team at the time.

We're boring, and lucky, and dirty, and petulant, and rich, and mean, and have been, as far as I can tell, since the 1930s. That was when the greatest football manager of all time, Herbert Chapman, introduced an extra defender and changed the way football was played, thus founding Arsenal's reputation for negative, unattractive football; yet successive Arsenal teams, notably the Double team in 1971, used an intimidatingly competent defence as a springboard for success. (Thirteen of our league games that year ended nil–nil or 1–0, and it is fair to say that none of them were pretty.) I would guess that 'Lucky Arsenal' was born out of 'Boring Arsenal', in that sixty years of 1–0 wins tend to test the credulity and patience of opposing fans.

West Ham, on the other hand, like Tottenham, are famous for their poetry and flair and commitment to good, fluent ('progressive', in the current argot, a word which for those of us in our thirties is distressingly reminiscent of Emerson, Lake and Palmer and King Crimson) football. Everyone has a soft spot for Peters and Moore and Hurst and Brooking and the West Ham 'Academy', just as everyone loathes and despises Storey and Talbot and Adams and the whole idea and purpose of Arsenal. No matter that the wild-eyed Martin Allen and the brutish Julian Dicks currently represent the Hammers, just as Van Den Hauwe and Fenwick and Edinburgh represent Spurs.

No matter that the gifted Merson and the dazzling Limpar play for Arsenal. No matter that in 1989 and 1992 we scored more goals than anyone else in the First Division. The Hammers and the Lilleywhites are the Keepers of the Flame, the Only Followers of the True Path; we are the Gunners, the Visigoths, with King Herod and the Sheriff of Nottingham as our twin centre-halves, their arms in the air appealing for offside.

West Ham, Arsenal's opponents in the 1980 Cup Final, were in the Second Division that season, and their lowly status made people drool over them even more. To the nation's delight, Arsenal lost. Saint Trevor of England scored the only goal and slew the odious monster, the Huns were repelled, children could sleep safely in their beds again. So what are we left with, us Arsenal fans, who for most of our lives have allowed ourselves to become identified with the villains? Nothing; and our sense of stoicism and grievance is almost thrilling.

The only things anyone remembers about the game now are Brooking's rare headed goal, and Willie Young's monstrous professional foul on Paul Allen, just as the youngest player to appear in a Cup Final was about to score one of the cutest and most romantic goals ever seen at Wembley. Standing on the Wembley terraces among the silent, embarrassed Arsenal fans, deafened by the boos that came from the West Ham end and the neutrals in the stadium, I was appalled by Young's cynicism.

But that night, watching the highlights on TV, I became aware that a part of me actually enjoyed the foul – not because it stopped Allen from scoring (the game was over, we'd lost, and that hardly mattered), but because it was so comically, parodically *Arsenalesque*. Who else but an Arsenal defender would have clattered a tiny seventeen-year-old member of the Academy? Motson or Davies, I can't remember which, was suitably disgusted and pompous about it all; to me, sick of hearing about how the goodies had put the baddies to flight, his righteousness sounded provocative. There was something about it that reminded me of Bill Grundy winding up the Sex

Pistols on television in 1976 and then expressing his outrage about their behaviour afterwards. Arsenal, the first of the true punk rockers: our centre-halves were fulfilling a public need for harmless pantomime deviancy long before Johnny Rotten came along.

LIFE AFTER FOOTBALL

ARSENAL v VALENCIA
14.5.80

Football teams are extraordinarily inventive in the ways they find to cause their supporters sorrow. They lead at Wembley and then throw it away; they go to the top of the First Division and then stop dead; they draw the difficult away game and lose the home replay; they beat Liverpool one week and lose to Scunthorpe the next; they seduce you, half-way through the season, into believing that they are promotion candidates and then go the other way . . . always, when you think you have anticipated the worst that can happen, they come up with something new.

Four days after losing one cup final, Arsenal lost another, to Valencia in the European Cup-Winners Cup, and the seventy-game season came to nothing. We outplayed the Spanish team, but couldn't score, and the game went to penalties; Brady and Rix missed theirs (some say that Rix was never the same again after the trauma of that night, and certainly he never recaptured his form of the late seventies, even though he went on to play for England), and that was that.

As far as I am aware, there isn't another English club that has lost two finals in a week, although in the years to come, when losing in a final was the most that Arsenal supporters dared to hope, I wondered why I felt quite so stricken. But that week also had a beneficially purgative side effect: after six solid weeks of semi-finals and finals, of listening to the radio and looking for Wembley tickets, the football clutter was gone and there was nothing with which to replace it. Finally I had to think about what I was going to do, rather than what the Arsenal manager was going to do. So I applied for teacher training college back in London, and vowed, not for the last time, that I would never allow football to replace life completely, no matter how many games Arsenal played in a year.

PART OF THE GAME

ARSENAL v SOUTHAMPTON
19.8.80

The first match of the season, so you're always that bit keener to get along. And over the summer there was an extraordinary bit of transfer business, when we bought Clive Allen for a million pounds, didn't like the look of him in a couple of pre-season friendlies, and swapped him for Kenny Sansom (a striker for a full-back; that's the Arsenal way) before he'd even played a game. So even though Liam had gone, and Southampton were not the most attractive of opponents, there was a forty-thousand-plus crowd.

Something went wrong – they hadn't opened enough turn-stiles, or the police had made a pig's ear of controlling the crowd flow, whatever – and there was a huge crush outside the North Bank entrances on the Avenell Road. I could pick both my legs up and remain pinioned and, at one stage, I had to put my arms in the air to give myself just that little bit more room and to stop my fists digging into my chest and stomach. It wasn't anything that special, really; fans have all been in situations where for a few moments things have looked bad. But I remember struggling for breath when I approached the front of the queue (I was so constricted that I couldn't fill my lungs properly) which means that it was a little bit worse than usual; when I finally got through the turnstile I sat down on a step for a while, gave myself time to recover, and I noticed that a lot of other people were doing the same.

But the thing was, I trusted the system: I knew that I could not be squashed to death, because that never happened at football matches. The Ibrox thing, well that was different, a freak combination of events; and in any case that was in Scotland during an Old Firm game, and everyone knows that these are especially problematic. No, you see, in England somebody, somewhere, knew what they were doing, and there was this *system*, which nobody ever explained to us, that prevented accidents of this kind. It might *seem* as though the authorities, the club and the police were pushing their luck on occasions, but that was because we didn't understand properly how they were organising things. In the mêlée in Avenell Road that night some people were laughing, making funny strangled faces as the air was pushed out of them; they were laughing because they were only feet away from unconcerned constables and mounted officers, and they knew that this proximity ensured their safety. How could you die when help was that close?

But I thought about that evening nine years later, on the afternoon of the Hillsborough disaster, and I thought about a lot of other afternoons and evenings too, when it seemed as though there were too many people in the ground, or the crowd had been unevenly distributed. It occurred to me that I could have died that night, and that on a few other occasions I have been much closer to death than I care to think about. There was no plan after all; they really had been riding their luck all that time.

MY BROTHER

ARSENAL v TOTTENHAM
30.8.80

There must be many fathers around the country who have experienced the cruellest, most crushing rejection of all: their children have ended up supporting the wrong team. When I contemplate parenthood, something I do more and more as my empathetic biological clock ticks nearer to midnight, I am aware that I am genuinely fearful of this kind of treachery. What would I do if my son or daughter decided, at the age of seven or eight, that Dad was a madman, and that Tottenham or West Ham or Manchester United were the team for them? How would I cope? Would I do the decent parental thing, accept that my days at Highbury were over, and buy a couple of season-tickets at White Hart Lane or Upton Park? Hell, no. I am myself too childish about Arsenal to defer to the whims of a child; I would explain to him or her that, although I would respect any decision of this kind, obviously if they wished to see their team then they would have to take themselves, with their own money, under their own steam. That should wake the little sod up.

I have more than once fantasised about Arsenal playing Tottenham in the Cup Final; in this fantasy my son, as rapt and tense and unhappy as I was when I first supported Arsenal, is a Spurs fan, and as we could not get tickets for Wembley we are watching the game at home on TV. In the last minute the old warhorse Kevin Campbell scores the winner . . . and I explode into a frenzy of joy, leaping around the sitting room, punching the air, *jeering at, jostling, tousling the head of my own traumatised child*. I fear that I am capable of this, and therefore the mature, self-knowing thing to do would be to see the vasectomist this afternoon. If my father had been a Swindon Town fan in 1969, on that awful afternoon at Wembley, and had reacted appropriately, we would not have spoken for twenty-two years.

I have already successfully negotiated one hurdle of this kind. In August 1980 my father and his family came back to England after more than ten years abroad in France and America. My half-brother Jonathan was thirteen, and crazy about soccer – partly due to my influence, partly because he had been in the States while the now-defunct North American Soccer League was at its zenith. And so, as quickly as possible, before he had a chance to work out that what was happening at White Hart Lane with Hoddle and Ardiles was infinitely more interesting than what was going on at Highbury with Price and Talbot, I took him to Arsenal.

He'd been once before, in 1973 when, as a six-year-old, he'd shivered uncontrollably through, and stared uncomprehendingly at, a third-round Cup match against Leicester, but he'd long forgotten that, so this early-season local derby was a fresh start. It wasn't a bad game, and certainly no indicator of the desperate times ahead: Pat Jennings, the Tottenham reject, kept out Crooks and Archibald for most of the first half, and then whichever of Spurs' terrible post-Pat keepers (Daines? Kendall?) let in a soft one before Stapleton finished them off with a wonderful lob.

But it wasn't the football that captivated Jonathan. It was the violence. All around us, people were fighting – on the North Bank, on the Clock End, in the Lower East Stand, in the Upper West. Every few minutes a huge gash would appear somewhere in the tightly woven fabric of heads on the terraces as the police separated warring factions, and my little brother was beside himself with excitement; he kept turning round to look at me, his face shining with a disbelieving glee. 'This is *incredible*,' he said, over and over again. I had no trouble with him after that: he came to the next game, a drab, quiet League Cup match against Swansea, and to most of the others that season. And now we have season-tickets together, and he drives me to away games, so it's all worked out OK.

Is he an Arsenal fan simply because for a long time he expected to see people attempt to kill each other? Or is it just because he looked up to me, as I know he did for a while, inexplicably, when he was younger, and therefore trusted me and my choice of team? Either way, I probably didn't have the right to inflict Willie Young and John Hawley and the Arsenal offside trap on him for the rest of his days, which is what I have ended up doing. So I feel responsible, but not regretful: if I had not been able to secure his allegiance to the cause, if he had decided to look for his footballing pain elsewhere, then our relationship would have been of an entirely different and possibly much cooler nature.

Here's a funny thing, though: Jonathan and I sit there, at Highbury, week after week, partly because of the distressing circumstances that led to his existence. My father left my mother in order to set up home with his mother, and my half-brother was born, and somehow all this turned me into an Arsenal fan; how odd, then, that my peculiar kink should have been transferred on to him, like a genetic flaw.

CLOWNS

ARSENAL v STOKE CITY
13.9.80

How many games like this did we watch, between Brady's departure and George Graham's arrival? The away team are struggling, unambitious also-rans; their manager (Ron Saunders, or Gordon Lee, or Graham Turner, or, in this case, Alan Durban) wants a draw at Highbury, and plays five defenders, four midfielders who used to be defenders, and a hopeless centre-forward standing on his own up front, ready to challenge for punts from the goalkeeper. Without Liam (and, after this season, without Frank Stapleton), Arsenal didn't have the wit or the imagination to break the opposition down, and maybe we won (with a couple of goals from near-post corners, say, or a deflected long-shot and a penalty), or maybe we drew (nil–nil), or maybe we lost 1–0 to a goal on the break, but it didn't really matter anyway. Arsenal were nowhere near good enough to win the League, yet were much too competent to go down; week after week, year after year, we turned up knowing full well that what we were about to witness would depress us profoundly.

This game against Stoke was very much in the mould – a goalless first half, and then, amid rising discontent, two late goals (ironically, given the towering height of Stoke's several centre-halves, headed in by the two smallest players on the pitch, Sansom and Hollins). Nobody, not even someone like me, would have been able to remember the game had it not been for the post-match press conference, when Alan Durban became angered by the hostility of the journalists towards his team and his tactics. 'If you want entertainment,' he snarled, 'go and watch clowns.'

It became one of the most famous football quotes of the decade. The quality papers in particular loved it for its effortless summary of modern football culture: here was conclusive proof that the game had gone to the dogs, that nobody cared about anything other than results any more, that the Corinthian spirit was dead, that hats were no longer thrown in the air. One could see their point. Why should football be different from every other branch of the leisure industry? You won't find too many Hollywood producers and West End theatre impresarios sneering at the public's desire to be diverted, so why should football managers get away with it?

Over the last few years, however, I have come to believe that Alan Durban was right. It was not his job to provide entertainment. It was his job to look after the interests of the

Stoke City fans, which means avoiding defeat away from home, keeping a struggling team in the First Division, and maybe winning a few cup games to alleviate the gloom. The Stoke fans would have been happy with a nil–nil draw, just as Arsenal fans are happy enough with nil–nil draws at Spurs or Liverpool or Manchester United; at home, we expect to beat more or less everyone, and we don't particularly care how it is done.

This commitment to results means, inevitably, that fans and journalists see games in a profoundly different way. In 1969 I saw George Best play, and score twice, for Manchester United at Highbury. The experience should have been profound, like seeing Nijinsky dance, or Maria Callas sing, and though I do talk about it in that way sometimes, to younger fans, or those who missed out on Best for other reasons, my fond account is essentially phoney: I hated that afternoon. Every time he got the ball he frightened me, and I wished then, as I suppose I wish now, that he had been injured. And I have seen Law and Charlton, Hoddle and Ardiles, Dalglish and Rush, Hurst and Peters, and the same thing happened: I have not enjoyed anything these players have ever done at Highbury (even though I have, on occasions, grudgingly admired things they have done against other teams). Gazza's free kick against Arsenal in the FA Cup semi-final at Wembley was simply astonishing, one of the most remarkable goals I have ever seen . . . but I wish with all my heart that I had not seen it, and that he had not scored it. Indeed, for the previous month I had been praying that Gascoigne would not be playing, which emphasises the separateness of football: who would buy an expensive ticket for the theatre and hope that the star of the show was indisposed?

Neutrals loved the glorious theatre of that Gascoigne moment, of course, but there were very few neutrals in the stadium. There were Arsenal fans, who were as horrified as I was, and Tottenham fans, who were just as thrilled with the second goal, a two-yard Gary Lineker tap-in after a scramble – in fact, they went even more berserk then, because at 2–0 after ten minutes Arsenal were dead and buried. So where is the relationship between the fan and entertainment, when the fan has such a problematic relationship with some of the game's greatest moments?

There *is* such a relationship, but it is far from straightforward. Tottenham, generally regarded as being the better footballing team, are not as well-supported as Arsenal, for example; and teams with a reputation for entertaining (West Ham, Chelsea, Norwich) don't get queues around the block. The way our team plays is beside the point for most of us, just as winning cups and championships is beside the point. Few of us have *chosen* our clubs, they have simply been presented to us; and so as they slip from the Second Division to the Third, or sell their best players, or buy players who you know can't play, or bash the ball for the seven hundredth time towards a nine foot centre-forward, we simply curse, go home, worry for a fortnight and then come back to suffer all over again.

For my own part, I am an Arsenal fan first and a football fan second (and, yes, again, I know all the jokes). I will never be able to enjoy the Gazza goal, and there are countless other similar moments. But I know what entertaining football is, and have loved the relatively few occasions when Arsenal have managed to produce it; and when other teams who are not in competition with Arsenal in any way play with flair and verve, then I can appreciate that, too. Like everyone, I have lamented long and loud the deficiencies of the English game, and the permanently depressing ugliness of the football that our national team plays, but really, deep down, this is pub-speak, and not much more. Complaining about boring football is a little like complaining about the sad ending of *King Lear*: it misses the point somehow, and this is what Alan Durban understood: that football is an alternative universe, as serious and as stressful as work, with the same worries and hopes and disappointments and occasional elations. I go to football for loads of reasons, but I don't go for entertainment, and when I look

135

around me on a Saturday and see those panicky, glum faces, I see that others feel the same. For the committed fan, entertaining football exists in the same way as those trees that fall in the middle of the jungle: you presume it happens, but you're not in a position to appreciate it. Sports journalists and armchair Corinthians are the Amazon Indians who know more than we do – but in another way they know much, much less.

SAME OLD ARSENAL

ARSENAL v BRIGHTON
1.11.80

A nothing game, between two nothing teams; I doubt if anyone else who was there remembers anything about it at all, unless it was their first time, or their last time, and doubtless my two companions for the afternoon, my dad and my half-brother, had forgotten the occasion by the following day. I recall it only because (only because!) it was the last time I was at Highbury with my dad, and though we might well go again sometime (he has made a couple of very small noises recently) the game now has an end-of-an-era aura about it.

The team were in much the same state as we had found them twelve years before, and I am sure that he must have complained about the cold, and Arsenal's ineptitude, and I am sure that I felt responsible for both, and wanted to apologise. And I wasn't much different in important ways, either. I was still as gloomy, somehow, as I had been when I was a boy, although because I was now aware of this gloom, understood what it was, it seemed darker and more threatening than it had ever done before. And, of course, the team were still in there, mixed in with it all, leading these lows from the front or trailing them from behind, I don't know which.

But other things had changed, permanently and for the

better, particularly in my dealings with my 'other' family. My stepmother had long ceased to be the Enemy – there was a real warmth in our relationship that neither of us could have anticipated years before – and there had never been any problem with the kids; but most important of all, my father and I, almost imperceptibly, had reached the stage where football was no longer the chief method of discourse between us. I lived with him and his family in London for the whole of the 80/81 season, my teacher training year; this was the first time we had had such an arrangement since I was a child, and it was fine. We had other stuff going on by now, as we have done ever since. The failure of his first marriage must still be mixed in there somehow, I suppose, but we have managed to fashion something that works well in its own way; and though there are still frustrations and difficulties, I don't think that these are ruinous, or that the problems we have are any worse than my friends have with their fathers – indeed, we get along much better than most.

I didn't think all that at the time, of course, because as far as I knew, a 2–0 home victory over Brighton had no particular significance, and there would be another last game for us some other time – but then, our début together had been equally inauspicious. It's best just to leave us there, the three of us – Dad topping up his tea with the contents of his hip flask and grumbling about still watching the same old bloody Arsenal, me shifting around uncomfortably in my seat, hoping that somehow things would get better, and Jonathan, still small and pale with cold and, for all I know, wishing that his brother and his father had found a different way to sort out their problems in 1968.

A TRIVIAL PURSUIT

ARSENAL v MANCHESTER CITY
24.2.81

I got lost around this time, and stayed lost for the next few years. Between one home game (against Coventry) and the next (a midweek game against Manchester City), I split up with my girlfriend, all the things that had been rotting away inside me for who knows how many years oozed out for the first time, I started my teaching practice in a difficult west London school, and Arsenal got a draw at Stoke and a beating at Forest. It was strange to see the same players trotting out that evening as they had trotted out three weeks before: I felt that they should have had the decency to reinvent themselves, accept that the faces and physiques and shortcomings they had had in the Coventry game belonged to another period entirely.

If there had been a match every weekday evening and week-end afternoon I would have gone, because the games acted as punctuation marks (if only commas) between bleak periods, when I drank too much and smoked too much and weight fell off me gratifyingly quickly. I remember this one so clearly simply because it was the first of them – they all began to merge into each other a little after this; Lord knows nothing much happened on the pitch, apart from Talbot and Sunderland trundling in a couple of goals.

But football had taken on yet another meaning now, connected with my new career. It had occurred to me – as I think it occurs to many young teachers of a similar ilk – that my interests (football and pop music in particular) would be an advantage in the classroom, that I would be able to 'identify' with 'the kids' because I understood the value of the Jam and Laurie Cunningham. It had not occurred to me that I was as childish as my interests; and that although, yes, I knew what my pupils were talking about most of the time, and that this gave me an entrée of sorts, it didn't help me to teach them any better. In fact the chief prob-

lem I had – namely, that on a bad day there was uproarious mayhem in my classroom – was actually exacerbated by my
partisanship. 'I'm an Arsenal fan,' I said in my best groovy
teacher voice, as a way of introducing myself to some difficult
second years. 'Boo!' they replied, noisily and at great length.

On my second or third day, I asked a group of third years to
write down on a piece of paper their favourite book, favourite
song, favourite film and so on, and went around the class talking
to them all in turn. This was how I discovered that the bad boy
at the back, the one with the mod haircut and the permanent
sneer (and the one, inevitably, with the biggest vocabulary and
the best writing style), was completely consumed by all things
Arsenal, and I pounced. But when I had made my confession,
there was no meeting of minds, or fond, slow-motion embrace;
instead, I received a look of utter contempt. 'You?' he said.
'You? What do *you* know about it?'

For a moment I saw myself through his eyes, a pillock in a
tie with an ingratiating smile, desperately trying to worm my
way into places I had no right to be, and understood. But then
something else – a rage born out of thirteen years of Highbury
hell, probably, and an unwillingness to abandon one of the
most important elements of my self-identity to chalky, tweedy
facelessness – took over, and I went mad.

The madness took a strange form. I wanted to grab that kid
by his lapels and bang him against the wall, and yell at him,
over and over again, 'I know more than you ever will, you
snotty little fuckwit!' but I knew that this was not advisable. So
I spluttered for a few seconds, and then to my surprise (I
watched them as they spewed forth) a torrent of quiz questions
gushed out of me. 'Who scored for us in the '69 League Cup
Final? Who went in goal when Bob Wilson got carried off in
'72 at Villa Park? Who did we get from Spurs in exchange for
David Jenkins? Who . . . ?' On and on I went; the boy sat
there, the questions bouncing off the top of his head like snow-
balls, while the rest of the class watched in bemused silence.

It worked, in the end – or at least, I managed to convince the boy that I was not the man he had taken me for. The morning after the Manchester City game, the first home game following my trivia explosion, the two of us talked quietly and cordially about the desperate need for a new midfield player, and I never had any trouble with him for the remainder of my practice. But what worried me was that I hadn't been able to let it go, that football, the great retardant, hadn't let me act like a grown-up in the face of a young lad's jibe. Teaching, it seemed to me, was by definition a job for grown-ups, and I appeared to have got stuck somewhere around my fourteenth birthday – stuck in the third year, in fact.

COACH

MY SCHOOL v THEIR SCHOOL
January 1982

I'd seen *Kes*, of course; I'd laughed at Brian Glover dribbling around kids and pushing them over, awarding himself penalties, doing the commentary. And my friend Ray, the deputy head of the school in Cambridge where I was now a Scale 1 English teacher (Cambridge because a job came up there, because I still had friends there, and because my teacher training year in London had taught me that I should avoid London schools if at all possible) had an endless fund of true stories about headmasters who appointed themselves referees for important matches, and sent the fifteen-year-old star striker of the opposing team off in the first two minutes of the match. I was well aware, therefore, of the way schools football encouraged teachers to behave in an astonishingly foolish manner.

But what would you do, if your fifth years were 2–0 down at half-time in a local derby (although admittedly schools football does tend to throw up a number of local derbies), and you made an astute tactical switch at half-time, and the boys pulled one back, and then, bang on ninety minutes, when your voice is hoarse with frustration and impotence, they equalise? You would probably find yourself, as I did, two feet up in the air, fists punching the sky, letting rip with an undignified and certainly unteacherly howl . . . and just before your feet hit the touchline, you would remember who you were supposed to be, and how old these kids were, and you would start to feel daft.

ON THE PITCH

ARSENAL v WEST HAM
1.5.82

Looking back, it was quite clear that the stuff on the terraces was getting worse and that sooner or later something was going to happen that would change it all, somehow. In my experience there was more violence in the seventies – that is to say, there was fighting more or less every week – but in the first half of the eighties, with Millwall's F-Troop, West Ham's Inter-City Firm (and the calling cards that these factions were reputed to leave on the battered bodies of their victims), the England fans and their alleged National Front agenda – it was less predictable and much nastier. Police confiscated knives and machetes and other weapons I did not recognise, things with spikes coming out of them; and there was that famous photograph of a fan with a dart sticking from his nose.

One beautiful spring morning in 1982 I took Ray's son Mark, then a teenager, down to Highbury to see the West Ham game, and explained to him in an insufferably old-hand way how and where the trouble, if any, would start. I pointed to the top right-hand corner of the North Bank and told him that there were probably West Ham fans up there, without colours, who would either find themselves surrounded by police, and thus rendered harmless, or who would attempt to force their way under the roof and drive out the Arsenal fans gathered there; which was why we were safe on the bottom left-hand side, where I had been standing for a few years now. He was duly grateful, I felt, for my guidance and protection.

In the event I was able, by casting an expert eye over the area, to reassure him that there were no Hammers fans there, and we settled down to watch the game; and about three minutes after the kick-off, there was a huge roar immediately behind us and that terrible, eerily muffled sound of boot on denim. Those behind us pushed forward, and we found ourselves being forced towards the pitch – and then there was another roar, and we looked round and saw billowing clouds of thick yellow smoke. 'Fucking tear gas!' somebody shouted, and, although thankfully it wasn't, the alarm inevitably induced panic. There were now so many people pouring out of the North Bank that we were being driven right down against the low wall which separated us from the pitch, and in the end we had no option: Mark and I, and hundreds of others, jumped over it and on to the holy turf just as West Ham were about to take a corner. We stood there for a few moments, feeling rather self-conscious about standing in the penalty-area during a First Division match, and then the referee blew the whistle and took the players off. And that was more or less the end of our involvement in the incident. We were all escorted the length of the pitch down to the Clock End, from where we watched the rest of the game in fairly subdued silence.

But there is a horrible and frightening irony here. At Highbury there is no perimeter fencing. If there had been, then those of us pushed towards the pitch that afternoon would have been in serious trouble. A couple of years later, during an FA Cup semi-final between Everton and Southampton at Arsenal, a few hundred stupid Everton fans ran on to the pitch after their team scored a late winner, and the FA (although they have changed their minds again now) decided that Highbury should no longer be used as a semi-final venue unless the club fenced the fans in. To their eternal credit, the club refused (leaving aside the safety aspects, it obstructs the view), despite the loss of revenue incurred. Hillsborough, however, had the fences, and thus until 1989 was deemed suitable for these games; and it was in an FA Cup semi-final between Liverpool and Nottingham Forest that all those people died. It was the fencing, the very feature which allowed the game to take place there, that killed them, prevented them from getting out of the crush and on to the pitch.

After the West Ham match, a young Arsenal fan was stabbed in one of the streets near the ground, and died where he lay: a sickening end to a dismal afternoon. When I went back to school on Monday morning I ranted and raved at a class of baffled second years about the whole culture of violence. I tried to argue to them that their hooligan paraphernalia – their Doctor Martens and their green flying jackets and their spiky haircuts – all fed the process, but they were too young, and I was too incoherent. And anyway there was something pretty nauseating, although I didn't appreciate it at the time, about me of all people explaining to a whole load of provincial kids that dressing hard didn't mean you were hard, and that wanting to be hard in the first place was kind of a pathetic ambition.

THE MUNSTERS AND QUENTIN CRISP

SAFFRON WALDEN v TIPTREE
May 1983

I will watch any football match, any time, any place, in any weather conditions. Between the ages of eleven and twenty-five I was an occasional visitor to York Road, home of Maidenhead United of the Athenian, later the Isthmian League; occasionally I even travelled to see them in away games. (I was there on the great day in '69 when they won the Berks and Bucks Senior Cup, beating Wolverton 3–0 in the final played at, I think, Chesham United's ground. And at Farnborough once, a man came out of the club house and told the travelling fans to keep the noise down.) In Cambridge, when United or Arsenal weren't playing, I went to Milton Road, home of Cambridge City, and when I started teaching I went with my friend Ray to watch his son-in-law Les, whose good looks and impeccable behaviour gave him the air of a non-league Gary Lineker, play for Saffron Walden.

Part of the fascination of non-league football is the rest of the crowd: some, though by no means all, of the people who attend the games are hideously mad, perhaps driven so by the quality of the football they have spent years watching. (There are lunatics on the First Division terraces too – my friends and I spent years on the North Bank trying to avoid one who stood near us every week – but they are less noticeable among all the casual consumers.) At Milton Road there was an old man we called Quentin Crisp, because of the disarming femininity of his white hair and wrinkled face: he wore a crash helmet throughout the entire ninety minutes, and spent his afternoons buzzing round and round the stadium like an ageing greyhound (you could see him on his own at the far end of the ground where there was no terracing, picking his way through mud and over debris, gamely determined to complete his circuit), hurling abuse at the linesmen – 'I'm going to write to the FA about you' – when he got anywhere near them. At York Road there was (and perhaps still is) an entire family, known to everyone as the Munsters due to a somewhat outlandish and unfortunate physical appearance, who had taken it upon themselves to act as stewards to a crowd of two hundred who really had no need of such services; there was also Harry Taylor, a very old and slightly simple man who couldn't stay to see the end of midweek games on a Tuesday because Tuesday was bath night, and whose entrance was greeted by a chant of 'Harry Harry, Harry

Harry, Harry Harry, Harry Taylor' to the tune of the old Hare Krishna chant. Non-league football, perhaps by its very nature, attracts these people, and I say this in the full knowledge that I am one of the people attracted.

What I have always wanted is to find a place where I could lose myself in the patterns and rhythms of football without caring about the score. I have this idea that in the right circumstances the game could serve as a kind of New Age therapy, and the frantic movement before me would somehow absorb and then dissolve everything inside me, but it never works that way. First I become diverted by the eccentricities – the fans, the shouts of the players ('Put him in the tea bar!' urged Maidenhead's Micky Chatterton, our hero, to a team-mate faced with a particularly tricky winger one afternoon), the peculiar, ramshackle presentation of the entertainment (Cambridge City took the field to the theme from *Match of the Day*, but frequently the music wound down with a pitiful groan just at the crucial moment). And then once I have been engaged thus, I start to care; and before long Maidenhead and Cambridge City and Walden start to mean more than they should do, and once again I am involved, and then the therapy cannot work.

Saffron Walden's tiny ground is one of the nicest places I have ever watched football, and the people there always seemed startlingly normal. I went because Ray, Mark and Ben their dog went, and I went because Les was playing; and, after a little while, when I got to know the players, I went to watch a gifted, idle striker called, improbably, Alf Ramsey, rumoured to be a heavy smoker, who in classic Greaves style did nothing apart from score once or twice a game.

When Walden beat Tiptree 3–0 and won something or other – the Essex Senior Cup? – on a mild May evening, there was a warmth to the occasion that professional football will never be able to match. A small, partisan crowd, a good game, a team of players with a genuine affection for their club (Les didn't play for anyone else throughout his career, and like most of his team-mates lived in the town) . . . and when, at the end of the game, the crowd went on to the pitch, it wasn't intended as an act of aggression, or bravado, or scene-stealing, as pitch invasions so frequently are, but to congratulate the team, all of them brothers or sons or husbands of nearly all of the spectators. There is a sourness that is central to the experience of supporting a big team, and you can't do anything about it apart from live with it and accept that professional sport has to be sour if it is to mean anything at all. But sometimes it's nice to have a little holiday from it, and wonder what it would be like if Arsenal players all came from London N4 or N5, and had other jobs, and played only because they loved the game and the team they played for. This is sentimental, but teams like Walden inspire sentiment; sometimes, you feel, it would be nice if the theme from the *A-Team* that marks Arsenal's entrance on to the pitch wound down horribly, as the tapes did at Cambridge City, and the players looked at each other and laughed.

CHARLIE NICHOLAS

ARSENAL v LUTON
27.8.83

How can you *not* see omens everywhere? In the summer of 1983, after two years, I packed up my teaching job to be a writer; and a couple of weeks later Arsenal signed, against all odds, the hottest property in British football – Charlie Nicholas, the Cannonball Kid, the Celtic player who had scored fifty-something goals in Scotland the previous season. *Now* we were going to see something. And with Charlie around, I felt that there was no way I could fail with my witty yet sensitive plays, the first of which – oh, the unfathomable mysteries of creativity – was about a teacher who becomes a writer.

It is easy to see now that I should not have linked Charlie's career to my own, but at the time I found it irresistible to do so. The optimism of Terry Neill and Don Howe and the press swept me along, and as the Charlie hype became more and more feverish during the summer of '83 (he had, in truth, made a bit of an idiot of himself in the tabloids even before he kicked a ball), it became very easy to believe that the newspapers were talking about me. It was distinctly possible, I felt, that I was on the verge of becoming the Cannonball Kid of television drama, and then of the West End theatre (even though I knew nothing about either, and indeed had frequently expressed my contempt for the stage).

The neat and obvious synchronism of it all still baffles me. The last new dawn, back in '76 when Terry Neill took over and Malcolm Macdonald came to the club, I was about to depart for university. And the one after Charlie's arrival, just a year later (when we were top of the First Division for a couple of months, and playing as well as anyone could remember), came right after I walked out of various terrible messes I had made in Cambridge and moved back to London to start a new life. Maybe football teams and people are always having fresh starts; maybe Arsenal and I have more than most, and therefore we are suited to each other.

In the event, Charlie proved to be a pretty accurate indicator of my fortunes. I was there for this, his first game, of course, along with a good forty thousand others, and he was OK: he didn't score, but he played his part, and we won 2–1. And though he got two in the next game, away at Wolves, that was it in the League until after Christmas (he got one League Cup goal at Tottenham in November). The next game at home, against Manchester United, he looked slow and out of touch, and the team were outclassed – we lost 3–2, but we were never really in the game. (In fact he didn't score at all at Highbury until 27th December, with a penalty against Birmingham which we greeted with the fervour of a hat-trick against Tottenham.)

His first season was, in short, a disaster, as it was for the whole team, and the manager, Terry Neill, got the sack after a dismal run of results in November and early December.

The other Cannonball Kid, the literary version, finished his imaginative play and got a kind and encouraging rejection letter back; then started another, which was also rejected, a little less kindly. And he was doing the most dismal sorts of work – private tuition, proof reading and supply teaching – to pay the rent. He showed no signs of scoring before Christmas either, or for a few more Christmases to come; if he had supported Liverpool, and tied his fortunes to Ian Rush, he would have won a Booker prize by May.

I was twenty-six in 1983, and Charlie Nicholas was just twenty-one; it suddenly occurred to me over the next few weeks, as I looked at the hundreds of Charlie haircuts and earrings on the terraces and regretted that my already thinning hair would not allow me to participate, that my heroes were not going to age as I did. I will reach thirty-five, forty, fifty, but the players never will: Paul Merson, Rocky, Kevin Campbell . . . I am more than a decade older than the people I love in the current Arsenal team. I am even a year older than David O'Leary, the veteran, the Old Man, whose pace is patently no longer what it was, whose first-team outings are limited to protect his creaking joints and his waning stamina. It doesn't make any difference, however. To all intents and purposes, I am still twenty years younger than O'Leary, and ten years younger than all the 24-year-olds. In one important sense, I really am: they have done things that I never will, and sometimes I feel that if I could just score once into the North Bank end and run behind the goal to the fans, then I could at last leave behind all childish things.

A SEVEN-MONTH HICCUP

CAMBRIDGE UNITED v OLDHAM ATHLETIC
1.10.83

It was the beginning of another typical Cambridge season. They'd won one, drawn a couple, lost a couple, but they always started like this; at the beginning of October my friends and I watched them beat Oldham (whose team, incidentally, included Andy Goram, Mark Ward, Roger Palmer and Martin Buchan) 2–1; they moved into comfortable mid-table obscurity, their natural habitat, and we went home fully and happily prepared for another season of nothingness.

And that was it. Between 1st October and 28th April they failed to beat Palace at home, Leeds away, Huddersfield at home, Portsmouth away, Brighton and Derby at home, Cardiff away, Middlesbrough at home, Newcastle away, Fulham at home, Shrewsbury away, Manchester City at home, Barnsley away, Grimsby at home, Blackburn away, Swansea and Carlisle at home, Charlton and Oldham away, Chelsea at home, Brighton away, Portsmouth at home, Derby away, Cardiff and Wednesday at home, Huddersfield and Palace away, Leeds at home, Middlesbrough away, Barnsley at home and Grimsby away. Thirty-one games without a win, a Football League record (you can look it up), seventeen of them at home . . . and I saw all seventeen, as well as a fair few games at Highbury. I missed only United's home defeat by Derby in the FA Cup third round – the girl I was living with took me to Paris for the weekend as a Christmas present. (When I saw the date on the tickets, I was unable, shamingly, to hide my disappointment, and she was understandably hurt.) My friend Simon managed only sixteen of the seventeen League games – he smashed his head on a bookshelf in London a few hours before the Grimsby game on the 28th of December; his girlfriend had to take his car keys away from him because he kept making dazed attempts to drive from Fulham up to the Abbey.

It would, however, be absurd to pretend that my allegiance was sorely tested: I never once thought of abandoning the team simply because they were incapable of beating anyone at all. In fact this long losing-run (which resulted, inevitably, in relegation) became charged with a drama all of its own, a drama which would have been entirely absent in the normal course of events. After a while, when winning a game appeared to be an option that had somehow become impossible, we began to adjust to a different order, and look for things that would replace the satisfaction of winning: goals, draws, a brave performance in the face of overwhelmingly hostile fortune (and the team were terribly, terribly unlucky on occasions, as a team that does not win for six whole months would have to be) . . . these all became causes for quiet, if occasionally self-mocking, celebration. And in any case Cambridge developed a certain infamy over the course of the year. Whereas previously their results had been deemed unworthy of note, they now always got a mention on *Sports Report*; telling people that I was there for the duration, even seven years later, has a certain social cachet in some quarters.

In the end I learned, from this period more than any other in my footballing history, that it simply doesn't matter to me how bad things get, that results have nothing to do with anything. As I have implied before, I would like to be one of those people who treat their local team like their local restaurant, and thus withdraw their patronage if they are being served up noxious rubbish. But unfortunately (and this is one reason why football has got itself into so many messes without having to clear any of them up) there are many fans like me. For us, the consumption is all; the quality of the product is immaterial.

COCONUTS

CAMBRIDGE UNITED v NEWCASTLE UNITED
28.4.84

At the end of April, Newcastle, with Keegan and Beardsley and Waddle, came to the Abbey. They were near the top of the Second Division, and they needed a win badly if they were going to make sure of promotion, and Cambridge were already long down by then. Cambridge were awarded a penalty in the first few minutes and scored, though given their recent history this was not in itself enthralling – as we had learned over the previous months that there were countless ways to convert a lead into a defeat. But there were no further goals in the game; in the last five minutes, with Cambridge thumping the ball as far into the allotments as possible, you would have thought that they were about to win the European Cup. At the final whistle the players (most of whom, bought or pulled out of the reserves to stop the rot, had never played in a winning team) embraced each other and waved happily to the ecstatic home fans; and for the first time since October the club DJ was able to play 'I've Got a Lovely Bunch of Coconuts'. It didn't mean a thing in the long run, and the next season they got relegated again, but after that long, bleak winter it was a memorable couple of hours.

This was the last time I went to the Abbey; that summer I decided to run away from Cambridge and United, and back to London and Arsenal. But the afternoon – eccentric, funny, joyful from one perspective and heartbreaking from another, private in a way that football usually isn't (there were probably less than three thousand Cambridge fans in the crowd for the Newcastle game) – was a perfect end to my relationship with the club. And sometimes, when it seems to me that supporting a First Division team is a thankless and indefensible chore, I miss them a lot.

PETE

'You must meet my friend,' I am always being told. 'He's a big Arsenal fan.' And I meet the friend, and it turns out that, at best, he looks up the Arsenal score in the paper on Sunday morning or, at worst, he is unable to name a single player since Denis Compton. None of these blind dates ever worked; I was too demanding, and my partners simply weren't interested in commitment.

So I wasn't really expecting very much when I was introduced to Pete in the Seven Sisters Road before the Stoke game; but it was a perfect, life-changing match. He was (and still is) as stupid as I am about it all – he has the same ludicrous memory, the same propensity to allow his life to be dominated for nine months of the year by fixture lists and TV schedules. He is gripped by the same stomach-fizzing fear before big games, and the same dreadful glooms after bad defeats. Interestingly, I think he has had the same tendency to let his life drift along a little, the same confusions about what he wants to do with it, and I think that, like me, he has allowed Arsenal to fill gaps that should have been occupied by something else, but then we all do that.

I was twenty-seven when I met him, and without his influence I suppose I might have drifted away from the club over the next few years. I was approaching the age at which drifting sometimes begins (although the things that one is supposed to drift towards – domesticity, children, a job I really cared about – just weren't there), but with Pete the reverse happened. Our desire for all things football sharpened, and Arsenal began to creep back deep into both of us.

Maybe the timing helped: at the beginning of the 84/85 season Arsenal led the First Division for a few weeks. Nicholas was playing with breathtaking skill in midfield, Mariner and Woodcock looked like the striker partnership we'd been lacking for years, the defence was solid, and yet another of those little sparks of optimism lit me up and led me to believe once again that if things could change for the team then they could change for me. (By Christmas, after a disappointing string of results for me and the team, we were all back in the Slough of Despond.) Maybe if Pete and I had met at the beginning of the following dismal season, things would not have turned out the same way – maybe we would not have had the same incentive to make the partnership work during those crucial first few games.

I suspect, though, that the quality of Arsenal's early-season football had very little to do with anything. There was another agenda altogether, involving our shared inability to get on with things away from Highbury and our shared need to carve out a little igloo for ourselves to protect us from the icy winds of the mid-eighties and our late twenties. Since I met Pete in 1984, I have missed fewer than half a dozen games at Arsenal in seven years (four in that first year, all connected with the continuing upheaval in my personal life, and none at all for four seasons), and travelled to more away games than I had ever done before. And though there are fans who haven't missed any games, home or away, for decades, I would have been amazed by my current attendance record if I had known about it in, say, 1975, when I grew up for a few months and stopped going, or even in 1983, when my relationship with the club was polite and cordial but distant. Pete pushed me over the edge, and sometimes I don't know whether to thank him for that or not.

HEYSEL

LIVERPOOL v JUVENTUS
29.5.85

When I ran away from Cambridge and came to London in the summer of 1984, I found work teaching English as a foreign language at a school in Soho, a temporary post that somehow lasted four years, in the same way that everything I fell into through lethargy or chance or panic seemed to last much longer than it should have done. But I loved the work and loved the students (mostly young western Europeans taking time out from degree courses); and though the teaching left me plenty of time to write, I didn't do any, and spent long afternoons in coffee bars in Old Compton Street with other members of staff, or a crowd of charming young Italians. It was a wonderful way to waste my time.

They knew, of course, about the football (the topic somehow seemed to crop up in more than one conversation class). So when the Italian students started to complain, on the afternoon of the 29th of May, that they had no access to a television, and therefore could not watch Juve beat Liverpool in the European Cup Final that night, I offered to come down to the school with the keys so that we could watch the match together.

There were scores of them when I arrived, and I was the only non-Italian in the place; I was pushed, by their cheerful antagonism and my own vague patriotism, into becoming an honorary Liverpool fan for the night. When I turned the TV on, Jimmy Hill and Terry Venables were still talking, and I left the sound down so that the students and I could talk about the game, and I put a little bit of technical vocabulary up on the board while we were still waiting. But after a while, when conversation started to flag, they wanted to know why the game hadn't started and what the Englishmen were saying, and it wasn't until then that I understood what was going on.

So I had to explain to a group of beautiful young Italian boys and girls that in Belgium, the English hooligans had caused the deaths of thirty-eight people, most of them Juventus supporters. I don't know how I would have felt watching the game at home. I would have felt the same rage that I felt that night in the school, and the same despair, and the same terrible sick shame; I doubt if I would have had the same urge to apologise, again and again and again, although perhaps I should have done. I would certainly have cried, in the privacy of my own front room, at the sheer stupidity of it all but in the school I wasn't able to. Maybe I thought it would be a bit rich, an Englishman weeping in front of Italians on the night of Heysel.

All through 1985, our football had been heading unstoppably for something like this. There was the astonishing Millwall riot at Luton, where the police were routed, and things seemed to go further than they ever have done at an English football ground (it was then that Mrs Thatcher conceived her absurd ID card scheme); there was the Chelsea v Sunderland riot, too, where Chelsea fans invaded the pitch and attacked players. These incidents took place within weeks of each other, and they were just the pick of the bunch. Heysel was coming, as inevitably as Christmas.

In the end, the surprise was that these deaths were caused by something as innocuous as running, the practice that half the juvenile fans in the country had indulged in, and which was intended to do nothing more than frighten the opposition and amuse the runners. The Juventus fans – many of them chic, middle-class men and women – weren't to know that, though, and why should they have done? They didn't have the intricate knowledge of English crowd behaviour that the rest of us had absorbed almost without noticing. When they saw a crowd of screaming English hooligans running towards them, they panicked, and ran to the edge of their compound. A wall collapsed and, in the chaos that ensued, people were crushed to death. It was a horrible way to die and we probably watched people do it: we all remember the large bearded man, the one who looked a little like Pavarotti, imploring with his hand for a way out that nobody could provide.

Some of the Liverpool fans who were later arrested must have felt genuinely bewildered. In a sense, their crime was simply being English: it was just that the practices of their culture, taken out of its own context and transferred to somewhere that simply didn't understand them, killed people. 'Murderers! Murderers!' the Arsenal fans chanted at the Liverpool fans the December after Heysel, but I suspect that if exactly the same circumstances were to be recreated with any group of English fans – and these circumstances would include a hopelessly inadequate local police force (Brian Glanville, in his book *Champions of Europe*, reports that the Belgian police were amazed that the violence began before the game started, when a simple phone call to any metropolitan constabulary in England could have put them right), a ludicrously decrepit stadium, a vicious set of opposing fans, and pitifully poor planning on the part of the relevant football authorities – then the same thing would surely happen.

I think this is why I felt quite so ashamed by the events of that night. I knew that Arsenal fans might have done the same, and that if Arsenal had been playing in the Heysel that night then I would certainly have been there – not fighting, or running at people, but very much a part of the community that spawned this sort of behaviour. And anyone who has ever used football in the ways that it has been used on countless occasions, for the great smell of brute it invariably confers on the user, must have felt ashamed too. Because the real point of the tragedy was this: it was possible for football fans to look at TV coverage of, say, the Luton–Millwall riot, or the Arsenal–West Ham stabbing, and feel a sense of sick horror but no real sense of connection or involvement. The perpetrators were not the kind of people that the rest of us understood, or identified with. But the kids' stuff that proved murderous in Brussels belonged firmly and clearly on a continuum of apparently harmless but obviously threatening acts – violent chants, wanker signs, the whole petty hard-act works – in which a very large minority of fans had been indulging for nearly twenty years. In short, Heysel was an organic part of a culture that many of us, myself included, had contributed towards. You couldn't look at those Liverpool fans and ask yourself, as you had been able to do with the Millwall fans at Luton, or the Chelsea fans in their League Cup match, 'Who *are* these people?'; you already knew.

I am still embarrassed by the fact that I watched the game; I should have turned the TV off, told everyone to go home, made a unilateral decision that football no longer mattered, and wouldn't for quite a while. But everyone I know, more or less, wherever they were watching, stuck with it; in my school room, nobody really cared who won the European Cup any more, but there was still a last, indelible trace of obsession left in us that made us want to talk about the dubious penalty decision which gave Juventus their 1–0 win. I like to think I have an answer for most irrationalities connected with football, but this one seems to defy all explanation.

DYING ON ITS FEET

ARSENAL v LEICESTER
31.8.85

The season following Heysel was the worst I can remember – not just because of Arsenal's poor form, although that didn't help (and I regret to say that if we had won the League or the Cup, then I'm sure I would have been able to put all those deaths into some kind of *perspective*), but because everything seemed poisoned by what had gone on in May. Gates, which had been falling imperceptibly for years, were down even further, and the whacking great holes in the terraces were suddenly noticeable; the atmosphere at games was subdued; without the European competitions, second, third or fourth place in the League was useless (a high position had previously guaranteed a team a place in the UEFA Cup), and as a consequence, most First Division fixtures in the second half of the season were even more meaningless than usual.

One of my Italian students, a young woman with a Juventus season-ticket, found out that I was a football fan and asked if she could come with me to Highbury for the Leicester game. And though she was good company, and the chance of talking to a female European obsessive about the difference between her obsession and mine doesn't come along too frequently, I was hesitant about it. It definitely wasn't because I couldn't take a young lady to stand on the North Bank among the thugs (even an Italian, a Juventus fan, three and a half months after Heysel): as we had seen in May, the people she spent her time with on Sunday afternoons were familiar with the symptoms of the English disease, and she had already waved away my clumsy and pious apologies on behalf of the Liverpool fans. It was more because I was ashamed of the whole thing – the desperate quality of Arsenal's football, the half-empty stadium, the quiet, uninterested crowd. In the event, she said she enjoyed herself, and even claimed that Juventus were just as bad early-season (Arsenal scored after quarter of an hour and spent the rest of the match trying to keep out a dismal Leicester team). I didn't bother to tell her that this was as good as we ever got.

In my previous seventeen years of fandom, going to football had always held something above and beyond its complicated and distorted personal meanings. Even if we weren't winning, there had always been Charlie George or Liam Brady, big, noisy crowds or fascinating sociopathic disturbances, Cambridge United's gripping losing runs or Arsenal's endless cup replays. But looking at it all through the Italian girl's eyes, I could see that post-Heysel there was simply nothing going on at all; for the first time, football seemed to have been stripped right down to its subtext, and without it I would surely have been able to give it all up, as thousands of others seemed to be doing.

DRINKING AGAIN

ARSENAL v HEREFORD
8.10.85

There is, I think, a distinction to be made between the type of hooliganism that takes place in this country, and the type involving English fans that takes place abroad. Most fans I have talked to argue that drink hasn't ever had a very large influence on the domestic violence (there has been trouble even at games with morning kick-offs, a scheme designed to stop people going to the pub before the match); travelling abroad, however, with the duty-free ferry crossings, the long, boring train journeys, the twelve hours to kill in a foreign city . . . this is a different problem altogether. There were eyewitness reports of widespread drunkenness among the Liverpool fans before Heysel (although one must bear in mind that the Yorkshire police tried, shamefully, to argue that drink had been a factor at Hillsborough), and there is a suspicion that many of the England riots of the early eighties, in Berne and Luxembourg and Italy, were alcohol-fuelled (although probably not alcohol-induced) too.

There was a lot of anguished and long overdue self-flagellation after Heysel; drink, inevitably, was the focus for a great deal of it, and before the start of the new season its sale was banned inside our stadia. This angered some fans, who argued that as drink had only a tenuous connection with hooliganism, the real purpose of this move was to obviate the need for any radical action. Everything was wrong, people said – the relationship between clubs and fans, the state of the grounds and the lack of facilities therein, the lack of fan representation in any decision-making process, the works – and banning the sale of alcohol when everybody did their drinking in pubs (it is, as many fans have pointed out, impossible to get drunk inside a stadium anyway, given the number of people waiting to be served) wasn't going to help a bit.

I agree, as anybody would, with all of this, but it is still difficult to claim that, even with a few more toilets and a sup-porters' representative on the board of directors at every club, Heysel wouldn't have happened. The point was that banning the sale of alcohol didn't, couldn't possibly, do any harm: it wasn't going to cause any violence, and may even have stopped one or two fights. And, if nothing else, it showed that we were serious about our repentance. The ban could have been taken as a small but felt token towards those in Italy who might have lost loved ones because a few silly boys had had too much to drink.

And what happened? The clubs whined because it affected their relationship with their more affluent fans, and the ban was lifted. On 8th October, seventeen weeks after Heysel, Pete and I and a couple of others decided to buy ourselves a seat in the Lower West Stand for a League Cup game on a miserable night, and to our astonishment were able to buy a round of shorts to keep the cold out: the rule had been changed from 'No alcohol' to 'No alcohol within sight of the pitch', as if it were the heady combination of grass and whisky that enraged us all and turned us into lunatics. So where had all the hair-shirt penitence gone? What, practically, were the clubs doing to prove that we were capable of getting a grip on ourselves, and that one day we would be able to play other European teams without wiping out half their supporters? The police were doing things, and the fans were doing things (it was this post-Heysel climate of despair that produced the lifesaving *When Saturday Comes* and all the club fanzines, and the Football Supporters' Association, whose Rogan Taylor was such an accomplished, impassioned and intelligent spokesman in the weeks after Hillsborough, four years later); but the clubs, I'm afraid to say, did nothing; this one poignant little gesture would have cost them a few bob, so they scrapped it.

THE PITS

ASTON VILLA v ARSENAL
22.1.86
ARSENAL v ASTON VILLA
4.2.86

Away at Villa in the quarter-final of the League Cup in January '86 was one of the best nights I can remember: fantastic away support in a magnificent stadium I hadn't visited since I was a kid, a good game and a reasonable result (1–1 after a first-half Charlie Nicholas goal and an early second-half period of domination when Rix and Quinn missed unmissable chances). There was also an interesting historical element to the evening: the freezing January air, near us at least, was thick with marijuana smoke, the first time I had really noticed that there was some sort of different terrace culture emerging.

Over Christmas there had been a mini-revival of sorts: we beat Liverpool at home and Manchester United away on consecutive Saturdays, just when things were beginning to look really bad. (In the run-up to the Liverpool game we lost 6–1 at Everton, and then went three consecutive Saturdays without even scoring. On the middle Saturday we drew nil–nil at home to Birmingham, who were relegated, in what must surely have been the worst game ever played in the history of First Division football.) We began to allow ourselves to hope a little – always a foolish thing to do – but from February through to the end of the season everything fell apart.

Home to Villa in the League Cup quarter-final replay was probably my worst-ever night, a new low in a relationship already studded with them. It wasn't just the manner of the defeat (this was the night that Don Howe played Mariner in midfield and left Woodcock on the bench); it wasn't just that there was really nobody left in the League Cup, and we should at least have gone on to Wembley (if we had beaten Villa then it was Oxford in the semis); it wasn't even that we weren't going to win anything, for the sixth year in succession. It was more than all these things, although they were in themselves bleak enough.

Part of it was my own latent depression, permanently looking for a way out and liking what it saw at Highbury that night; but even more than that, I was as usual looking to Arsenal to show me that things did not stay bad for ever, that it *was* possible to change patterns, that losing streaks did not last. Arsenal, however, had other ideas: they seemed to want to show me that troughs could indeed be permanent, that some people, like some clubs, just couldn't ever find ways out of the rooms they had locked themselves into. It seemed to me that night and for the next few days that we had both of us made too many wrong choices, and had let things slide for far too long, for anything ever to come right; I was back with the feeling, much deeper and much more frightening this time, that I was chained to the club, and thus to this miserable half-life, forever.

I was stunned and exhausted by the defeat (2–1, although the one came in the last minute, and we were well beaten by then): the next morning a girlfriend phoned me at work, and, hearing the tired dejection in my voice, asked me what was wrong. 'Haven't you heard?' I asked her pitifully. She sounded worried and then, when I told her what had happened, I could hear, just for a second, relief – so it wasn't, after all, the things she had momentarily feared for me – before she remembered who she was talking to, and the relief was replaced by all the sympathy she could muster. I knew she didn't really understand this sort of pain, and I wouldn't have had the courage to explain it to her; because this idea, that there was this log-jam, this impasse, and that until Arsenal sorted themselves out then neither could I . . . this idea was stupid and reprehensible (it gave a whole new meaning to relegation) and, worse than that, I knew now that I really did believe it.

FREEING THE LOG-JAM

ARSENAL v WATFORD
31.3.86

It wasn't just the few results after the Villa game, I suspect, that enabled the Arsenal board to see that something had to be done, even though they were bad enough: the particularly pathetic 3–0 FA Cup defeat at Luton has been cited (on the *History of Arsenal 1886–1986* video, for example) as the game that provoked manager Don Howe's resignation, but everyone knows that's not true. Howe actually resigned after a 3–0 victory over Coventry, because he found out that chairman Peter Hill-Wood had approached Terry Venables behind his back.

We had heard a few 'Howe Out' chants on the North Bank, in between the Villa game and his resignation; when he did resign, however, the managerless team fell apart, and the chants then became directed against the chairman, although I couldn't join in. I know the board went about things in a pretty underhand way, but something had to be done. That Arsenal team – full of cliques and overpaid, over-the-hill stars – would never be bad enough to go down, but never good enough to win anything, and the stasis made you want to scream with frustration.

The girlfriend who had tried, and failed, to get any sense out of me on the morning after the Villa match came with me to the Watford game, her first experience of live football. In a way it was a ludicrous introduction: there were less than twenty thousand in the ground, and most of those that were there had come simply to register their disapproval with everything that had taken place. (I belonged to the other category: those that were there because they were always there.)

After the players had bumbled around for an hour or so, and had gone two down, something strange happened: the North Bank switched allegiance. Each Watford attack was greeted by a roar of encouragement, each near miss (and there were hundreds of them) given an 'Oooh!' of commiseration. It was funny, in a way, but it was also desperate. Here were fans who had been completely disenfranchised, who could think of no more hurtful way to express their disgust than to turn their back on the team; it was, in effect, a form of self-mutilation. It was obvious, now, that the bottom had been reached, and it was a relief. We knew that whoever the manager was (Venables quickly made it clear that he didn't want to get involved in this sort of mess), things could not get any worse.

After the game there was a demonstration outside the main entrance, although it was difficult to ascertain precisely what people wanted; some were chanting for the reinstatement of Howe, others simply giving vent to a vague but real anger. We wandered along to have a look, but none of my crowd could muster the requisite rage needed to participate. From my own point of view, I could still remember my childish, melodramatic behaviour on the telephone the morning after the Villa game, and the demonstration was oddly comforting – the girl who had had to tolerate my sulk could see that I was not the only one, that there was this whole community who cared about what was happening to their Arsenal more than they cared about anything else. The things that I have often tried to explain to people about football – that it is not an escape, or a form of entertainment, but a different version of the world – were clear for her to see; I felt vindicated, somehow.

1986–1992

GEORGE

ARSENAL v MANCHESTER UNITED
23.8.86

My mother has two cats, one called O'Leary and the other called Chippy, Liam Brady's nickname; the walls of her garage still bear the graffiti I chalked up there twenty years ago: 'RADFORD FOR ENGLAND!' 'CHARLIE GEORGE!' My sister Gill can still, when pushed, name most of the Double team.

Sometime in May 1986 Gill called me at the language school during my midmorning break. She was then working at the BBC, and the Corporation announces big news as it comes in over the tannoy for the benefit of all staff.

'George Graham,' she said, and I thanked her and put the phone down.

This is how things have always worked in my family. I feel bad that Arsenal has intruded into their lives, too.

It wasn't a very imaginative appointment, and it was obvious that George was second or even third choice for the job, whatever the chairman says now. It is possible that if he hadn't played for the club, with great distinction, around the time that I started going then he wouldn't even have been considered for the position. He came from Millwall, whom he had rescued from relegation and then led to promotion, but I can't remember him setting the world on fire there; I worried that his lack of experience would lead to him treating Arsenal as another Second Division team, and that he would think small, buy small, concentrate on keeping his job rather than attacking the other big teams and, at first, these fears seemed well-founded – the only new player he bought in his first year was Perry Groves from Colchester for £50,000, yet he sold Martin Keown immediately, and Stewart Robson not long after, and these were young players we knew and liked. So the squad got smaller and smaller: Woodcock and Mariner had gone, Caton went, and nobody replaced them.

He won his first game, at home against Manchester United, with a late Charlie Nicholas goal, and we went home cautiously positive. But he lost the next two, and by the middle of October he was in a little trouble. There was a nil–nil draw at home to Oxford which was as poor as anything we had seen in the previous six years, and already the people around me were yelling abuse at him, outraged at his perceived parsimony. In mid-November, however, after thumping Southampton 4–0 (admittedly all four of our goals were scored after the Southampton goalkeeper had been carried off), we went top of the League, and stayed there for a couple of months, and there was more, lots more, to come on top of that. He turned Arsenal into something that anyone under the age of fifty could never have seen before at Highbury, and he saved, in all the ways the word implies, every single Arsenal fan. And goals . . . where we had come to expect 1–0 wins at Highbury, suddenly fours and fives, even sixes, became commonplace; I have seen five hat-tricks, by three different players, in the last seven months.

The Manchester United game was significant for another reason: it was my first as a season-ticket holder. Pete and I bought terrace tickets that summer, not because we expected the new manager to change anything, really, but because we had come to terms with the hopelessness of our addiction. It was no use pretending any longer that football was a passing fancy, or that we were going to be selective with our games, so I flogged a pile of old punk singles that had somehow acquired value, and used the money to tie myself to the fortunes of George, and have often bitterly regretted it, but never for very long.

The most intense of all footballing relationships is, of course, between fan and club. But the relationship between fan and manager can be just as powerful. Players can rarely alter the whole tone of our lives like managers can, and each time a new one is appointed it is possible to dream bigger dreams than the previous one ever allowed. When an Arsenal manager resigns or is sacked, the occasion is as sombre as the death of a monarch: Bertie Mee quit around the same time as Harold Wilson, but there is no question that the former resignation signified more to me than the latter. Prime Ministers, however manic or unjust or wicked, simply do not have the power to do to me what an Arsenal manager can, and it is no wonder that when I think about the four I have lived with and through, I think about them as relatives.

Bertie Mee was a grandfather, kindly, slightly otherworldly, a member of a generation I didn't understand; Terry Neill was a new stepfather, matey, jocular, dislikeable however hard he tried; Don Howe was an uncle by marriage, dour and stolid yet probably and unpredictably good for a couple of card tricks at Christmas. But George . . . George is my dad, less complicated but much more frightening than the real one. (Disconcertingly, he even looks a little bit like my dad – an upright, immaculately groomed, handsome man with an obvious taste for expensive, well-cut formal clothes.)

I dream about George quite regularly, perhaps as often as I dream about my other father. In dreams, as in life, he is hard, driven, determined, indecipherable; usually he is expressing disappointment in me for some perceived lapse, quite often of a sexual nature, and I feel guilty as all hell. Sometimes, however, it is the other way around, and I catch him stealing or beating someone up, and I wake up feeling diminished. I do not like to think about these dreams or their meanings for too long.

George ended his fifth year with Arsenal just as he had begun his first, with a home game against Manchester United, but this time Highbury was awash with self-congratulation rather than sceptical anticipation: we had won the 1991 Championship some forty-five minutes before the kick-off, and the stadium was replete with noise and colour and smiles. There was a large banner draped over the edge of the West Stand Upper Tier which read, simply, 'George Knows', and which in a peculiar way isolated and defined my filial relationship with the man. He *did* know, in a way that fathers very rarely do, and on that enchanted evening every one of his mystifying decisions (the sale of Lukic, the purchase of Linighan, even the persistence with Groves) began to look unfathomably wise. Perhaps little boys want fathers to be this way, to act but never to explain the actions, to triumph on our behalf and then to be able to say, 'You doubted me but I was right, and now you must trust me'; it is one of football's charms that it can fulfil this kind of impossible dream.

A MALE FANTASY

ARSENAL v CHARLTON ATHLETIC
18.11.86

Typically, I remember her first game and she doesn't: a moment ago I poked my head round the bedroom door and asked her the name of the opponents, score and scorers, but all she could tell me was that Arsenal won and Niall Quinn got one. (2–0, and the other goal came courtesy of a Charlton defender.)

It is fair to say that back then, in the first few months of our relationship, we were having trouble (trouble caused by me), and I don't think either of us thought that we were going to last much longer. The way she tells it now, she thought that the end was coming sooner rather than later, and chose Charlton on a wet and cold November night because she thought she wasn't going to get too many more opportunities to come to Highbury with me. It wasn't a great game, but it was a good time to come, because Arsenal were slap-bang in the middle of a tremendous twenty-two-game unbeaten run, and crowds were up, spirits were up, young players (Rocky, Niall, Adams, Hayes, who later became her inexplicable favourite) were in the team and playing well, and the previous Saturday we'd all been down to Southampton to see the new League leaders.

She craned her neck and watched what she could see, and after the game we went to the pub and she said that she'd like to come again. This is what women always say and it usually means that they would like to come again in another life, and not even the next life but the one after that. I said, of course, that she would be welcome whenever; immediately she asked whether there was another home game on the Saturday. There was, and she came to that too, and to most home games for the rest of the season. She has travelled to Villa Park and Carrow Road and other London grounds, and one year she bought a season-ticket. She still comes regularly, and can recognise every member of the Arsenal squad without any difficulty, although there is no doubt that her enthusiasm is on the wane now, and that my perpetual intensity irritates her more as we both get older.

I wouldn't like to think that it was all this that saved the relationship – in fact, I know it wasn't. But it certainly had a lubricious effect, initially, and her sudden interest complicated things that were already confused. On New Year's Day 1987, when she and I went to watch a 3–1 win over Wimbledon, I began to realise why the woman who not only tolerates but actively participates in the football ritual has become for many men something of a fantasy figure: some men I knew, who had wrecked the previous night's jollities and the bank holiday's traditional familial calm by dragging themselves off to Goodison or somewhere to watch a morning kick-off, would return home to tensions and baleful glances all of their own making, whereas I was in the fortunate position of being at Highbury because it was an organic part of our day.

Later, however, I began to wonder whether this Arsenal-sharing really was what I wanted. Once, during the height of her sudden passion, we were watching a father struggling into the stadium with a very young child, and I remarked in passing that I wouldn't take a child of mine to a game until he or she was old enough to want to go; this led on to a conversation about future child-care arrangements on Saturday afternoons, a conversation that haunted me for weeks, months, afterwards. 'Alternate home games, I suppose,' she said, and for a while I presumed she meant that she would try to get along to every other match at Highbury, that our children could be left somewhere once a month but no more frequently than that, and that she would come when she could. But what she meant was that we would *take it in turns* to go, that for half the home games every year I would be at home listening to *Sport on Five* or Capital Gold (Capital Gold is less authoritative, somehow, but keeps you bang up-to-date with all the London clubs) while she sat in *my seat* watching *my team*, the team to which I had introduced her just a few years before. So now where is the advantage? Friends with partners who loathe football get to go to every game; meanwhile I – who have an apparently ideal relationship with a woman who knows why Arsenal aren't the same without Smithy leading the line – I'm looking at a future sitting in my living room with a pile of *Postman Pat* videos and the window open, mournfully hoping that a gust of wind will blow a roar my way. It wasn't what I had anticipated, that evening against Charlton when she said she wanted to go again.

There's more. All my footballing life I have lived with people – my mum, my dad, my sister, girlfriends, flatmates – who have had to learn to tolerate football-induced moods, and they have all of them, more or less, done so with good humour and tact. Suddenly I found myself living with someone who was attempting to claim moods for herself, and I didn't like it. Her elation after the 1987 Littlewoods Cup Final . . . that was her *first season.* What right did she have to swagger into the pub that Sunday evening with an Arsenal hat on? No right at all. For Pete and me, this was the first trophy since 1979, and how could she, who had only been going for the previous four months, understand what that felt like? 'They don't win things every season, you know,' I kept telling her, with all the point-less and bilious envy of a parent whose Mars Bar-munching child has never experienced the deprivations of wartime rationing.

I soon found that the only way to claim all the emotional territory for myself was to go on a sort of sulk war, confident in the knowledge that when it came to football I could pout and grump any pretender to the Football Pain throne right off the terraces, and eventually I beat her, as I knew I would. It happened at the end of the 88/89 season when, after a home defeat by Derby, it looked as though we were going to miss out on the Championship after having led the First Division for most of the season. And though I was genuinely inconsolable (that evening we went to see Eric Porter in *King Lear* at the Old Vic, and the play didn't engage me because I couldn't see what Lear's problem was), I nurtured every bit of the misery until it grew to monstrous, terrifying proportions, I behaved badly in order to prove a point, and inevitably we had an argu-ment (about going to see some friends for a cup of tea), and once it had started I knew that Arsenal was all mine once again: she was left with no alternative but to say that it was only a game (she didn't use those words, thankfully, but the implication was, I felt, clear), that there was always next year, that even this year all hope was not lost, and I leaped on these words triumphantly.

'*You don't understand,*' I shouted, as I had wanted to shout for months, and it was true – she didn't, not really. And I think that once I had been given this opportunity, once I had uttered the words that most football fans carry around with them like a kidney donor card, it was all over. What was she left with? She could attempt, or pretend, to behave even worse than I had done; or she could withdraw, yield ground, leave the agony and the ecstasy more or less entirely to me and use her own distress merely to buttress mine. She is much too gentle a person to attempt to out-tantrum me, so she chose the latter course, and I can safely and smugly say that I am top Arsenal dog in this house, and that when and if we have children it will be my bottom exclusively that fills our season-ticket seat. I'm ashamed, of course I'm ashamed, that I have had to play dirty like this, but for a while back then I was beginning to worry.

FROM NW3 TO N17

TOTTENHAM v ARSENAL
4.3.87

If this book has a centre, then it is here, on the Wednesday night in March 1987 that I travelled from a psychiatrist's office in Hampstead to White Hart Lane in Tottenham to see a Littlewoods Cup semi-final replay. I didn't plan it that way, of course: the trip to Hampstead had been arranged well before a replay became necessary. But now, when I am attempting to explain why football has managed to slow me down and speed me up, and how Arsenal and I got all mixed up together in my head, this particular conjunction looks implausibly neat.

It is easier to explain why Arsenal and Spurs needed a replay than it is to explain why I needed a psychiatrist, so I shall begin there. The two legs of the semi-final had produced an aggregate score of 2–2, and even extra time on the Sunday at White Hart

Lane had failed to push one of the teams over the edge and out of the competition, although four measly goals in three and a half hours of football is an inadequate indicator of the draining drama of the two games. In the first one, at Highbury, Clive Allen celebrated his typically predatory piece of finishing in the first half by leaping into the air and landing flat on his back from a height of about five feet, one of the most eccentric expressions of joy I have ever seen; and Paul Davis missed an open goal from less than six inches, and Hoddle hit the bar with a brilliant curling free kick, and poor Gus Caesar (Arsenal's thin squad was being stretched to the point of disaster), tormented beyond all dignity by Waddle, had to be replaced by the only other player we had available, a young man called Michael Thomas, who had never played in the first team before.

In the second game Allen scored again early on, so Spurs were 2–0 up on aggregate, and had four other one-on-ones with Lukic as Arsenal pushed forward, and missed them all; and at half-time the Spurs announcer told the Spurs fans how they could apply for tickets for the Final at Wembley, a misguided and provocative moment of extreme smugness that served to awaken and enrage the subdued Arsenal fans (and, we heard later, the team, who heard the tannoy message in the dressing room) to the extent that when our players came out for the second half, they were met with a proud and defiant roar; thus inspired, the team bravely inched their way back into the game and, even though on paper Adams, Quinn, Hayes, Thomas and Rocastle were no match for Waddle, Hoddle, Ardiles, Gough and Allen, first Viv Anderson, scrappily, and then Niall, refulgently, scored to push the game into extra time. We should have won in the extra thirty minutes – Tottenham were in pieces, and both Hayes and Nicholas could have finished them off – but given the number of chances Tottenham had had over the two games, and our two-goal deficit with three-quarters of the tie gone, a replay was better than anything we had dared hope for. After the game George came on to the pitch and tossed a coin to settle the venue for the deciding match, and when he looked over towards us and pointed straight down at the White Hart Lane mud to indicate that he had lost the call, the Arsenal fans roared again: we'd beaten Spurs twice at their place in the space of a few weeks (the League game at the beginning of January finished 2–1) and had only managed a draw and a defeat against them at Highbury. We would all be back on Wednesday.

This, then, is how the replay came about – football is easy like that. And if you want to know how we came to be in the Littlewoods Cup semi-final, then that's easy too: we'd beaten Forest at Highbury in the quarter-final, and before that Manchester City, Charlton and Huddersfield over two legs in the second round, and before Huddersfield there was nothing at all. The contrast between the strong, clean, straight lines of a cup run and the messy, tangled, overgrown paths of a life is plangent: I wish I could draw one of those big knock-out trophy diagrams to show how I'd ended up playing on the unfamiliar turf of a Hampstead psychiatrist's carpet.

The best I can do is as follows. In the spring of 1986, I had become frustrated beyond patience by my inability to find, even seven years after leaving college, a job I wanted to do, and by my failure, six years after losing the Lost Girl, to hold down any kind of permanent, healthy relationship, although temporary and sickly relationships, usually involving some kind of third party, were a dime-a-dozen. And as I had spent a lot of time talking to the principal of my language school, a man who was then training to become a Jungian therapist, and had become interested in what he had to say about the value of therapy, I somehow ended up going to see a lady in Bounds Green once a week.

Huge parts of me didn't like going. Had Willie Young ever bothered with therapy? Or Peter Storey? Or Tony Adams? Yet every Thursday I sat in a big armchair, flicking the leaves of

the rubber plant that dangled over my head, trying to talk about
my family and my jobs and my relationships and, as often as
not, Arsenal; after a few months of this leaf-flicking, some sort
of lid blew off, and I lost the last few pieces of the spurious
muddle-through optimism that had been sustaining me for the
previous few years. Like most depressions that plague people
who have been more fortunate than most, I was ashamed of
mine because there appeared to be no convincing cause for it;
I just felt as though I had come off the rails somewhere.

I had no idea at what point this might have happened.
Indeed, I wasn't even sure which rails these were. I had loads
of friends, including girlfriends, I was in work, I was in regular
contact with all the members of my immediate family, I had
suffered no bereavements, I had somewhere to live . . . I was
still on all the tracks that I could think of; so what, precisely,
was the nature of the derailment? All I know is that I felt,
inexplicably, *unlucky*, *cursed* in some way that would not be
immediately apparent to anyone without a job or a lover or a
family. I knew myself to be doomed to a life of dissatisfactions:
my talents, whatever they were, would go permanently unre-
cognised, my relationships wrecked by circumstances entirely
beyond my control. And because I knew this beyond any doubt,
then there was simply no point in attempting to rectify the
situation by looking for work that would stimulate me, or for
a personal life that would make me happy. So I stopped writing
(because if you are born under a bad sign, as I had been,
there is simply no point in persisting with something that will
inevitably bring with it only the humiliation of perpetual rejection), and involved myself in as many miserable and debilitating
triangular relationships as I possibly could, and settled down
to the remainder of my allotted three-score years and ten of
unrelieved and terrible nothingness.

It wasn't, in truth, a future I could regard with a great deal
of enthusiasm, and even though it was the therapy that seemed
to have brought most of this bleakness on, or out, it seemed to

me that I needed more of it: the last shred of common sense I had left suggested that many of these problems were in me rather than in the world, that they were of a psychological rather than an actual nature, that I hadn't been born under a bad sign at all but that I was some sort of self-destructive nutcase, that I literally needed my head seeing to. Except I was flat broke and couldn't afford to see any more of my lady in Bounds Green, so she sent me to see the man in Hampstead, who had the power to refer me back to her at a preferential rate if he was convinced that I was sick enough. And so it came to pass – and there are a number of Arsenal-loathing football fans all over the country who might find the episode gloriously and hilariously significant – that this Arsenal fan was obliged to preface his attendance at the Littlewoods Cup semi-final replay by visiting a psychiatrist, in order to persuade him that I was round the twist. I got the referral I needed, and I didn't even have to produce my season-ticket.

I travelled from Hampstead down to Baker Street, from Baker Street to King's Cross, from King's Cross to Seven Sisters, and got a bus the rest of the way up the Tottenham High Road; and from Baker Street onwards, the point at which my return journey from the psychiatrist became an outward journey to a football match, I felt better, less isolated, more purposeful (although on the final stage of the journey I felt bad again, but this was a comforting pre-match bad, my stomach churning and my body weary at the thought of the emotional effort to come); I no longer had to try to explain to myself where I was going or where I had been, and I was back in the mainstream. The value of the herd instinct, again: I was only too happy to experience the loss of identity that crowds demand. It was then that it occurred to me that I would never really be able to explain or even remember precisely how the evening had started as it had, and that in some ways, football isn't a very good metaphor for life at all.

*

I usually hate games between Arsenal and Tottenham, especially the away games, when the hostile territory brings out the
very worst in the Arsenal fans, and I have stopped going to
White Hart Lane now. 'I hope your wife dies of cancer,
Roberts,' a man behind me shouted a few years back. And in
September 1987, just before David Pleat was forced to resign
his position as Tottenham manager, but just after unsavoury
allegations about his personal life had appeared in the tabloids,
I sat among several thousand people roaring 'Sex case! Sex
case! HANG HIM HANG HIM HANG HIM!', and felt, perhaps understandably, that I was much too delicate a soul for this
sort of entertainment; the blow-up dolls being tossed around
merrily at our end, and the hundreds of pairs of amusing breast
spectacles that were *de rigueur* for the committed Arsenal fan
that afternoon, hardly helped to make the sensitive liberal feel
any more at ease. And in 1989, when Spurs beat us at White
Hart Lane for the first time for four years, there was an awful
and disturbing ugliness in the Arsenal end after the final
whistle, and seats were broken, and that was enough for me.
The anti-Semitic chanting, even though Arsenal have just as
many Jewish fans as Tottenham, is obscene and unforgivable,
and over the last few years the rivalry between the two sets of
fans has become intolerably hateful.

A cup-tie is different, however. The older season-ticket
holders, those who hate Tottenham, but not with the drooling
and violent rage of some of the twenty and thirtysomethings, are
sufficiently motivated to travel, and so some of the bile is diluted.
And the result, and the football, matters more than it does in
many of the League games between Arsenal and Spurs, who for
most seasons over the last twenty or thirty years have found
themselves in mid-table, and consequently there is some sort of
a focus for the aggression. Paradoxically, when the game means
something then the identity of the opponents signifies less.

Anyway, I know that my middle-class sensibilities were not
unduly disturbed, and that there were no chanted sex-case or

cancer references to sour my memory of the evening. The game was fast and open, just as it had been on the Sunday, and once again we seemed to spend the whole of the first half watching Clive Allen bear down on the unprotected goal in front of us, but the longer it went on the more I feared for Arsenal. The team was getting younger and younger with each match (Thomas, a full-back replacement for Caesar in the first leg, was playing his first full match, in midfield) and though it was nil–nil at half-time, Allen finally scored, right at the beginning of the second half; shortly afterwards Nicholas was stretchered off, and Ian Allinson, a tryer but hardly the man to save the match, had to come on, and it was all up.

A couple of rows in front of me, a line of middle-aged men and women, blankets over their legs, soup flasks twinkling, started singing the Irish song that the older fans in the seats – I have never heard a North Bank rendition – often used to sing on big nights, and everyone who knew the words ('And then he got up and he sang it again/Over and over and over again') joined in. So I thought, with, what, six or seven minutes left, that at least I would remember the occasion with some fondness, even though it was to have a bitter and dismal conclusion; and then Allinson, jinking unconvincingly down the left, put in a feeble shot on the turn that totally deceived Clemence and snuck in guiltily at the near post, and there was this enormous explosion of relief and unhinged joy. And Tottenham fell apart, just as they had on Sunday: over the next two minutes Hayes intercepted a bad back-pass and shot into the side netting, Thomas grooved his way through to the edge of the area, with the sort of insouciance we later came to love and hate, and shot just past the post. On my video, you can see, as Anderson goes to take a throw-in, the Arsenal fans literally bouncing with excitement. And there was more to come. As Tottenham's digital clock stopped on ninety minutes, Rocky picked up a loose cross, chested it down, and hit it through Clemence and into the net; and almost immediately the referee blew the final whistle, and the rows of people disappeared and were replaced by one shuddering heap of ecstatic humanity.

It was the second of three or four lifetime football moments where my delirium was such that I had no idea what I was doing, where everything went blank for a few moments. I know that an old man behind me grabbed me around the neck and wouldn't let go, and that when I returned to a state approaching normal consciousness the rest of the stadium was empty save for a few Tottenham fans who stood watching us, too stunned and sick to move (in my mind I see white faces, but we were too far away to be able to detect shock-induced pallor), and the Arsenal players were cavorting beneath us, as overjoyed and probably as baffled by their win as we were.

We were all still in the stadium twenty minutes after the final whistle, and then we roared out on to the street, and Pete and I drove back to the Arsenal Tavern, where we were locked in after closing time so that we could watch the highlights of the game on their big TV screen, and so that I could drink much too much.

The depression that I had been living with for the best part of the 1980s packed up and started to leave that night, and within a month I was better. Inevitably part of me wishes that it had been something else that effected the cure – the love of a good woman, or a minor literary triumph, or a transcendent realisation during something like Live Aid that my life was blessed and worth living – something worthy and real and meaningful. It embarrasses me to confess that a decade-long downer lifted because Arsenal won at Spurs in the Littlewoods Cup (I would be slightly less embarrassed if it had been an FA Cup win, but the *Littlewoods*!), and I have often tried to work out why it happened like this. The win meant a lot to all Arsenal fans, of course: for seven years our team hadn't even come very close to winning a semi-final, and the decline had begun to look terminal. And there might even be a medical explanation. It could be that the monstrous surge of adrenalin released by a last-minute winner at Tottenham in a semi-final when you were one down with seven minutes left, all hope abandoned, maybe this surge corrects some kind of chemical imbalance in the brain or something.

The only convincing explanation I can come up with, however, is that I stopped feeling unlucky that night, and that the log-jam that had provoked such despair just over a year before had been sorted, not by me, predictably, but by Arsenal; and so I jumped on to the shoulders of the team and they carried me into the light that had suddenly shone down on all of us. And the lift they gave me enabled me to part company from them, in some ways: though I am still one of Arsenal's most devoted fans, and though I still go to every home game, and feel the same tensions and elations and glooms that I have always felt, I now understand them to have an entirely separate identity whose success and failure has no relationship with my own. That night, I stopped being an Arsenal lunatic and relearnt how to be a fan, still cranky, and still dangerously obsessive, but only a fan nonetheless.

JUST ANOTHER SATURDAY

CHELSEA v ARSENAL
7.3.87

Everyone went to Chelsea on the Saturday to continue the party, and it lasted for about another fifteen minutes, until something – a Hayes miss, or a Caesar back-pass, I can't remember now – provoked the howls of frustration and irritation that you could have heard on any Saturday of the previous few years. The average football fan is notoriously, almost savagely unsentimental.

It has to be said, however, that Stamford Bridge is not a

place where moist-eyed affection or indulgent forgiveness will ever thrive. Games at Chelsea are inevitably dismal – it is no coincidence that the only league fixture Arsenal lost during their otherwise all-conquering '91 Championship season was this one. The track around the outside of the pitch distances the fans from the players, and affects the atmosphere; and as most supporters on the terraces at both ends are completely in the open (and thus liable for a good soaking if there's one in the offing) there is no noise anyway. In my experience the home fans' reputation for vicious thuggery and for witless and ugly racism, although there has been a little less of both over the last couple of years, is well deserved, and everyone knows that you're safer standing, thus receiving the benefit of well-organised and thorough police protection, than you are sitting, and leaving yourself prone to isolation, recognition and ultimately demolition, the very process that did for a friend a few years back.

And the game went on, and the sky darkened, and Arsenal got worse, eventually conceding a goal, which in their hangover listlessness was one goal too many. And you stand there on the huge crumbling terrace, your feet stiffening and then actually burning in the cold, with the Chelsea fans jeering and gesturing at you, and you wonder why you bothered, when you knew, not only in your heart of hearts but with your head as well, that the game would be dull, and the players would be inept, that the feelings engendered on the Wednesday would have dribbled away to a flat nothingness before twenty minutes of the Saturday game had passed when, if you had stayed at home or gone record shopping, you could have kept the embers glowing for another week longer. But then, these are the games, the 1–0 defeats at Chelsea on a miserable March afternoon, that give meaning to the rest, and it is precisely because you have seen so many of them that there is real joy to be had from those others that come once every six, seven, ten years.

At the end of the game the away fans managed a respectful

and muted gratitude for their team, a recognition of recent past achievements, but it had been a dismal afternoon, a piece of dues-paying, spadework, absolutely nothing more than that. And yet as we were waiting to be let out (another thing about Chelsea: you are kept behind for a good thirty minutes while the streets outside are cleared of their menace) the sheer awfulness of it all deepened and thus the experience was lent a perverse kind of glory, so that those of us there became entitled to award themselves a campaign medal.

Two things happened. First, it began to snow and the discomfort was such that you wanted to laugh at yourself for tolerating this fan's life any longer; and secondly, a man came out with a rolling machine and proceeded to drive up and down the pitch with it. He was not the irascible old git of football club legend, but an enormous young man with a monstrous skinhead haircut, and he obviously hated Arsenal with all the passion of his employers' followers. As he drove towards us on his machine, he gave us the finger, a delighted and maniacal smile on his face; and on his return visit he gave us the finger again, and so it went on – up, back, and the finger. Up, back and the finger. And we had to stand and watch him do it, over and over again, in the dark and the freezing cold, while the snow fell on us in our concrete compound. It was a proper, thorough restoration of normal service.

GOLDEN

ARSENAL v LIVERPOOL
(at Wembley) 11.4.87

And on the other hand, some days are just golden. My depression had gone completely now; all I could feel was the place where the ache had been, and that was a pleasurable sensation, just as when you are recovering from food poisoning

and eating again, the soreness of the stomach muscles is pleasurable. I was six days off my thirtieth birthday, and I had the
idea that everything had pulled round for me just in time; that
thirty was the falls at the end of the river and if I had still been
down when I got there I would have gone right over the edge.
So I felt good about that, and Arsenal back at Wembley felt
good, because with a young team and a new manager the
Littlewoods Cup seemed like an unimaginably delicious hors
d'oeuvre, rather than a meal in itself. I had just turned twenty-
three when we were last all there together, and for me and
the team, the seven intervening years had been unpredictably
horrible; but now we had come out of the dark and into the
light.

There *was* light, too, a glorious and gloriously apposite April
sunshine. And though you are always aware of how it feels
when the winter is over, however long that winter might have
been, there is nothing like a football stadium, especially Wembley, to remind you, because you stand there in the shadowed
dark looking down into the light, on to the brilliant lush green
and it's as if you are in a cinema watching a film about another
and more exotic country. It was as sunny outside the stadium
as in it, of course, but it didn't seem that way, because of this
trick football grounds have of using just a rectangle of the
sunshine so that you can see it and understand it.

So there was all that already, even before the game started.
And though we were playing Liverpool (admittedly Liverpool
in one of their less mighty guises, pre-Beardsley and Barnes,
but post-Dalglish, although he was their sub that day), and thus
could only be expected to lose, I really had convinced myself
that it wouldn't matter, and that me being back, and the team
being back, was enough. So when Craig Johnston put Rush
through, and he paused for a moment, took his time, and
smashed the ball neatly and authoritatively past our goalkeeper
Lukic's groping left hand, I was stung but not surprised, and
determined not to let the goal and the defeat that was bound

to follow spoil my recuperation or my new, springy optimism.

But Charlie equalised before half-time, after he had hit the post and caused a massive scramble in the Liverpool penalty area; and in a wonderful second half of football, when both teams played with grace and skill and desire, our substitute, the poor, maligned Perry Groves, skipped past Gillespie, crossed, Charlie swung, the ball hit a defender and rolled gently past the deceived Grobbelaar and into the goal. It all seemed so languid, and the ball trundled in so slowly, that I feared that it would not have the strength to cross the line completely, or it would be cleared before the referee had spotted that it had indeed gone over, but in the end it found just enough puff to touch the net. Nicholas and Groves, one of whom had come from Celtic for nearly three-quarters of a million pounds, the other of whom had come from Colchester United for about one-fifteenth of that sum, ran behind the goal and did a little dance of joy, just the two of them, in front of us; they could not ever have imagined dancing together before, and they never would again, but there they were, yoked just for one tiny moment in the one-hundred-and-one-year history of the club by their unrepeatable and frankly fortuitous collaboration. And that is how Arsenal came to win the Littlewoods Cup, not the most prestigious trophy I know, but much more than Pete and I and the rest of us could have dared hope for two years previously. It was some kind of reward for blind persistence.

One thing I know for sure about being a fan is this: it is not a vicarious pleasure, despite all appearances to the contrary, and those who say that they would rather do than watch are missing the point. Football is a context where watching *becomes* doing – not in the aerobic sense, because watching a game, smoking your head off while doing so, drinking after it has finished and eating chips on the way home is unlikely to do you a whole lot of Jane Fonda good, in the way that chuffing up and down a pitch is supposed to. But when there is some kind of triumph, the pleasure does not radiate from the players outwards until it reaches the likes of us at the back of the terraces in a pale and diminished form; our fun is not a watery version of the team's fun, even though they are the ones that get to score the goals and climb the steps at Wembley to meet Princess Diana. The joy we feel on occasions like this is not a celebration of others' good fortune, but a celebration of our own; and when there is a disastrous defeat the sorrow that engulfs us is, in effect, self-pity, and anyone who wishes to understand how football is consumed must realise this above all things. The players are merely our representatives, chosen by the manager rather than elected by us, but our representatives nonetheless, and sometimes if you look hard you can see the little poles that join them together, and the handles at the side that enable us to move them. I am a part of the club, just as the club is a part of me; and I say this fully aware that the club exploits me, disregards my views, and treats me shoddily on occasions, so my feeling of organic connection is not built on a muddle-headed and sentimental misunderstanding of how professional football works. This Wembley win belonged to me every bit as much as it belonged to Charlie Nicholas or George Graham (does Nicholas, who was dropped by Graham right at the start of the following season, and then sold, remember the afternoon as fondly?), and I worked every bit as hard for it as they did. The only difference between me and them is that I have put in more hours, more years, more decades than them, and so had a better understanding of the afternoon, a sweeter appreciation of why the sun still shines when I remember it.

BANANAS

ARSENAL v LIVERPOOL
15.8.87

Because my partner is small, and therefore disadvantaged when it comes to watching football from the terraces, I gave my season-ticket away for the afternoon and bought seats high up in the West Stand for the first game of the new season. It was the afternoon that Smith made his début for Arsenal, and Barnes and Beardsley theirs for Liverpool, and it was hot, and Highbury was heaving.

We were level with the penalty spot at the Clock End of the ground, so we had a perfect view of the Davis diving header that equalised Aldridge's opening goal, and a perfect view of the astonishing twenty-five-yard header from Nichol that gave Liverpool their winner in the very last minute; we could also see, with terrible clarity, the extraordinary behaviour of the Liverpool fans beneath us and to our right.

In his book on Barnes and race issues in Liverpool, *Out of His Skin*, Dave Hill only mentions that first game in passing ('Liverpool's travelling supporters went home delighted, any doubts about the wisdom of the manager's summer shopping spree already on the retreat.'). He pays more attention to Liverpool's game a few weeks later against Everton at Anfield in the Littlewoods Cup, during which the away supporters chanted 'Niggerpool! Niggerpool', and 'Everton are white!'. (Everton, mysteriously, still haven't managed to find a black player good enough for their team.)

Yet Barnes's first game did throw up information that Hill could have used, because we could see quite clearly, as the teams warmed up before the kick-off, that banana after banana was being hurled from the away supporters' enclosure. The bananas were designed to announce, for the benefit of those unversed in codified terrace abuse, that there was a monkey on the pitch; and as the Liverpool fans have never bothered to bring bananas to previous Arsenal matches, even though we have always had at least one black player in the side since the turn of the decade, one can only presume that John Barnes was the monkey to whom they were referring.

Those who have seen John Barnes, this beautiful, elegant man, play football, or give an interview, or even simply walk out on to a pitch, and have also stood next to the grunting, overweight orang-utans who do things like throw bananas and make monkey noises, will appreciate the dazzling irony of all this. (There may well be attractive, articulate and elegant racists, but they certainly never come to football matches.) And maybe the bananas were not intended as an expression of racial hatred, but as a grotesque form of welcome – maybe these Liverpudlians, with their famous quick and ready wit, merely wanted to welcome Barnes in a way that they thought he could understand, just as the Spurs supporters gave Ardiles and Villa an Argentinian tickertape welcome in '78. (This latter theory is hard to believe, but it is no harder than believing that so many fans could be so poisonously angry about the arrival at their club of one of the best players in the world.) Yet however hysterically ironic the scene might have been, and whatever the Liverpool fans might have meant, it was a revolting, nauseating sight.

Arsenal, by and large, have no problems with this kind of filth any more, although they have problems with other kinds, particularly anti-Semitism. There are black fans, on the terraces and in the seats, and our best players – Rocastle, Campbell, Wright – are black, and enormously popular. You can still, even now, occasionally hear idiots who jeer the black players on opposing teams. (One night I turned round angrily to confront an Arsenal fan making monkey noises at Manchester United's Paul Ince, and found that I was abusing a blind man. A blind racist!) And sometimes, when an opposing black player commits a foul, or misses a good chance, or doesn't miss a good

chance, or argues with the referee, you sit quivering in a panic
of liberal foreboding. 'Please don't say anything, anybody,' you
sit muttering to yourself. 'Please don't ruin it all for me.' (For
me, please note, not for the poor bastard who has to play just
feet away from some evil fascist stormtrooper – such is the
indulgent self-pity of the modern free-thinker.) Then some
neanderthal rises to his feet, points at Ince, or Wallace, or
Barnes, or Walker, and you hold your breath . . . and he calls
him a cunt, or a wanker, or something else obscene, and you
are filled with an absurd sense of metropolitan sophisticate
pride, because the adjectival epithet is missing; you know that
this would not be the case if you were watching a game on
Merseyside or in the West Country or in the North-East, or
anywhere that has no real multiracial community. It's not much
to be grateful for, really, the fact that a man calls another man
a cunt but not a black cunt.

It seems lame to say that I loathe the baiting of black players
that takes place as a matter of routine inside some football
grounds, and if I had had any guts I would have either (a)
confronted some of the worst perpetrators or (b) stopped going
to games. Before remonstrating with the blind racist I was
making some frantic calculations – how hard is he? How hard
are his mates? How hard are my mates? – until I heard something, a certain whininess in his voice, maybe, that led me
to conclude that I wasn't about to get a pasting, and acted
accordingly, but this is rare. More usually I take the view that
these people, like the people who smoke on tube trains, know
what they're doing, and their abuse is intended to intimidate
anyone, black or white, who feels like doing something about
it. And as for not going . . . what I'm supposed to say is that
football grounds are for everyone, not just for racist thugs, and
when decent people stop going then the game is in trouble.
And part of me believes that (Leeds fans have done amazing
things to conquer the foul atmosphere that used to engulf their

ground); part of me, however, knows that I can't stop because of the strength of my obsession.

I wish all the things that other fans like me wish: I wish that football commentators would express outrage more than they do; I wish Arsenal really did insist on the ejection of fans who sing songs about Hitler gassing Jews, instead of forever threatening to do so; I wish all players, black and white, would do more to make their disgust known. (If, say, Everton's goalkeeper Neville Southall simply walked off the pitch in protest every time his own fans made these noises, then the problems at Goodison Park would stop almost overnight, but I know that things are not done this way.) But most of all, I wish I were enormous and of a violent disposition, so that I could deal with any problem that arises near me in a fashion commensurate with the anger I feel.

THE KING OF KENILWORTH ROAD

LUTON v ARSENAL
31.8.87

Non-footballing friends and family have never met anyone madder than I; indeed, they are convinced that I am as obsessed as it is possible to be. But I know that there are people who would regard the level of my commitment – every home game, a handful of away games, and one or two reserve or youth games each season – as inadequate. People like Neil Kaas, a Luton fan who took me and my half-brother to watch Arsenal at Kenilworth Road as his guest in the days when Luton's ban on away fans was in operation, are obsessives with all traces of timidity or self-doubt removed; they make me look like the faint-hearted dilettante they suspect me of being.

Eight things you didn't know about Neil Kaas:

(1) He would, of course, travel to Plymouth on a Wednesday night, thus using up a precious day's holiday. (He has travelled to Wigan, and Doncaster, and everywhere else; and on the way back from a mid-week game in Hartlepool, the coach broke down, and he and his party watched *Police Academy 3* seven times.)

(2) When I first met him, he had just returned from a kibbutz, although when I got to know him better I was amazed that he had managed to tear himself away from the Hatters for any length of time. He explained that he had gone because the Luton fans were about to organise a boycott of all home games in protest against a planned move to Milton Keynes; Neil knew that even though he had given the boycott his sincere backing, he would be unable to maintain it unless he took himself off to the other side of the world.

(3) After a bizarre chain of circumstances too complicated to relate here, he watched a game against QPR from the directors' box, having been introduced by David Evans to the rest of the Luton board as 'the next Chairman of Luton Town'.

(4) He has single-handedly driven Mike Newell and a number of other players away from the club, by ensuring that he is always positioned near the players' tunnel to abuse viciously and incessantly anybody he believes is not good enough to tread the Kenilworth Road turf.

(5) A report in the *Independent* once made some reference to a loudmouth with a foghorn voice who sits in the main stand at Luton, said loudmouth precluding enjoyment for anyone in his immediate vicinity; having watched with Neil I can only conclude, regretfully, that he is the man.

(6) He attends every open evening at Luton, occasions which enable the fans to talk to the manager and the directors, although recently he has begun to suspect that they will no longer allow him to ask questions. He is mystified by this, although some of the questions I know him to have asked are

not really questions at all, but slanderous and noisy allegations of impropriety and incompetence.

(7) He has written to Luton Council proposing that they commission a statue commemorating Raddy Antic, whose last-minute goal at Maine Road prevented Luton dropping into Division Two.

(8) On Sunday mornings, just a few hours after he has returned from wherever he has been on the Saturday afternoon, he plays for Bushey 'B' (a team which suffered the misfortune of having two points deducted when the goalkeeper's dog stopped a shot on the line) in the Maccabi League, although he has had disciplinary problems of late, both with his manager and with referees, and at the time of writing is sidelined.

This litany contains *a* truth about Neil, but not *the* truth, which is that he has a cheerful and ironic perspective on his own excesses, and talks about them as if they were the property of someone else – his younger brother, maybe. And away from Kenilworth Road he is charming, interested, and unflaggingly polite, at least to strangers, so the rage that invariably afflicts him on Saturdays is induced exclusively by Luton.

Luton are not a big club, and they don't have many fans – their home crowds are between a third and a quarter the size of Arsenal's. What was memorable about watching this game with him was not the football, which ended up a drab 1–1 draw after Davis had put us into the lead, but the sense of proprietorship that emanates from someone who has to his own satisfaction taken the club over. It seemed, as we walked to our seats, that Neil knew maybe one in three of the crowd, and stopped for a chat with half of those. And when he travels to away games, it is not as a mote in some huge invading army, but as a visible and recognisable face in a ragged crowd of a couple of hundred, maybe even less than that for some of the more problematic midweek fixtures.

Yet this is part of the attraction for him: he is the Lord of

Luton, the King of Kenilworth Road. So when his friends hear
the results on a Saturday, on national radio and television, or
on the tannoys of other League grounds, they think, simply,
'Neil Kaas' when they hear the Luton score. Neil Kaas 0 Liverpool 2, Neil Kaas saved from relegation with last-minute goal,
Neil Kaas wins Littlewoods Cup . . .

And this too is an appeal that football has for me, although
I could never claim to be a definition of Arsenal in the way that
Neil and Luton define each other. This appeal is one that has
emerged slowly over the years, but it is a powerful attraction
nevertheless: *I like the thought of people remembering me on a
regular basis.*

I know that this happens. On the night of the 26th of May
1989 I came back to my flat after carousing deep into the night
to find fourteen or fifteen phone messages from friends all over
Britain and Europe, some of whom I hadn't spoken to for
months; often, on the day after an Arsenal calamity or triumph,
I receive phone calls from friends, even non-footballing friends,
who have been reminded to contact me by a newspaper or a
chance idle glance at a sports round-up at the end of a news
bulletin. (To prove the point: I just went downstairs to pick up
the mail, and there was a postcard, a thank-you note from a
friend whom I assisted in a banal and unspectacular way some
weeks ago, and whom I haven't heard from since. At first I was
puzzled as to why she should thank me now, long after the
event in question – I wasn't expecting her to do so – but the PS
at the end, 'Sorry about the Arse', serves as an explanation.)

Even though you know that anything – Mickey Rourke or
Brussels sprouts or Warren Street underground station or
toothache, the associations that people might have for you are
endless and private – can set somebody off on a train of thought
which will end up with you sitting in one of its carriages, you
have no idea when this might happen. It is unpredictable and
haphazard. With football, there is none of this randomness:
you know that on nights like the '89 Championship night, or

on afternoons like the afternoon of the 1992 Wrexham disaster, you are in the thoughts of scores, maybe even hundreds, of people. And I love that, the fact that old girlfriends and other people you have lost touch with and will probably never see again are sitting in front of their TV sets and thinking, momentarily but *all at the same time*, Nick, just that, and are happy or sad for me. Nobody else gets that, only us.

MY ANKLE

ARSENAL v WIMBLEDON
19.9.87

I can't remember how it happened – probably I trod on the ball or something equally graceless. And I didn't realise the implication of it straight away. I just knew, when I hobbled off the five-a-side court, that my ankle hurt like hell and was swelling like a bastard in front of my eyes. But when I was sitting in my flatmate's car on the way back to our flat, I began to panic: it was a quarter to one, I couldn't walk, and I had to be at Highbury by three.

At home, I sat with a bag of frozen peas balanced on the end of my leg while I contemplated the options. My flatmate, his girlfriend and my girlfriend suggested that, since I was completely immobile and in obvious pain, I should sit at home listening to the radio, but obviously that wasn't possible; and once I realised that I was going to the game somehow, that there were taxis and seats in the Lower West Stand and friends' shoulders to lean on if necessary, the panic subsided and it became a simple matter of logistics.

It wasn't so bad, in the end. We got the tube to Arsenal instead of Finsbury Park – not as far to walk – and we all stood outside, not in our usual spot under the North Bank roof, even though it pelted down for the whole of a goalless second half, so that I could lean against a crush barrier and avoid any tumbles down the North Bank when Arsenal scored. But still. Getting soaked to the skin (and insisting that everyone else got soaked to the skin with me), shivering with the pain and trebling my journey time to and from the ground didn't seem like too bad a price to pay. Not when you consider the cataclysmic alternative, anyway.

THE MATCH

COVENTRY v ARSENAL
13.12.87

Pete and I left around twelve, I guess, for a three p.m., Sunday afternoon kick-off, and got there just in time. It was an awful game, unspeakable, a nil–nil draw in freezing conditions . . . and it was live on television, so we could have stayed at home. My powers of self-analysis fail me completely here: I don't know why we went. We just did.

I didn't see a live League game on television until 1983, and neither did anyone else of my generation. When I was a kid there wasn't so much football on TV: an hour on Saturday night, an hour on Sunday afternoon, sometimes an hour mid-week, when our clubs had European games. We got to see an entire ninety minutes only very rarely. Occasional England games were shown live; then there was the FA Cup Final, and maybe the European Cup Final . . . two or three live club games a year, maximum.

That was obviously ridiculous. Even Cup semi-finals, or Championship deciders, weren't televised live; sometimes the stations weren't even allowed to show us highlights. (When Liverpool just pipped QPR for the Championship in 1976, we got to see the goals on the news, but that was all; there was a whole set of incomprehensible rules about TV coverage that no one understood.) So despite satellite technology, and colour televisions, and 24-inch screens, we had to sit with our ears pressed against transistor radios. Eventually the clubs realised that there was big money to be made, and the TV companies were happy to give it to them; the behaviour of the Football League thereafter has resembled that of the mythical convent girl. The League will let anybody do anything they want – change the time of the kick-off, or the day of the game, or the teams, or the shirts, it doesn't matter; nothing is too much trouble for them. Meanwhile the fans, the paying customers, are regarded as amenable and gullible idiots. The date advertised on your ticket is meaningless: if ITV or BBC want to change the fixture to a time more convenient to them, they will do so. In 1991, Arsenal fans intending to travel to the crucial match at Sunderland found that after a little television interference (kick-off was changed from three to five), the last train to London left before the game finished. Who cared? Just us, nobody important.

I will continue to attend televised games at Highbury, mostly because I've already paid for my ticket. But, sod it, I'm not going to travel to Coventry or Sunderland or anywhere else if I can sit at home and watch the match, and I hope lots of other people do the same. Television will notice our absence, one day. In the end, however much they mike up the crowd, they will be unable to create any atmosphere whatsoever, because there will be nobody there: we'll all be at home, watching the box. And when that happens, I hope that the managers and the chairmen spare us the pompous and embittered column in the programme complaining about our fickleness.

NO APOLOGY NECESSARY

ARSENAL v EVERTON
24.2.88

I know that I have apologised a great deal during the course of these pages. Football has meant too much to me, and come to represent too many things, and I feel that I have been to watch far too many games, and spent too much money, and fretted about Arsenal when I should have been fretting about something else, and asked for too much indulgence from friends and family. Yet there are occasions when going to watch a game is the most valid and rewarding leisure pursuit I can think of, and Arsenal against Everton, another second-leg Littlewoods Cup semi-final, was one of those times.

It came four days after another huge game, against Manchester United in the FA Cup, a game which Arsenal won 2–1 but only after McClair had sent a penalty high over the bar and into an ecstatic North Bank with the last kick of the game (and Nigel Winterburn pursued him relentlessly and unpleasantly back to the half-way line after he had done so, one of the first hints of this Arsenal team's embarrassing indiscipline); so it was an enormous week, with gigantic crowds – fifty-three thousand on the Saturday, fifty-one thousand on the Wednesday.

We beat Everton 3–1 that night, 4–1 on aggregate, a comfortable enough win which Arsenal fully deserved, but we had to wait for it. Four minutes before half-time Rocastle beat Everton's offside trap, went round Southall, and stroked the ball well wide of a completely empty goal; and then three minutes later Hayes was through too, only this time Southall brought him down six inches from the goal-line. Hayes took the penalty himself, and, like McClair, booted it well over the bar. And the crowd is going spare with frustration and worry; you look around and you see faces working, completely absorbed, and the susurration that spreads around the ground after particularly dramatic incidents lasts all the way through half-time because there is so much to talk about but, at the beginning of the second half, Thomas chips Southall and scores, and you want to burst with relief, and the noise that greets the goal has a special depth to it, a bottom that you only get when everyone in the stadium except for the away supporters gives the roar everything they've got, even people right up the top in the fifteen quid seats. And though Heath equalises soon after, Rocky then makes up for his earlier miss, and Smith gets another one, and the whole of Highbury, all four sides of the ground, is alive, yelling and hugging itself with delight at the prospect of another Wembley final, and the manner in which it has been achieved. It's extraordinary, knowing that you have a role to play in all this, that the evening wouldn't have been the same without you and thousands like you.

Absurdly, I haven't yet got around to saying that football is a wonderful sport, but of course it is. Goals have a rarity value that points and runs and sets do not, and so there will always be that thrill, the thrill of seeing someone do something that can only be done three or four times in a whole game if you are lucky, not at all if you are not. And I love the pace of it, its lack of formula; and I love the way that small men can destroy big men (watch Beardsley against Adams) in a way that they can't in other contact sports, and the way that the best team does not necessarily win. And there's the athleticism (with all due respect to Ian Botham and the England front row, there are very few good fat footballers), and the way that strength and intelligence have to combine. It allows players to look beautiful and balletic in a way that some sports do not: a perfectly-timed diving header, or a perfectly-struck volley, allow the body to achieve a poise and grace that some sportsmen can never exhibit.

But there's even more to it than all that. During matches like the Everton semi-final, although nights like that are inevitably rare, there is this powerful sensation of being exactly in the right place at the right time; when I am at Highbury on a big night, or, of course, Wembley on an even bigger afternoon, I feel as though I am at the centre of the whole world. When else does this happen in life? Maybe you've got a hot ticket for the first night of an Andrew Lloyd Webber show, but you know that the show is going to run for years and years, so you'd actually have to tell people afterwards that you saw it before they did, which is kind of uncool and in any case completely ruins the effect. Or maybe you saw the Stones at Wembley, but then even something like that is repeated for night after night nowadays, and consequently doesn't have the same one-off impact of a football match. It's not *news*, in the same way that an Arsenal *v* Everton semi-final is news: when you look at your newspaper the next day, whichever one you read, there will be extensive space given over to an account of *your* evening, the evening to which you contributed simply by turning up and shouting.

You just can't find this outside a football ground; there is nowhere else you can be in the entire country that will make you feel as though you are at the heart of things. Because whichever nightclub you go to, or play, or film, or whichever concert you see, or restaurant you eat at, life will have been going on elsewhere in your absence, as it always does; but when I am at Highbury for games like these, I feel that the rest of the world has stopped and is gathered outside the gates, waiting to hear the final score.

WELCOME TO ENGLAND

ENGLAND v HOLLAND
March 1988

In 1988 I began working for a Far Eastern trading company. I started out as a teacher, but it soon became clear that my middle-management pupils were more perplexed by the bizarre requests they received from their head office than they were by the English language. So the teaching vanished, and instead I did what I can only describe as Other Things, since a generic description of my duties is beyond me. I wrote countless letters to solicitors, and a long essay on Jonathan Swift which was translated and faxed back to base; I ascertained to my employers' satisfaction what constituted drinking water; I pored over the landscape plans for Hampton Court and took photographs of Beaulieu Motor Museum; I went to see Directors of Social Services to talk about orphanages; I became involved in protracted negotiations for equestrian centres in Warwickshire and pedigree dogs in Scotland. It was varied work.

The managers worked astonishingly hard: their contracted hours were from 8 a.m. to 8 p.m. on Monday to Friday, and from 8 a.m. to 2 p.m. on Saturday, but these were nominal – a twelve-hour day, like Gordon Gekko's lunch, was for wimps. But when I told three of my students that Gullit and Van Basten were coming to town to pit their wits against Lineker and Shilton, the temptation was too much even for them, and I was instructed to buy tickets and act as their chaperon and inductor for the evening.

Every couple of years I forget what a miserable experience it is to go to Wembley to watch England play, and give it another try. In '85 I went to watch a World Cup qualifier a couple of weeks after Scotland's Jock Stein had died, and listened to the most mind-bogglingly obscene celebratory songs; four years later I went to another one, and sat among people who gave drunken Nazi salutes during the National Anthem. Why I thought that things would be any different for a friendly against Holland I can't remember, but it turned out to be an embarrassing misapprehension.

Our timing was just right. We were walking down Wembley Way about fifteen minutes before kick-off, with reserved seats in our pockets, and I was feeling pleased with my expert organisation. As we approached our entrance, however, we were met by a determined and indiscriminate mounted police charge, and we were forced back down the road with hundreds of other ticket holders, and my colleagues began to panic. We regrouped and started again; this time our £12.00 tickets were regarded, reluctantly, as certificates of legitimate interest, and we were allowed to approach the stadium. As we did so, the game kicked off and England scored almost immediately, but we missed all that – we were still negotiating admission. One of the entrance doors was hanging off its hinges, and an official told us that large numbers of people had forced their way into the ground.

Once inside, it was obvious that our seats had gone. The gangways were packed with people like us, all clutching now-worthless ticket stubs, all too afraid to confront the crop-headed, thick-necked people sitting in our seats. There wasn't a steward in sight. 'Here come the fucking Wongs', remarked one of a group of young men, as I led my charges down the steps to find a position from which we could see at least a square of the pitch. I didn't bother translating. We stood and watched for about half an hour, during which time Holland took a 2–1 lead; the dreadlocked Gullit, the main reason why the game had sold out in the first place, provoked monkey noises every time he touched the ball. Just before half-time we gave up and went home. I got back to my flat just in time to watch the highlights on TV.

People have told me that they're beginning to turn things round at Wembley now, and post-Italia '90, what with Gazzamania and Lineker charm, the composition of the average England crowd is changing. This often happens when a team is doing well, and in itself it doesn't offer much cause for hope, because when they play badly again you lose that lot. It seems to me, and this is not a theory that I can support with any hard evidence, but never mind, that bad teams attract an ugly following.

Only boneheads entertain serious doubts nowadays about the link between social and economic conditions and football violence, but why is it that, say, Birmingham City fans have a markedly worse reputation than Sunderland fans? Even if we accept, for the sake of argument, that the West Midlands suffers from the same kind of social and economic deprivation that plagues the North-East, then how does one explain the impeccable behaviour of the Villa supporters? Two teams from the same city; but one plays in the First Division, and the other languishes in the Third. When Leeds, Chelsea and Manchester United were in the Second Division their fans terrified everybody; when Millwall came up to the First their reputation for monstrous, evil violence evaporated a little. And I don't think that poor football actually changes the way people behave; it's not that, although there is an element of compensatory pride involved ('We might not be much good at football, but we can give you a good kicking'); it's more that – how can I put this tactfully? – there is a higher proportion of nutters among the never-say-die, we'll-support-you-evermore hardcore than among the sod-that-for-a-lark floating punter.

So among crowds of twenty-five thousand, you'll find a few hundred troublemakers; when you're getting crowds of five or six thousand, the same few hundred will still be turning up, and suddenly the tiny minority have become much more significant, and the club are landed with a reputation. And once you've got a reputation, you start to appeal to those who are attracted by the promise of violence inherent in that reputation. That, I think, is what happened with Chelsea and Millwall in the late seventies and early eighties; it is also what happened with England between elimination from the World Cup in 1974 and qualification for Italy in 1990. For most of that time they were a desperate side, and they attracted a pretty desperate crowd.

The problem here is that unless a team is playing well, winning things, filling their stadia, clubs simply cannot afford to alienate the very people they are supposed to be purging. I can think of at least one club chairman who has in the past been conspicuously ambivalent about some of the unpleasant characters that keep his club afloat, and I have not been aware of any particularly strident campaigning on the part of the England authorities to drive out one crowd and bring in another (any campaigning of that kind has been done by the fans themselves); they know, deep down, which side their bread is buttered on.

I tried to compensate for the evening by offering to take my new workmates to Highbury, where I knew that we would be left undisturbed whether we stood on the terraces or sat in the seats. But every time I suggested it, they just looked at me and smiled, as if the invitation was an extreme example of the famously incomprehensible English sense of humour. I guess they still think I spend every Saturday afternoon being charged by police horses and then cowering in a gangway somewhere, too frightened to claim the seat I have paid for, and on the evidence of the Holland game it would be an obvious assumption to make; in their position, I would have been on the phone back to Head Office first thing on Thursday morning, begging and pleading for a posting somewhere, anywhere, else in the world.

GUS CAESAR

ARSENAL v LUTON
(at Wembley) 24.4.88

The Littlewoods Cup Final that year was a disaster, and sometimes I still find myself drifting back to it: 2–1 up with ten minutes left, and at the end of one of the most one-sided periods of football I have ever seen (Hayes hits the post, Smith hits the bar, Smith one-on-one with Dibble but doesn't beat him), the ball is on the penalty spot after Rocky has been brought down and Winterburn is about to . . .

No. He's missed it again, for the fortieth or fiftieth time since that April afternoon. My daydreams are so vivid that I really do find it hard to believe that he won't get another chance sometime, and my re-emergence back into my underground journey, or the book I am reading, is ludicrously slow, only achievable once I have forced myself to recognise, sometimes by saying the words under my breath, that the game is over, finished, and will never be played again. But you see, if Winterburn had scored (and why did none of the others volunteer to take it? A Wembley final isn't the place to take your first one), we would have won 3–1, no question, and retained the Cup we had won the year before; but he didn't, and Luton went up the other end and scored twice in the last seven minutes and won 3–2. Fairly or unfairly, the Arsenal fans I have spoken to blame one man: Augustus Caesar.

There have been so many players that the crowd have rubbished over the years, and not all of them were bad: Ure, Sammels, Blockley, Rix, Chapman, Hayes, Groves, even Michael Thomas for the second half of the first Championship season and a good chunk of the following year. But Gus was different. There was no debate whatsoever about his talents. Hayes, Groves, Thomas, and Rix all had their defenders among the fans, but Gus had none, or none that I ever came across; the nadir of his Arsenal career was probably during a horrible 1–0 defeat at Wimbledon in January 1990, when every back-pass or clearance he accomplished without disaster was greeted with ironic cheers and applause for the entire game. I can't begin to imagine how anyone could ever cope with that kind of public humiliation.

Soon after I had stopped teaching and begun to try to write, I read a book called *The Hustler* by Walter Tevis. I was much taken by Fast Eddie, the character played by Paul Newman in the film, just as I had been much taken with the notion that I was the Cannonball Kid when Charlie Nicholas moved down from Celtic. And as the book seemed to be about anything you wanted to do that was difficult – writing, becoming a footballer, whatever – I paid it extra special attention. At one point (oh God oh God oh God) I typed these words out on a piece of paper and pinned it above my desk:

> 'That's what the whole goddamned thing is: you got to commit yourself to the life you picked. And you picked it – most people don't even do that. You're smart and you're young and you've got, like I said before, talent.'

As the rejection slips piled up, these words comforted me; and as I began to panic about the way things that everybody else had, like careers and nice flats and a bit of cash for the weekend, seemed to be slipping out of arm's reach, friends and family began to try to reassure me. 'You know you're good,' they said. 'You'll be OK. Just be patient.' And I *did* know I was good, and I *had* committed myself to the life I had picked, and my friends, and Fast Eddie's friends, couldn't all be wrong, so I sat back and waited. I know now that I was wrong, stupid, to do so, and I know because Gus Caesar told me so.

Gus is living proof that this self-belief, this driven sense of vocation (and I am not talking about arrogance here, but the simple healthy self-confidence that is absolutely necessary for survival), can be viciously misleading. Did Gus commit himself to the life he had picked? Of course he did. You don't get anywhere near the first team of a major First Division football club without commitment. And did he know he was good? He must have done, and justifiably so. Think about it. At school he must have been much, much better than his peers, so he gets picked for the school team, and then some representative side, South London Boys or what have you; and he's still better than anyone else in the team, by miles, so the scouts come to watch, and he's offered an apprenticeship not with Fulham or Brentford or even West Ham but with the mighty Arsenal. And it's still not over, even then, because if you look at any First Division youth team of five years ago you won't recognise most of the names, because most of them have disappeared. (Here's the Arsenal youth team of April 1987, from a randomly plucked programme: Miller, Hannigan, McGregor, Hillier, Scully, Carstairs, Connelly, Rivero, Cagigao, S. Ball, Esqulant. Of those, only Hillier has come through, although Miller is still with us as a highly rated reserve goalkeeper; Scully is still playing professional football somewhere, though not for Arsenal or any other First Division team. The rest have gone, and gone from a club famous for giving its own players a fair crack.)

But Gus survives, and goes on to play for the reserves. And suddenly, it's all on for him: Don Howe is in trouble, and flooding the first team with young players – Niall Quinn, Hayes, Rocastle, Adams, Martin Keown. And when Viv Anderson is suspended over Christmas 1985 Gus makes his début, as a right-back, at of all places Old Trafford, and we win 1–0 up there, so he's part of a back four that's kept a clean sheet away at Manchester United.

Howe gets the sack, and George Graham keeps him on, and he's used as a sub in quite a few games over George's first season, so things are still going well for him – not as well as they are for Rocky and Hayes and Adams and Quinn, but then these players are having an exceptional first full season, and when the squad for the England Under-21s is announced it's full of Arsenal players, *and Gus Caesar is one of them*. The England selectors, like the Arsenal fans, are beginning to trust Arsenal's youth policy implicitly, and Gus gets a call-up even though he isn't in the first team regularly. But never mind why, he's in, he's recognised as one of the best twenty or so young players in the whole country.

Now at this point Gus could be forgiven for relaxing his guard a little. He's young, he's got talent, he's committed to the life he's picked, and at least some of the self-doubt that plagues everyone with long-shot dreams must have vanished by now. At this stage you have to rely on the judgement of others (I was relying on the judgements of friends and agents and anyone I could find who would read my stuff and tell me it was OK); and when those others include two Arsenal managers and an England coach then you probably reckon that there isn't much to worry about.

But as it turns out, they are all wrong. So far he has leaped over every hurdle in his path comfortably, but even at this late stage it is possible to be tripped up. Probably the first time we notice that things aren't right is in January 1987, in that first-leg semi-final against Tottenham: Caesar is painfully, obviously, out of his depth against those Spurs forwards. In truth he looks like a rabbit caught in headlights, frozen to the spot until Waddle or Allen or somebody runs him over, and then he starts to thrash about, horribly and pitifully, and finally George and Theo Foley put him out of his misery by substituting him. He doesn't get another chance for a while. The next time I remember him turning out is against Chelsea at Stamford Bridge in a 1–1 draw, a week or two before the Luton final, but again there is a moment in the first half where Dixon runs at him, turns him one way, then the other, then back again, like your dad used to do to you when you were a really little kid in the back garden, and eventually strolls past him and puts the ball just the wrong side of the post. We knew that there was going to be trouble at Wembley, when O'Leary was out injured and Gus was the only candidate to replace him. Caesar leaves it late, but when the ball is knocked into the box seven minutes from time, he miskicks so violently that he falls over; at this point he looks like somebody off the street who has won a competition to appear as a centre-half in a Wembley final, and not like a professional footballer at all, and in the ensuing chaos Danny Wilson stoops to head the ball over the line for Luton's equalising goal.

That's it. End of story. He's at the club for another three or four years, but he's very much the last resort centre-back, and he must have known, when George bought Bould and then Linighan and then Pates, with Adams and O'Leary already at the club, that he didn't have much of a future – he was the sixth in line for two positions. He was given a free transfer at the end of the 90/91 season, to Cambridge United; but within another couple of months they let him go too, to Bristol City, and a couple of months after that Bristol City let him go to Airdrie. To get where he did, Gus Caesar clearly had more talent than nearly everyone of his generation (the rest of us can only dream about having his kind of skill) and it still wasn't quite enough.

Sport and life, especially the arty life, are not exactly analogous. One of the great things about sport is its cruel clarity: there is no such thing, for example, as a bad one-hundred-metre runner, or a hopeless centre-half who got lucky; in sport, you get found out. Nor is there such a thing as an unknown genius striker starving in a garret somewhere, because the scouting system is foolproof. (*Everyone* gets watched.) There are, however, plenty of bad actors or musicians or writers making a decent living, people who happened to be in the right place at the right time, or knew the right people, or whose talents have been misunderstood or overestimated. Even so, I think there is a real resonance in the Gus Caesar story: it contains a terrifying lesson for any aspirants who think that their own unshakeable sense of destiny (and again, this sense of destiny is not to be confused with arrogance – Gus Caesar was not an arrogant footballer) is significant. Gus must have known he was good, just as any pop band who has ever played the Marquee know they are destined for Madison Square Garden and an *NME* front cover, and just as any writer who has sent off a completed manuscript to Faber and Faber knows that he is two years away from the Booker. You trust that feeling with your life, you feel the strength and determination it gives you coursing through

your veins like heroin . . . and it doesn't mean anything
at all.

WALKING DISTANCE

ARSENAL v SHEFFIELD WEDNESDAY
21.1.89

It made sense to move into the area, for other reasons too:
your money goes a lot further in decrepit areas of north London
than it does in Shepherd's Bush or Notting Hill, and the public
transport up here is good (five minutes from King's Cross, two
tube lines, millions of buses). But really, living within walking
distance of the ground was the fulfilment of a pitiful twenty-year
ambition, and it's no use trying to dress it up in logic.

It was fun looking. One flat I saw had a roof terrace which
overlooked a section of the front of the stadium, and you could
see these huge letters, 'RSEN', no more than that but just
enough to get the blood pumping. And the place we got
gazumped on was on the route that the open-top bus takes
when we win something. The rooms were smaller and darker
than the ones we have now, but the living-room window framed
the entire West Stand; I would have been able to pause, during
the writing of this book, look out, and return to the Amstrad
refreshed.

In the end we had to settle for somewhere a little less spiritual
overlooking Finsbury Park, and even if you stand on a stool
and stick your head out of the window you can't see anything,
not even the Barclays League pennant which at the time of
writing (although not, I fear, for much longer) is still ours to
flutter. But still! People park their cars in our road before the
game! And on a windy day the tannoy is clearly audible, even
from inside the flat, if the windows are open! (I don't know
about the audibility of roars, obviously, because I am never at

home when the team are, but I would like to think that the noisier celebrations make it this far. Maybe one day I will borrow my brother-in-law's smart Sony recorder, place it on the chair by the TV under the window and let it run, just out of interest.) And best of all, just a few days after moving in, I was walking down the road – *this really happened* – and I found, just lying there, filthy dirty and somewhat torn but there none-theless, a twenty-year-old Peter Marinello bubblegum card. You cannot imagine how happy this made me, to know that I was living in an area so rich in archaeological interest, so steeped in my own past.

As we turned the corner into our new street, the rental-van radio brought us news of a Kevin Richardson goal at Goodison Park, the third in an eventual 3–1 win (*and* Everton's goal never crossed the line), which seemed like a pretty good omen. But I was waiting for the following Saturday, my first ever *home* home game against Sheffield Wednesday, when finally, at the age of thirty-one, I would walk down Avenell Road, through the turnstiles and on to the North Bank as a north Londoner.

What was I expecting to find, when I opened the front door on to the street at twenty to three (twenty to three!) that Saturday afternoon and turned right towards the ground? I imagine I thought it was going to be like one of those sitcom depictions of suburbia, with all the identical front doors opening at pre-cisely the same time, and identically dressed men marching down the street together, clutching identical briefcases, brollies and newspapers. In my street, of course, it would be Arsenal supporters, rather than commuters, who emerged, and they would all be wearing flat caps and faded bar-type red-and-white scarves. And they would see me and smile and wave, and I would immediately become a much-loved and valued member of a happy, working-class Arsenal community.

But no doors opened. Nobody supports Arsenal in my street. Some of my neighbours are what used to be known, years ago, as yuppies, and they have no interest in football; others are transients, squatters or short-lease tenants, never around for long enough to acquire the taste for it. The rest of them . . . I don't know. You can't come up with a theory for everyone, and there's no accounting for taste. All I know is that there used to be one other fan in our street, a young lad who wandered around in an away shirt, but he moved soon after we got here; and apart from him I could have been back in Maidenhead, were it not for the cars cruising up and down, looking for a matchday parking space.

I suspect that I moved here a good twenty years too late, and that for the last couple of decades the local support has dwindled away steadily. According to the club's information, a huge percentage of fans live in the Home Counties (when I travelled down from Cambridge, the trains were packed with Arsenal supporters by the time we got to Hatfield). Football in London – at Spurs, Chelsea, Highbury and, to a lesser extent, West Ham – has become a suburban afternoon out. The demographics have changed now, and all those people who used to walk to the game from Islington and Finsbury Park and Stoke Newington have gone: they're either dead or they've sold up, moved out to Essex or Hertfordshire or Middlesex. And though you see a fair few people walking around with club shirts on, and some of the shopkeepers take an interest in the results (one of the guys who runs the news-stand inside the station is a committed and knowledgeable fan, although his brother supports Chelsea), I'm more alone here than I ever thought I would be at the end of the sixties, all those years ago, when I used to pester my dad to buy a house on Avenell Road, and he said I'd get fed up with it.

TYRANNY

I'm writing about me, now. The boy who fretted his way through the first part of this book has gone; the young man who spent most of his twenties twisted in on himself isn't around either. I can no longer use age, or rather youth, to explain myself in the way I have been able to do elsewhere.

As I get older, the tyranny that football exerts over my life, and therefore over the lives of people around me, is less reasonable and less attractive. Family and friends know, after long years of wearying experience, that the fixture list always has the last word in any arrangement; they understand, or at least accept, that christenings or weddings or any gatherings, which in other families would take unquestioned precedence, can only be plotted after consultation. So football is regarded as a given disability that has to be worked around. If I were wheelchair-bound, nobody close to me would organise anything in a top-floor flat, so why would they plan anything for a winter Saturday afternoon?

Like everyone, I have a peripheral role to play in the lives of most of the people I know, however, and these people are often uninterested in the forthcoming First Division programme. So there have been wedding invitations that I have reluctantly but unavoidably had to turn down, although I am always careful to provide a socially acceptable excuse involving family problems or work difficulties; 'Home to Sheffield United' is deemed an inadequate explanation in situations like these.

And then there are the unpredictable Cup replays, the rearranged midweek fixtures, the games transferred from Saturday to Sunday at short notice in order to accommodate the television schedules, so I have to refuse invitations that clash with potential fixtures, as well as those which clash with actual fixtures. (Or I do arrange something, but warn the parties involved that I might have to pull out at the last moment, which sometimes doesn't go down too well.)

But it gets harder and harder, and sometimes hurting someone is unavoidable. The Charlton game was rearranged for the same night as a very close friend's birthday party, a party to which only five people had been invited. Once I realised that there was a conflict of interest, there was the usual brief panic as I contemplated a home game taking place without me; and then I phoned her with a heavy heart and told her what had happened. I was hoping for a laugh and absolution, but I got neither, and from the sound of her voice, from the disappointment and tired impatience it contained, I understood that I wasn't going to. Instead, she said one of those awful things, 'You must do what you think is right', or 'You must do what you want to do', something like that; one of those chilling deliverances designed to find you out, and I said that I'd have to think about it, but we both knew that I wasn't going to think about it at all, that I had been exposed as the worthless, shallow worm I was, and I went to the game. I was glad I went, too. Paul Davis scored one of the best goals I have ever seen at Highbury, a diving header after he'd sprinted the length of the pitch following a Charlton attack.

There are two points that arise from incidents like this. Firstly, I have begun to suspect that my relationship is with Highbury, rather than with the team: if the match had taken place at the Valley or Selhurst Park or Upton Park, none of them inaccessible, you might have thought, to a man as obsessive as this one, then I wouldn't have gone. So what's this all about? Why am I hell-bent on seeing a match involving Arsenal in one part of London, but not another? What, in the jargon of the therapist, is the fantasy here? What do I imagine would happen to me if I didn't go to Highbury just for one evening, and missed a game that might have been crucial to the eventual outcome of the Championship race but hardly promised unmissable entertainment? The answer, I think, is this: I am frightened that in the next game, the one after the one I have missed, I won't understand something that's going on, a chant or the crowd's antipathy to one of the players; and so the place I know best in the world, the one spot outside my own home where I feel I belong absolutely and unquestionably, will have become alien to me. I missed the game against Coventry in 1991, and the game against Charlton in 1989, but I was abroad at the time. And though the first of those absences felt odd, the fact that I was several hundred miles from the stadium assuaged the panic and made it tolerable; the only time I have ever been somewhere else in London while Arsenal were at home (I was at Victoria, queuing for a ticket on Freddie Laker's Skytrain, while we were beating QPR 5–1 in September 1978, and my recall of both score and opponents signifies something), I felt squirmingly uncomfortable.

But one day, soon, it's going to have to happen again, I know that. Illness (but I've been to Highbury with flu and sprained ankles and more or less anything that didn't require access to a toilet), a future child's first football match or school play (surely I'd go to the school play . . . but I fear that I'm daft enough to pass it over and thus ensure that the child spends hours on some Hampstead couch in the year 2025 explaining to a disbelieving shrink that throughout his or her childhood I always put Arsenal first), family bereavement, work . . .

Which brings me to the second point arising from these rearranged game problems: work. My brother now has a job which demands more than a nine-to-five routine, and though I can't recall him missing a game through work hitherto, it is only a matter of time. One day soon, this season or next, someone will call an impromptu meeting that won't end until half past eight or nine o'clock, and he will be sitting staring at a memo while three or four miles away the Merse is humiliating an opposing full-back. And he won't like it, but he won't have much choice, so he'll shrug and get on with it.

I don't think I could do that kind of job, for the reasons outlined above. But if I did, I hope I'd be able to shrug. I hope I wouldn't kick out, in my panic, and pout, and plead, and generally reveal myself as someone who has yet to come to terms with the demands of adult life. Writers are luckier than most, but one day, I suppose, I will have to do something at a time disastrously inconvenient to me – I'll have a one-off chance to interview somebody who can only fit me in on a Saturday afternoon, or there will be some impossible deadline which requires a Wednesday evening in front of the word-processor. Proper writers go on author tours, and appear as guests on *Wogan*, and all sorts of things fraught with perils, so maybe one day there will be all that to contend with. Not yet, though. The publishers of this book cannot reasonably expect me to write about this kind of neurosis and then ask me to miss a few games to help them publicise it. 'I'm mad, remember?' I will tell them. 'That's what this whole thing is about! No way can I do a reading in Waterstone's on a Wednesday night!' And so I survive a little longer.

Is it really a coincidence, blind luck, that I have not yet found myself in an unavoidable match-missing position in over a decade as a wage-earner? (Even my superiors at the Far Eastern company, usually completely mystified by the compulsion of a social life, were in no doubt that Arsenal came first.) Or has my obsession shaped and guided my ambition? I would prefer to think not, of course, because if it has then the implications are alarming: all those options that I thought were still mine during my teenage years have in that case never existed, and the Stoke game in 1968 effectively prevented me from becoming an entrepreneur or a doctor or a real journalist. (Like many fans, I have never even contemplated becoming a sports-writer. How could I report on Liverpool versus Barcelona when I would rather be at Highbury to watch Arsenal against Wimbledon? Being paid a lot of money to write about the game I love is one of my darkest, clammiest fears.) I prefer to think of my freedom to go to Highbury whenever there is a game as a fortuitous side-effect of my chosen path, and leave it at that.

HILLSBOROUGH

ARSENAL v NEWCASTLE
15.4.89

There were rumours emanating from those with radios, but we didn't really know anything about it until half-time, when there was no score given for the Liverpool–Forest semi-final, and even then nobody had any real idea of the sickening scale of it all. By the end of our game, a dull, distracted 1–0 win, everyone knew there had been deaths. And a few people, those who had been to Hillsborough for the big occasions, were able to guess whereabouts in the ground the tragedy had occurred; but then, nobody who runs the game has ever been interested in the forebodings of fans.

By the time we got home it was clear that this wasn't just another football accident, the sort that happens once every few years, kills one or two unlucky people, and is generally and casually regarded by all the relevant authorities as one of the hazards of our chosen diversion. The numbers of dead rose by the minute – seven, then a score, then fifty-something and eventually ninety-five – and you realised that if anybody had even a shred of common sense left available to them, nothing would ever be the same again.

It is easy to understand why bereaved families wish to see officers from the South Yorkshire police brought to trial: their error of judgement was catastrophic. Yet, though it is clear that the police messed up badly that afternoon, it would be terribly vengeful to accuse them of anything more than incompetence. Very few of us are unfortunate enough to be in a position where our professional mistakes kill people. The police at Hillsborough were never able to guarantee safety, however many gates they did or didn't open; no police force at any football ground in the country could do that. It could have happened anywhere. It could have happened at Highbury – on the concrete steps leading out of the North Bank down to the street, maybe (and it doesn't require a very elaborate fantasy to imagine that); or it could have happened at Loftus Road, where thousands of fans can only gain access to the away end through a *coffee bar*. And there would have been an enquiry, and newspaper reports, and blame attached to the police, or stewards, or drunken fans, or somebody. But that wouldn't have been right, not when the whole thing was based on such a ludicrous premise.

The premise was this: that football stadia built in most cases around a hundred years ago (Norwich City's ground, fifty-eight years old, is the youngest in the First Division) could accommodate between fifteen and sixty-three thousand people without those people coming to any harm. Imagine the entire population of a small town (my own home town has a population of around fifty thousand) trying to get into a large department store, and you will have some idea of the hopefulness of this. These people stood, in blocks of ten or twelve thousand, on steeply banked and in some cases crumbling concrete terracing, modified but essentially unchanged over several decades. Even in the days when the only missiles hurled into the air were flat hats, this patently wasn't safe: thirty-three people were killed at Burnden Park, Bolton, in 1946 when crush barriers collapsed, and the Ibrox disaster in 1971 was the second to take place there. By the time football became a forum for gang warfare, and containment rather than safety become a priority (those perimeter fences again), a major tragedy became an inevitability. How could anyone have hoped to get away with it? With sixty-thousand-plus crowds, all you can do is shut the gates, tell everyone to squash up, and then pray, very hard.

The Ibrox disaster in 1971 was an awful warning that wasn't heeded: there were specific causes for it, but ultimately what was responsible was the way we watch football, among crowds that are way too big, in grounds that are far too old.

These grounds had been built for a generation of fans that didn't drive, or even rely on public transport overly much, and so they were placed carefully in the middle of residential areas full of narrow streets and terraced houses. Twenty or thirty years after the catchment areas began to expand dramatically, and people started travelling from ten or twenty or fifty miles away, nothing has changed. This was the time to build new stadia, out of town, with parking facilities and improved safety provisions; the rest of Europe did, and as a consequence the grounds in Italy, Spain, Portugal and France are bigger, better and safer, but typically, in a country whose infrastructure is finally beginning to fall apart, we didn't bother. Here, tens of thousands of fans walk up narrow, winding underground tunnels, or double-park their cars in tiny, quiet, local streets, while the relevant football authorities seem content to carry on as if nothing at all – behaviour, the fan base, methods of transport, even the state of the grounds themselves, which like the rest of us start to look a bit tatty after the first half-century or so – had changed. There was so much that could and should have been done, and nothing ever was, and everyone trundled along for year after year after year, for a hundred years, until Hillsborough. Hillsborough was the fourth post-war British football disaster, the third in which large numbers of people were crushed to death following some kind of failure in crowd control; it was the first which was attributed to something more than bad luck. So you can blame the police for opening the wrong gate at the wrong time if you like, but in my opinion to do so would be to miss the point.

The Taylor Report, famously and I think rightly, recommended that every football ground should become all-seater. Of course this brings with it new dangers – a possible repeat of the Bradford fire disaster, for example, where people died because highly flammable rubbish had been allowed to accumulate under the stands. And seats in themselves are not going to eliminate hooliganism, and could, if the clubs are very stupid, exacerbate it. Seats can be used as weapons, and long rows of people can obstruct police intervention if trouble does break out, although all-seaters should give clubs greater control over who occupies which part of the ground. The real point is that the likelihood of dying in the way that people at Ibrox and Hillsborough died will be minimised if the clubs implement Lord Justice Taylor's recommendations properly, and that, as far as I can see, is all that matters.

At the time of writing, the Taylor Report is prompting noisy dissent among fans and among some clubs. The problems are manifold. Changing the stadia to make them safe will prove expensive, and many clubs haven't got the money. In order to raise the money, some of them will be charging much higher entrance fees, or introducing schemes like the Arsenal and West Ham Bonds, which may mean that many young working-class males, the traditional core of support, will be excluded. Some fans want to continue standing. (Not, I think, because standing is an inherently superior way of watching a game – it isn't. It's uncomfortable, and anyone under six feet two has a restricted view. Fans worry that the end of terrace culture will mean the end of noise and atmosphere and all the things that make football memorable, but the all-seated ends at Ibrox make more noise than the Clock End and the North Bank put together; seats in themselves do not turn football grounds into churches.) All ground capacities will be reduced, some to below current average attendance figures. And some clubs will have to close down altogether.

I have listened to and read the arguments of hundreds of fans who disagree with the Taylor Report, and who see the future of football as a modified version of the past, with safer terraces and better facilities, rather than as anything radically different. And what has struck me most is the conservative and almost neurotic sentimental attachments these arguments evince – in a sense, the same kind of neurotic sentimental attachment that informs this book. Every time a club mentions a new stadium, there is an outcry; when Arsenal and Tottenham mooted ground-sharing a few years back, at a projected site near, I think, Alexandra Palace, the protests were loud and long ('Tradition!'), and as a consequence we now find ourselves with an assortment of the tiniest stadia in the world. The Stadium of Light in Lisbon holds 120,000, the Bernabeu in Madrid 95,000, Bayern Munich's ground 75,000; but Arsenal, the biggest team in the biggest city in Europe, will be able to squeeze in less than forty thousand when their development is completed.

We didn't want new grounds, and now we don't want the old ones, not if they have to be modified to ensure our safety and the clubs have to charge more as a consequence. 'What if I want to take my kids to a game? I won't be able to afford it.' But neither can we afford to take our kids to Barbados, or to Le Manoir aux Quat' Saisons, or to the opera. Come the Revolution, of course, we will be able to do all those things as often as we like, but until then this seems a particularly poor argument, a whinge rather than a cogent objection.

'What about the little clubs who might go to the wall?' It will be very sad for Chester's couple of thousand fans if their team goes under – I would be devastated if I were one of them – but that in itself is absolutely no reason why clubs should be allowed to endanger the lives of their fans. If clubs have to close down because they do not have the money for the changes deemed necessary to avoid another Hillsborough, then so be it. Tough. If, like Chester and Wimbledon and scores of other teams, they are poor, it is in part because not enough people care whether they survive or go under (Wimbledon, a First Division team in a densely populated area, attracted tiny crowds even before they were forced to move to the other side of London), and that tells a story of its own. However, the converse of this is that there is absolutely no chance of being crushed on a terrace at these grounds; forcing clubs to install seating for fans who have their own back-garden-sized patch of concrete to stand on is ludicrous.

'What about the supporters who have followed the club through thick and thin, paid the players' wages? How can clubs really contemplate selling them up the river?' This is an argument that goes right to the heart of football consumption. I have explained elsewhere that if clubs erode their traditional fan base, they could find themselves in serious difficulties, and in my opinion they would be misguided to do so. Obviously the ground improvements have to be paid for somehow, and increased admission prices are inevitable; most of us accept that we will have to pay another couple of quid to watch our team. The bond schemes at Arsenal and West Ham go way beyond that, however: using these price increases to swap one crowd for another, to get rid of the old set of fans and to bring in a new, more affluent group, is a mistake.

Even so, it is a mistake that clubs are perfectly at liberty to make. Football clubs are not hospitals or schools, with a duty to admit us regardless of our financial wherewithal. It is interesting and revealing that opposition to these bond schemes has taken on the tone of a crusade, as if the clubs had a moral obligation to their supporters. What do the clubs *owe* us, any of us, really? I have stumped up thousands of pounds to watch Arsenal over the last twenty years; but each time money has changed hands, I have received something in return: admission to a game, a train ticket, a programme. Why is football any different from the cinema, say, or a record shop? The difference is that all of us feel these astonishingly deep allegiances, and that until recently we had all anticipated being able to go to watch every game that our team plays for the rest of our lives; now it is beginning to appear as though that will not be possible for some of us. But that won't be the end of the world. It could even be that increased admission prices will improve the quality of the football we watch; perhaps clubs will be able to play fewer games, the players will become injured less frequently, and there will be no need to play in rubbishy tournaments like the ZDS Cup in order simply to earn a few quid. Again, one must look to Europe: the Italians, the Portuguese and the Spanish have high ticket prices, but they can afford to pay for the best players in Europe and South America. (They are also less obsessed with lower league football than we are. There *are* third and fourth division clubs, but they are semi-professional, and do not influence the way the game is structured. The First Division takes precedence and the football climate is all the healthier for it.)

Over the years we have come to confuse football with something else, something more *necessary*, which is why these cries of outrage are so heartfelt and so indignant. We view everything from the top of this mountain of partisan passion; it is no wonder that all our perspectives are wrong. Perhaps it was time to climb down, and see what everyone else in the outside world sees.

For the most part, what the outside world saw made a lot of cold, harsh, practical sense. The cover of *The Economist* that week carried a picture of the extraordinary shrine of flowers, flags and banners that Liverpool and Everton fans and hundreds of others had created in the goalmouth beneath the Kop at Anfield; the headline, neatly placed just above the crossbar, was 'The game that died'. I bought the magazine, for the first and only time, and was shocked to realise how much I found myself agreeing with it. Perhaps it was predictable that a magazine entitled *The Economist* should be best equipped to penetrate the muddle that football had got itself into; here, after all, is a multi-million-pound industry which doesn't have two pennies to rub together.

The Economist on the inevitability of the disaster:

'Hillsborough was not just a calamitous accident. It was a brutal demonstration of systematic failure.' On the state of the grounds: 'Britain's football grounds now resemble maximum-security prisons, but only the feebleness of the regulations has allowed the clubs to go on pretending that crowd safety is compatible with prison architecture.' On the football authorities: 'For complacency and incompetence, there's nothing like a cartel; and of Britain's surviving cartels, the Football League is one of the smuggest and slackest.' On the people who own football clubs: 'Like old-fashioned newspaper magnates, they are willing to pay for prestige – which they see in terms of owning star players, rather than comfortable modern stadiums.' And on what needs to be done: 'Having fewer clubs, operating out of smarter stadiums, ought to revive the interest of those who have been driven away from football during the past ten years.'

These views and others in the same issue – well-informed, well-argued, devoid of the football authorities' dilatory self-interest, the Government's loathing for the game (if Hillsborough did nothing else, it wrecked Thatcher's ludicrously misbegotten ID-card scheme) and the distorting obsession of the fans – helped one to begin looking at the whole football débâcle with something approaching clarity. It was only after Hillsborough, when outsiders began to take an interest in the way football conducts itself, that it became clear just how deeply entrenched in the football way of looking at things we had all become. And that way, as parts of this book demonstrate, is not always the wisest.

On 1st May, two weeks and two days later, Arsenal played Norwich at Highbury, our first game since the disaster. It was a glorious Bank Holiday afternoon, and Arsenal played wonderfully well, and won 5–0; as far as everyone there that day, myself included, was concerned, everything seemed more or less all right with the world again. The mourning period was over, the TV cameras were there, the sun was out, Arsenal were scoring goals galore . . . after the bleakness of the previous fortnight, the match took on a celebratory air. It was a tired and muted celebration, but it was a celebration nonetheless, and from this distance that looks particularly bizarre now.

What were we all thinking of that afternoon? How on earth did the Forest–Liverpool game ever get replayed? It's all a part of the same thing, in a way. I went to the Arsenal–Norwich game, and loved it, for the same reasons I had watched the Liverpool–Juventus final after the Heysel disaster, and for the same reasons that football hasn't really changed that much in over a hundred years: because the passions the game induces consume everything, including tact and common sense. If it is possible to attend and enjoy a football match sixteen days after nearly a hundred people died at one – and it is possible, I did it, despite my new post-Hillsborough realism – then perhaps it is a little easier to understand the culture and circumstances that allowed these deaths to happen. Nothing ever matters, apart from football.

THE GREATEST MOMENT EVER

LIVERPOOL v ARSENAL
26.5.89

In all the time I have been watching football, twenty-three seasons, only seven teams have won the First Division Championship: Leeds United, Everton, Arsenal, Derby County, Nottingham Forest, Aston Villa and, a staggering eleven times, Liverpool. Five different teams came top in my first five years, so it seemed to me then that the League was something that came your way every once in a while, even though you might have to wait for it; but as the seventies came and went, and then the eighties, it began to dawn on me that Arsenal might never win the League again in my lifetime. That isn't as melodramatic as it sounds. Wolves fans celebrating their third championship in six years in 1959 could hardly have anticipated that their team would spend much of the next thirty years in the Second and Third Divisions; Manchester City supporters in their mid-forties when the Blues last won the League in 1968 are in their early seventies now.

Like all fans, the overwhelming majority of the games I have seen have been League games. And as most of the time Arsenal have had no real interest in the First Division title after Christmas, nor ever really come close to going down, I would estimate that around half of these games are meaningless, at least in the way that sportswriters talk about meaningless games. There are no chewed nails and chewed knuckles and screwed-up faces; your ear doesn't become sore from being pressed up hard against a radio, trying to hear how Liverpool are getting on; you are not, in truth, thrown into agonies of despair or eye-popping fits of ecstasy by the result. Any meanings such games throw up are the ones that you, rather than the First Division table, bring to them.

And after maybe ten years of this, the Championship becomes something you either believe in or you don't, like God. You concede that it's possible, of course, and you try to respect the views of those who have managed to remain credulous. Between approximately 1975 and 1989 I didn't believe. I hoped, at the beginning of each season; and a couple of times – the middle of the 86/87 season, for example, when we were top for eight or nine weeks – I was almost lured out of my agnostic's cave. But in my heart of hearts I knew that it would never happen, just as I knew that they were not, as I used to think when I was young, going to find a cure for death before I got old.

In 1989, eighteen years after the last time Arsenal had won the League, I reluctantly and foolishly allowed myself to believe it was indeed possible that Arsenal could win the Championship. They were top of the First Division between January and May; on the last full weekend of the Hillsborough-elongated season they were five points clear of Liverpool with three games left to play. Liverpool had a game in hand, but the accepted wisdom was that Hillsborough and its attendant strains would make it impossible for them to keep winning, and two of Arsenal's three games were at home to weaker teams. The other was against Liverpool, away, a game that would conclude the First Division season.

No sooner had I become a born-again member of the Church of the Latterday Championship Believers, however, than Arsenal ground to a catastrophic halt. They lost, dismally, at home to Derby; and in the final game at Highbury, against Wimbledon, they twice threw away the lead to draw 2–2 against a team they had destroyed 5–1 on the opening day of the season. It was after the Derby game that I raged into an argument with my partner about a cup of tea, but after the Wimbledon game I had no rage left, just a numbing disappointment. For the first time I understood the women in soap operas who have been crushed by love affairs before, and can't *allow* themselves to fall for somebody again: I had never before seen all that as a matter of choice, but now I too had left myself nakedly exposed when I could have remained hard and cynical. I wouldn't allow it to happen again, never, ever, and I had been a fool, I knew that now, just as I knew it would take me years to recover from the terrible disappointment of getting so close and failing.

It wasn't quite all over. Liverpool had two games left, against West Ham and against us, both at Anfield. Because the two teams were so close, the mathematics of it all were peculiarly complicated: whatever score Liverpool beat West Ham by, Arsenal had to halve. If Liverpool won 2–0, we would have to win 1–0, and so on. In the event Liverpool won 5–1, which meant that we needed a two-goal victory; 'YOU HAVEN'T

227

GOT A PRAYER, ARSENAL', was the back-page headline of the *Daily Mirror*.

I didn't go to Anfield. The fixture was originally scheduled for earlier in the season, when the result wouldn't have been so crucial, and by the time it was clear that this game would decide the Championship, the tickets had long gone. In the morning I walked down to Highbury to buy a new team shirt, just because I felt I had to do something, and though admittedly wearing a shirt in front of a television set would not, on the face of it, appear to offer the team an awful lot of encouragement, I knew it would make me feel better. Even at noon, some eight hours before the evening kick-off, there were already scores of coaches and cars around the ground, and on the way home I wished everyone I passed good luck; their positiveness ('Three–one', 'Two–nil, no trouble', even a breezy 'Four–one') on this beautiful May morning made me sad for them, as if these chirpy and bravely confident young men and women were off to the Somme to lose their lives, rather than to Anfield to lose, at worst, their faith.

I went to work in the afternoon, and felt sick with nerves despite myself; afterwards I went straight round to an Arsenal-supporting friend's house, just a street away from the North Bank, to watch the game. Everything about the night was memorable, right from the moment when the teams came on to the pitch and the Arsenal players ran over to the Kop and presented individuals in the crowd with bunches of flowers. And as the game progressed, and it became obvious that Arsenal were going to go down fighting, it occurred to me just how well I knew my team, their faces and their mannerisms, and how fond I was of each individual member of it. Merson's gap-toothed smile and tatty soul-boy haircut, Adams's manful and endearing attempts to come to terms with his own inadequacies, Rocastle's pumped-up elegance, Smith's lovable diligence . . . I could find it in me to forgive them for coming so close and blowing it: they were young, and they'd had a fantastic season and as a supporter you cannot really ask for more than that.

I got excited when we scored right at the beginning of the second half, and I got excited again about ten minutes from time, when Thomas had a clear chance and hit it straight at Grobbelaar, but Liverpool seemed to be growing stronger and to be creating chances at the end, and finally, with the clock in the corner of the TV screen showing that the ninety minutes had passed, I got ready to muster a brave smile for a brave team. 'If Arsenal are to lose the Championship, having had such a lead at one time, it's somewhat poetic justice that they have got a result on the last day, even though they're not to win it,' said co-commentator David Pleat as Kevin Richardson received treatment for an injury with the Kop already celebrating. 'They will see that as scant consolation, I should think, David,' replied Brian Moore. Scant consolation indeed, for all of us.

Richardson finally got up, ninety-two minutes gone now, and even managed a penalty-area tackle on John Barnes; then Lukic bowled the ball out to Dixon, Dixon on, inevitably, to Smith, a brilliant Smith flick-on . . . and suddenly, in the last minute of the last game of the season, Thomas was through, on his own, with a chance to win the Championship for Arsenal. 'It's up for grabs now!' Brian Moore yelled; and even then I found that I was reining myself in, learning from recent lapses in hardened scepticism, thinking, well, at least we came close at the end there, instead of thinking, please Michael, please Michael, please put it in, please God let him score. And then he was turning a somersault, and I was flat out on the floor, and everybody in the living room jumped on top of me. Eighteen years, all forgotten in a second.

What is the correct analogy for a moment like that? In Pete Davies's brilliant book about the 1990 World Cup, *All Played*

Out, he notices that the players use sexual imagery when trying to explain what it feels like to score a goal. I can see that sometimes, for some of the more workaday transcendent moments. Smith's third goal in our 3–0 win against Liverpool in December 1990, for example, four days after we'd been beaten 6–2 at home by Manchester United – that felt pretty good, a perfect release to an hour of mounting excitement. And four or five years back, at Norwich, Arsenal scored four times in sixteen minutes after trailing for most of the game, a quarter of an hour which also had a kind of sexual otherworldliness to it.

The trouble with the orgasm as metaphor here is that the orgasm, though obviously pleasurable, is familiar, repeatable (within a couple of hours if you've been eating your greens), and predictable, particularly for a man – if you're having sex then you know what's coming, as it were. Maybe if I hadn't made love for eighteen years, and had given up hope of doing so for another eighteen, and then suddenly, out of the blue, an opportunity presented itself . . . maybe in these circumstances it would be possible to recreate an approximation of that Anfield moment. Even though there is no question that sex is a nicer activity than watching football (no nil–nil draws, no offside trap, no cup upsets, *and* you're warm), in the normal run of things, the feelings it engenders are simply not as intense as those brought about by a once-in-a-lifetime last-minute Championship winner.

None of the moments that people describe as the best in their lives seem analogous to me. Childbirth must be extraordinarily moving, but it doesn't really have the crucial surprise element, and in any case lasts too long; the fulfilment of personal ambition – promotions, awards, what have you – doesn't have the last-minute time factor, nor the element of powerlessness that I felt that night. And what else is there that can possibly provide the *suddenness*? A huge pools win, maybe, but the gaining of large sums of money affects a different part of the psyche altogether, and has none of the *communal* ecstasy of football.

There is then, literally, nothing to describe it. I have exhausted all the available options. I can recall nothing else that I have coveted for two decades (what else *is* there that can reasonably be coveted for that long?), nor can I recall anything else that I have desired as both man and boy. So please, be tolerant of those who describe a sporting moment as their best ever. We do not lack imagination, nor have we had sad and barren lives; it is just that real life is paler, duller, and contains less potential for unexpected delirium.

When the final whistle blew (just one more heart-stopping moment, when Thomas turned and knocked a terrifyingly casual back-pass to Lukic, perfectly safely but with a coolness that I didn't feel) I ran straight out of the door to the off-licence on Blackstock Road; I had my arms outstretched, like a little boy playing aeroplanes, and as I flew down the street, old ladies came to the door and applauded my progress, as if I were Michael Thomas himself; then I was grievously ripped off for a bottle of cheap champagne, I realised later, by a shopkeeper who could see that the light of intelligence had gone from my eyes altogether. I could hear whoops and screams from pubs and shops and houses all around me; and as fans began to congregate at the stadium, some draped in banners, some sitting on top of tooting cars, everyone embracing strangers at every opportunity, and TV cameras arrived to film the party for the late news, and club officials leaned out of windows to wave at the bouncing crowd, it occurred to me that I was glad I hadn't been up to Anfield, and missed out on this joyful, almost Latin explosion on my doorstep. After twenty-one years I no longer felt, as I had done during the Double year, that if I hadn't been to the games I had no right to partake in the celebrations; I'd done the work, years and years and years of it, and I belonged.

SEATS

These are some of the things that have happened to me in my thirties: I have become a mortgage holder; I have stopped buying *New Musical Express* and the *Face*, and, inexplicably, I have started keeping back copies of *Q* Magazine under a shelf in my living room; I have become an uncle; I have bought a CD player; I have registered with an accountant; I have noticed that certain types of music – hip-hop, indie guitar pop, thrash metal – all sound the same, and have no tune; I have come to prefer restaurants to clubs, and dinners with friends to parties; I have developed an aversion to the feeling that a bellyful of beer gives you, even though I still enjoy a pint; I have started to covet items of furniture; I have bought one of those cork boards you put up in the kitchen; I have started to develop certain views – on the squatters who live in my street, for example, and about unreasonably loud parties – which are not altogether consistent with the attitudes I held when I was younger. And, in 1989, I bought a season-ticket for the seats, after standing on the North Bank for over fifteen years. These details do not tell the whole story of how I got old, but they tell some of it.

You just get tired. I got tired of the queues, and the squash, and tumbling half-way down the terrace every time Arsenal scored, and the fact that my view of the near goal was always partially obscured at big games, and it seemed to me that being able to arrive at the ground two minutes before kick-off without being disadvantaged in any way had much to recommend it. I didn't miss the terraces, really, and in fact I enjoyed them, the backdrop they provided, their noise and colour, more than I ever had when I stood on them. This Coventry game was our first in the seats, and Thomas and Marwood scored directly in front of us, at our end, and from our side.

There are five of us: Pete, of course, and my brother, and my girlfriend, although her place is usually taken by someone else nowadays, and me, and Andy, who used to be Rat when we were kids in the Schoolboys' Enclosure – I bumped into him on the North Bank in George's second season, a decade or so after I had lost touch with him, and he too was ready to leave the terraces behind.

What you're really doing, when you buy a seat season-ticket, is upping the belonging a notch. I'd had my own spot on the terraces, but I had no proprietorial rights over it and if some bloody big-game casual fan stood in it, all I could do was raise my eyebrows. Now I really do have my own home in the stadium, complete with flatmates, and neighbours with whom I am on cordial terms, and with whom I converse on topics of shared interest, namely the need for a new midfielder/striker/ way of playing. So I correspond to the stereotype of the ageing football fan, but I don't regret it. After a while, you stop wanting to live from hand to mouth, day to day, game to game, and you begin wanting to ensure that the remainder of your days are secure.

SMOKING

ARSENAL v LIVERPOOL
25.10.89

I remember the game for conventional reasons, for substitute Smith's late winner and thus a handy Cup win over the old enemy. But most of all I remember it as the only time in the 1980s and, hitherto, the 1990s, that I had no nicotine in my bloodstream for the entire ninety minutes. I have gone through games without smoking in that time: during the first half of the 83/84 season I was on nicotine chewing gum, but never managed to kick that, and in the end went back to the cigarettes. But in

October '89, after a visit to Allen Carr the anti-smoking guru, I went cold turkey for ten days, and this game came right in the middle of that unhappy period.

I want to stop smoking and, like many people who wish to do the same, I firmly believe that abstinence is just around the corner. I won't buy a carton of duty-frees, or a lighter, or even a household-sized box of matches because, given the imminence of my cessation, it would be a waste of money. What stops me from doing so now, today, this minute, are the things that have always stopped me: a difficult period of work up ahead, requiring the kind of concentration that only a Silk Cut can facilitate; the fear of the overwhelming domestic tension that would doubtless accompany screaming desperation; and, inevitably and pathetically, the Arsenal.

They do give me some leeway. There's the first half of the season, before the FA Cup begins, and before the Championship has warmed up. And there are times like now, when with my team out of everything by the end of January I am looking at almost five months of dull but tension-free afternoons. (But I've got this book to write, and deadlines, and . . .) And yet some seasons – the 88/89 Championship year, for example, or the chase for the Double in 90/91 where every game between January and May was crucial – I cannot contemplate what it would be like to sit there without a smoke. Two down against Tottenham in a Cup semi-final at Wembley with eleven minutes gone and no fag? Inconceivable.

Am I going to hide behind Arsenal forever? Will they always serve as an excuse for smoking, and never having to go away at weekends, and not taking on work that might clash with a home fixture? The Liverpool game was, I think, their way of telling me that it's not their fault, that it is I who control my actions, and not they; and though actually I do remember that I survived the evening without running on to the pitch and shaking the players silly, I have forgotten it all when the forthcoming fixtures convince me that now is not the right time to tackle my nicotine addiction. I have argued before that having Arsenal on my back, like a hump, year after year after year, is a real disability. But I use that disability too, I milk it for all it is worth.

SEVEN GOALS AND A PUNCH-UP

ARSENAL v NORWICH
4.11.89

For a match to be really, truly memorable, the kind of game that sends you home buzzing inside with the fulfilment of it all, you require as many of the following features as possible:

(1) *Goals:* As many as possible. There is an argument which says that goals begin to lose their value in particularly easy victories, but I have never found this to be a problem. (I enjoyed the last goal in Arsenal's 7–1 win over Sheffield Wednesday as much as I enjoyed the first.) If the goals are to be shared, then it is best if the other team get theirs first: I have a particular penchant for the 3–2 home victory, with a late winner after losing 2–0 at half-time.

(2) *Outrageously bad refereeing decisions:* I prefer Arsenal to be the victim, rather than the recipient, of these, as long as they don't cost us the match. Indignation is a crucial ingredient of the perfect footballing experience; I cannot therefore agree with match commentators who argue that a referee has had a good game if he isn't noticed (although like everybody else, I don't like the game stopped every few seconds). I prefer to notice them, and howl at them, and feel cheated by them.

(3) *A noisy crowd:* In my experience, crowds are at their best when their team is losing but playing well, which is one of the reasons why coming back for a 3–2 win is my favourite kind of score.

(4) *Rain, a greasy surface, etc:* Football in August, on a

perfect grassy-green pitch, is aesthetically more appealing, although I do like a bit of slithery chaos in the goalmouth. Too much mud and the teams can't play at all, but you can't beat the sight of players sliding ten or fifteen yards for a tackle or in an attempt to get a touch to a cross. There's something intensifying about peering through driving rain, too.

(5) *Opposition misses a penalty:* Arsenal's goalkeeper John Lukic was the penalty king, so I have seen a fair few of these; Brian McClair's last-minute horror in the fifth-round FA Cup-tie in 1988 – so wild that it nearly cleared the North Bank roof – remains my favourite. However, I retain a residual fondness for Nigel Clough's efforts, also in the last minute, during a League game in 1990, when he missed; the referee ordered the kick to be retaken, and he missed again.

(6) *Member of opposition team receives a red card:* 'It's dis-appointing to hear the reaction of the crowd,' remarked Barry Davies during the Portsmouth–Forest FA Cup quarter-final in 1992, when Forest's Brian Laws was sent off and the Portsmouth supporters went mad; but what does he expect? For fans, a sending-off is always a magic moment, although it is crucial that this doesn't happen too early. First-half dismissals frequently result either in boringly easy victories for the team with eleven men (c.f., Forest *v* West Ham, FA Cup semi-final, 1991), or in an impenetrable defensive reorganisation which kills the game dead; second-half sendings-off in a tight game are impossibly gratifying. If I had to plump for just one dismissal to take on to a desert island with me, it would have to be Bob Hazell of Wolves, sent off in the last minute of a fourth-round cup-tie at Highbury in 1978, when the score was 1–1. As I remember it, he took a swing at Rix, who was trying to get the ball off him so that we could take a corner quickly; from said corner, Macdonald, freed of his disgraced marker for the first time in the game and thus completely unmarked, headed us into a winning lead. I also enjoyed, enormously, Tony Coton's long and lonely march at Highbury in 1986 – there is something

special about seeing a goalkeeper go – and Massing's murderous assault on Caniggia, followed by his valedictory wave to the crowd, during the opening game of the 1990 World Cup.

(7) *Some kind of 'disgraceful incident' (aka 'silliness', aka 'nonsense', aka 'unpleasantness'):* We are entering doubtful moral territory here – obviously players have a responsibility not to provoke a highly flammable crowd. A brawl between Coventry and Wimbledon on a wet November afternoon in front of a stupefied crowd of ten thousand is one thing, but a brawl between Celtic and Rangers players, given the barely controllable sectarian bitterness on the terraces, is quite another. Yet one has to conclude, regretfully and with a not inconsiderable degree of Corinthian sadness, that there is nothing like a punch-up to enliven an otherwise dull game. The side-effects are invariably beneficent – the players and the crowd become more committed, the plot thickens, the pulse quickens – and as long as the match doesn't degenerate as a consequence into some kind of sour grudge-match, brawls strike me as being a pretty desirable feature, like a roof terrace or a fireplace. If I were a sportswriter or a representative of the football authorities, then no doubt I would purse my lips, make disapproving noises, insist that the transgressors be brought to justice – argy-bargy, like soft drugs, would be no fun if it were officially sanctioned. Luckily, however, I have no such responsibility: I am a fan, with no duty to toe the moral line whatsoever.

The Arsenal–Norwich game at the end of 1989 had seven goals, and Arsenal came back from 2–0 down and then 3–2 down to win 4–3. It had two penalties, one in the last minute with the score at 3–3 (both, incidentally, terrible decisions on the part of the referee) . . . and Norwich's Gunn saved it, the ball rolled back to Dixon, who scuffed it, and it trickled, very gently, into the empty net. And then, all hell broke loose, with more or less everyone bar the Arsenal keeper involved in a bout of fisticuffs which seemed to last forever but which was probably over in a matter of seconds. Nobody was sent off, but never mind: how was it not possible to enjoy a game like that?

The two teams were fined heavily, which was only right, of course. In situations like this, the FA could hardly send them a letter thanking the players for giving the fans what they want. And given Arsenal's later problems, discussed elsewhere, the fight has in retrospect lost some of its gloss. But it's this centre of the world thing again: after the game we went home knowing that what we had seen, live, was the most significant sporting moment of the afternoon, a moment which would be talked about for weeks, months, which would make the news, which everyone would be asking you about at work on Monday morning. So, in the end, one has to conclude that it was a privilege to be there, to see all those grown men make fools of themselves in front of thirty-five thousand people; I wouldn't have missed it for the world.

SADDAM HUSSEIN AND WARREN BARTON

ARSENAL v EVERTON
19.1.91

A little-known fact: football fans knew before anybody else that the Gulf War had started. We were sat in front of the TV, waiting for the highlights of the Chelsea–Tottenham Rumbelows Cup-tie just before midnight, when Nick Owen looked at his monitor, announced a newsflash, and expressed the hope that we would be able to go to Stamford Bridge shortly. (The report of the game in the *Daily Mirror* made peculiar reading the next morning, incidentally, given the circumstances: 'Wave after wave of attacks left Tottenham hanging on for grim life', that kind of thing.) ITV beat the BBC to the news by several minutes.

Like most people, I was frightened: by the possibility of nuclear and chemical weapons being used; of Israel's involvement; of hundreds of thousands of people dying. By three o'clock on the Saturday afternoon, sixty-three hours after the start of the conflict, I was more discombobulated than I can recall being at the start of a football match: I'd watched too much late-night television, and dreamed too many strange dreams.

There was a different buzz in the crowd, too. The North Bank chanted 'Saddam Hussein is a homosexual' and 'Saddam run from Arsenal'. (The first message is scarcely in need of decoding; in the second, 'Arsenal' refers to the fans rather than the players. Which makes the chant self-aggrandising, rather than ridiculing, and which paradoxically reveals a respect for the Iraqi leader absent in the speculation about his sexual preferences. A consistent ideology is probably too much to ask for.)

It was an interesting experience, watching a football match with the world at war; one I had never had before. How was Highbury to become the centre of the universe, with a million men preparing to kill each other a thousand miles away? Easy. Merse's goal just after half-time earned us a 1–0 win, which would not in itself have been enough to distract attention away from Baghdad; but when Warren Barton's free-kick got Wimbledon a result up at Anfield, and we went top of the League for the first time that season, everything became focused again. Eight points behind in December and one point clear in January . . . By a quarter to five, Saddam was forgotten, and Highbury was humming.

TYPICAL ARSENAL

ARSENAL v MANCHESTER UNITED
6.5.91

In May 1991 we won the League again, for the second time in three years and the third time in my whole life. In the end there was none of the drama of 1989: Liverpool collapsed ignominiously, and we were allowed to run away with it. On the evening of the 6th May, Liverpool lost at Forest before our home game against Manchester United, and the United game was thus transformed into a riotous, raucous celebration.

If ever a season has exemplified Arsenal, it was that one. It wasn't just that we lost only one League game all season, and conceded an astonishingly miserly eighteen goals, although these statistics are in themselves indicative of the team's traditional tenacity. It was that the Championship was achieved despite almost comical antagonism and adversity. We had two points deducted after becoming involved, in retrospect unwisely, in another brawl, less than a year after the exciting Norwich fracas; soon afterwards, our captain was imprisoned after a stupendously idiotic piece of drunken driving. And these incidents came on top of heaps of others, on and off the pitch – fights, tabloid reports of obnoxious drunken behaviour, mass displays of petulance and indiscipline (most notably at Aston Villa at the end of 1989, when most of the team surrounded an unhelpful linesman long after the final whistle, gesturing and shouting to the extent that those of us who had travelled to support them couldn't help but feel embarrassed), and so on and on and on. Each of these transgressions isolated the club and its devotees further and further from the lip-pursing, right-thinking, Arsenal-hating mainland; Highbury became a Devil's Island in the middle of north London, the home of no-goods and miscreants.

'You can stick your fucking two points up your arse,' the crowd sang gleefully, over and over again, throughout the Manchester United game, and it began to seem like the quintessential Arsenal song: take our points, imprison our captain, hate our football, sod the lot of you. It was our night, a show of solidarity and defiance that had no grey areas of vicarious pleasure for anyone else, an acclamation of the virtues of all things unvirtuous. Arsenal aren't a Nottingham Forest or a West Ham or even a Liverpool, a team that inspires affection or admiration in other football fans; we share our pleasures with nobody but ourselves.

I don't like the fact that for the last couple of years Arsenal have brawled and bitched their way through their seasons, of course I don't. And I would rather that Tony Adams hadn't skidded his way down a residential street after a bucketful of lager, that the club hadn't paid all of his wages while he was inside, that Ian Wright hadn't spat at Oldham fans, that Nigel Winterburn hadn't involved himself in a bizarre row with a supporter on the touchline at Highbury. These are, on the whole, Bad Things. But in a sense my feelings are beside the point. It is part of the essential Arsenal experience that they are loathed, and in an era in which more or less everybody plays with an offside trap and an extra defender, perhaps these distasteful incidents are the Arsenal way of upping the ante in order to stake sole claim to the territory.

So in the end, the question of why Arsenal behave like this is not a very interesting one. I suspect that the answer is that they behave like this because they are Arsenal, and they understand their allotted role in the football scheme of things. A more interesting question is this: what does it do to the fans? How is your psyche affected, when you commit yourself for a lifetime to the team that everybody loves to hate? Are football fans like the dogs that come to resemble their masters?

Emphatically, yes. The West Ham fans I know have an innate sense of underdog moral authority, the Tottenham fans give off an air of smug, ersatz sophistication, the Manchester United fans are imbued with a frustrated grandeur, Liverpool fans are simply grand. And as for Arsenal fans . . . It is impossible to believe that we have remained unaffected by loving what the rest of the world regards as fundamentally unlovable. Ever since 15th March 1969, I have been aware of the isolation my team induces, maybe even demands. My partner believes that my tendency to adopt an attitude of beleaguered defiance at each minor setback or perceived act of disloyalty has been learned from Arsenal, and she may be right. Like the club, I am not equipped with a particularly thick skin; my oversensitivity to criticism means that I am more likely to pull up the drawbridge and bitterly bemoan my lot than I am to offer a quick handshake and get on with the game. In true Arsenal style, I can dish it out but I can't take it.

So that second Championship win, though less enthralling than the first, was far more satisfying, and more truly indicative of the Arsenal way: the club and the fans closed ranks and overcame, with a magnificently single-minded sense of purpose, almost insurmountable difficulties all of their own making. It was a triumph not only for the team, but for what the team has come to represent, and by extension for what all Arsenal fans have become. The 6th May was our night, and everybody else could go hang.

PLAYING

FRIENDS v OTHER FRIENDS
every Wednesday night

I started playing football seriously – that is to say, I started to care about what I was doing, rather than simply going through the motions to appease a schoolteacher – at the same time as I started watching. There were the games at school with the tennis ball, and the games in the street with a punctured plastic ball, two- or three-a-side; there were the games with my sister in the back garden, games up to ten in which she received a nine-goal start and threatened to go indoors if I scored; there were games with the local aspirant goalkeeper in the nearby playing fields after *The Big Match* on a Sunday afternoon, where we would re-enact high-scoring League games and I would provide live commentary at the same time. I played five-a-side in the local sports centre before I went to university, and second- or third-team football at college. I played for the staff team when I was teaching in Cambridge, and a mixed game twice a week with friends during the summer, and for the last six or seven years, all the football enthusiasts I know have been gathering on a five-a-side court in West London once a week. So I have been playing for two-thirds of my life, and I would like to play throughout as many of the three or four decades remaining to me as possible.

I'm a striker; or rather, I am not a goalkeeper, defender or midfield player, and not only can I remember without difficulty some of the goals I scored five or ten or fifteen years ago, I still, privately, take great pleasure in doing so, although I am sure that this sort of indulgence will result in my eventual blindness. I'm no good at football, needless to say, although happily that is also true of the friends I play with. We are just good enough to make it worthwhile: every week one of us scores a blinding goal, a scorching right-foot volley or a side-foot into a corner that caps a mazy run through a bewildered opposition defence, and we think about it secretly and guiltily (this is not what grown men should dream about) until the next time. Some of us have no hair on the tops of our heads, although this, we remind each other, has never been a handicap to Ray Wilkins, or that brilliant Sampdoria winger whose name escapes me; many of us are a few pounds overweight; most of us are in our mid-thirties. And even though there is an unspoken agreement that we don't tackle very hard, a relief for those of us who never could, I have noticed in the last couple of years that I wake up on Thursday mornings almost paralysed by stiffening joints, pulled hamstrings and sore Achilles tendons; my knee is swollen and puffy for the next two days, a legacy of the medial ligament torn in a game ten years ago (the subsequent exploratory operation was the closest I ever got to being a real footballer); whatever pace I had has been eroded by my advancing years and my self-abusive lifestyle. By the end of our sixty minutes I am bright red with exertion, and my Arsenal replica away shirt (old model) and shorts are sopping wet.

This is how close I came to becoming a professional: at college, one or two of the first team (I was in the third team in my final year) played for the Blues, a team consisting of the eleven best players in the whole of the University. To my knowledge, two Blues players in my time went on to play at a professional level. The best one, the university god, a blond striker who seemed to glow with talent in the way stars do, played as sub a few times for Torquay United in the Fourth Division – he may even have scored for them once. Another played for Cambridge City – City, Quentin Crisp's team, the team with the wonky *Match of the Day* tape and a crowd of two hundred, not United – as a full-back; we went to see him, and he was way off the pace.

So . . . if I had ranked number one in my college, as opposed to number twenty-five or thirty, then I might have been able, if I had been lucky, to look bad in a very poor semi-professional team. Sport doesn't allow you to dream in the way that writing or acting or painting or middle-management does: I knew when I was eleven that I would never play for Arsenal. Eleven is too young to know something as awful as that.

Luckily, it is possible to be a professional footballer without walking on to a League pitch, and without being blessed with a footballer's physique or pace or stamina or talent. There are the grimaces and gestures – the screwed-up eyes and slumped shoulders when you miss a good chance, the high-fives when you score, the clenched fists and hand-claps when your team-mates require encouragement, the open arms and upturned palms indicating your superior positioning and your team-mate's greed, the finger pointing to where you would like a pass delivered, and, after the pass has been delivered just right and you have messed up anyway, the raised hand acknowledging both facts. And sometimes, when you receive the ball with your back to goal and knock a short pass out wide, you know you have done it just right, just so, and that were it not for your paunch (but then, look at Molby) and your lack of hair (Wilkins, that Sampdoria winger – Lombardo? – again), and your lack of height (Hillier, Limpar), were it not for all those *peripherals*, you would have looked just like Alan Smith.

A SIXTIES REVIVAL

ARSENAL v ASTON VILLA
11.1.92

There was a part of me that was afraid to write all this down in a book, just as a part of me was afraid to explain to a therapist precisely what it had all come to mean: I was worried that by so doing it would all go, and I'd be left with this great big hole where football used to be. It hasn't happened, not yet, anyway. What has happened is more disturbing: I have begun to relish the misery that football provides. I am looking forward to more Championships, and days out at Wembley, and last-minute victories over Tottenham at White Hart Lane, of course I am, and when they come I will go as berserk as anyone. I don't want them yet, though. I want to defer the pleasure. I have been cold and bored and unhappy for so long that when Arsenal are good, I feel slightly but unmistakably disoriented, but I shouldn't have worried. What goes around, comes around.

I started this book in the summer of 1991. Arsenal were the

runaway First Division champions, about to enter the European Cup for the first time in exactly twenty years. They had the biggest squad, the brightest prospects, the strongest defence, the deadliest attack, the most astute manager; after their final match of the 90/91 season, in which they crushed poor Coventry 6–1 with four goals in the last twenty-odd minutes, the papers were full of us. 'READY TO RULE EUROPE'; 'THEY'RE GUNNER RULE FOR FIVE YEARS'; 'WE'RE THE BEST EVER'; 'CHAMPIONS SET SIGHTS ON THE BIGGEST PRIZE OF ALL'. There had been nothing in my time to compare with this sort of rich optimism. Even Arsenal-haters among my friends were predicting a triumphant and stately procession through to the European Cup Final, as well as another League title for sure, no trouble.

There was a little hiccup at the beginning of the season, but the team had found their form by the time the European Cup started in the middle of September: they crushed the Austrian champions 6–1, a magnificent performance which we believed would scare the rest of the continent rigid. We drew Benfica of Portugal in the next round, and I travelled on one of the two supporters' club planes to Lisbon, where we hung on for a creditable 1–1 draw in front of eighty thousand Portuguese in the intimidating Stadium of Light. In the return at Highbury, however, we got stuffed, overrun, outplayed, and it was all over, maybe for another twenty years. Then we dropped out of the running for the Championship, after a string of terrible results over Christmas; and then, unbelievably and cataclysmically, we were knocked out of the FA Cup by Wrexham, who had the previous season finished bottom of the Fourth Division as Arsenal finished top of the First.

It was strange, trying to write about how miserable most of my footballing life has been in the midst of all that post-Championship hope and glory. So as the season crumbled to dust, and Highbury became a place for discontented players and unhappy fans once more, and the future began to look so dismal that it was impossible to remember why we thought it bright in the first place, I began to feel comfortable again. The Great Collapse of 1992 had a sort of sympathetic magic to it. Wrexham was a quite brilliant and entirely authentic recreation of Swindon, humiliating enough to enable me to relive childhood trauma; at the same time as I was trying to recall the old boring, boring Arsenal of the sixties, and seventies, and, yes, the eighties, Wright and Campbell and Smith and the rest obligingly stopped scoring, and began to look as inept as their historical counterparts had ever done.

Against Aston Villa, one week after Wrexham, my whole life flashed before my eyes. A nil–nil draw, against a nothing team, in a meaningless game, in front of a restive, occasionally angry but for the most part wearily tolerant crowd, in the freezing January cold . . . All that was missing was Ian Ure falling over his feet, and my dad, grumbling away in the seat next to me.

FOR THE BEST IN PAPERBACKS, LOOK FOR THE

In every corner of the world, on every subject under the sun, Penguin represents quality and variety—the very best in publishing today.

For complete information about books available from Penguin—including Puffins, Penguin Classics, and Arkana—and how to order them, write to us at the appropriate address below. Please note that for copyright reasons the selection of books varies from country to country.

In the United Kingdom: Please write to *Dept. JC, Penguin Books Ltd, FREEPOST, West Drayton, Middlesex UB7 0BR*.

If you have any difficulty in obtaining a title, please send your order with the correct money, plus ten percent for postage and packaging, to *P.O. Box No. 11, West Drayton, Middlesex UB7 0BR*

In the United States: Please write to *Consumer Sales, Penguin USA, P.O. Box 999, Dept. 17109, Bergenfield, New Jersey 07621-0120.* Visa and MasterCard holders call 1-800-253-6476 to order all Penguin titles

In Canada: Please write to *Penguin Books Canada Ltd, 10 Alcorn Avenue, Suite 300, Toronto, Ontario M4V 3B2*

In Australia: Please write to *Penguin Books Australia Ltd, P.O. Box 257, Ringwood, Victoria 3134*

In New Zealand: Please write to *Penguin Books (NZ) Ltd, Private Bag 102902, North Shore Mail Centre, Auckland 10*

In India: Please write to *Penguin Books India Pvt Ltd, 706 Eros Apartments, 56 Nehru Place, New Delhi 110 019*

In the Netherlands: Please write to *Penguin Books Netherlands bv, Postbus 3507, NL-1001 AH Amsterdam*

In Germany: Please write to *Penguin Books Deutschland GmbH, Metzlerstrasse 26, 60594 Frankfurt am Main*

In Spain: Please write to *Penguin Books S. A., Bravo Murillo 19, 1° B, 28015 Madrid*

In Italy: Please write to *Penguin Italia s.r.l., Via Felice Casati 20, I-20124 Milano*

In France: Please write to *Penguin France S. A., 17 rue Lejeune, F–31000 Toulouse*

In Japan: Please write to *Penguin Books Japan, Ishikiribashi Building, 2–5–4, Suido, Bunkyo-ku, Tokyo 112*

In Greece: Please write to *Penguin Hellas Ltd, Dimocritou 3, GR–106 71 Athens*

In South Africa: Please write to *Longman Penguin Southern Africa (Pty) Ltd, Private Bag X08, Bertsham 2013*

THE AUDACIOUS AUTOBIOGRAPHY OF AN OBSESSED SOCCER FAN

Nick Hornby fell in love with soccer as a morose eleven-year-old in 1968, the same year that his parents separated. He remembers the end of his first love affair because his beloved Arsenal had tied Spurs 2–2 the day before. And when another girlfriend took Nick for a weekend in Paris years later, he couldn't hide his disappointment— that he'd have to miss a crucial match.

Fortunately, however, Hornby did also manage to become a writer of singular intelligence and wit. And this touching, funny memoir in the guise of a series of match reports is more than a love letter to soccer and its players. It is also about families, identity, sports, sex, class, love, masculinity, depression, joy, and violence. Not since Roger Angell and Frederick Exley has anyone written with greater charm and perceptiveness about the intersection of sports and life.

Cover design by Cecelia Smith; Cover photograph by Hulton Deutsch

A PENGUIN BOOK
Sports

ISBN 0-14-023729-1

$10.95

Francesca Bondy